STORY ENGINEERING

MASTERING THE
6 CORE COMPETENCIES
OF SUCCESSFUL WRITING

LARRY BROOKS

WRITER'S DIGEST
BOOKS

**WRITER'S
DIGEST
BOOKS**

An imprint of Penguin Random House LLC
penguinrandomhouse.com

ISBN 978-1-58297-998-4

Printed in the United States of America

Edited by Scott Francis
Designed by Terri Woesner

DEDICATION

For Laura and Nelson

PRAISE FOR LARRY BROOKS AND *STORY ENGINEERING*

"Larry Brooks's *Story Engineering* is a brilliant instructional manual for fiction writers that covers what the author calls the 'Six Competencies of Successful Storytelling.' The author presents a story telling model that keeps the writer focused on creating a dynamic living and breathing story from concept to the 'beat sheet' plan, through story structure and writings scenes. It's a wonderful guide for the beginner and a great refresher for the pro. I guarantee this book will give you new ways to fire up your creativity."

> —Jim Frey, author of *How to Write a Damn Good Novel, How to Write a Damn Good Thriller,* and *Gift of the White Light*

"Larry Brooks' groundbreaking book offers both novelists and screenwriters a model for storytelling that is nothing short of brilliant in its simplicity, its depth, its originality and its universality. Following his unique process is guaranteed to elevate your writing to the highest professional level."

> —Michael Hauge, author of *Writing Screenplays That Sell,* and *Selling Your Story in 60 Seconds*

"Nobody on the planet teaches story structure better than Larry Brooks. Nobody."

> —Randy Ingermanson, author of *Writing Fiction For Dummies*

"A useful guide explaining how to transfer screenwriting techniques to the craft of novel-writing. Good for screenwriters, too, summarizing the essence of entertaining commercial storytelling with great clarity."

> —Christopher Vogler, author of *The Writer's Journey: Mythic Structure for Writers*

TABLE OF CONTENTS

PART FOUR

The Third Core Competency—Theme

PART FIVE

The Fourth Core Competency—Story Structure

PART SIX

The Fifth Core Competency—Scene Execution

PART SEVEN

The Sixth Core Competency—Writing Voice

PART EIGHT

The Story Development Process

INTRODUCTION

As a bit of a cynic—a result of actually having worked in the writing business—I asked myself if the world really needs another book about writing. Another how-to from an author who, frankly, isn't exactly a household name. A quick Google search reveals there are 128,000,000 available resources on the subject of *how to write a book*. (It also provides 1,380,000 hits on my name, but even after five published novels I'm not kidding myself.)

Maybe 128,000,001 won't make that much difference either way.

Unless, perhaps, it offers something original, clarifying, and empowering for writers who are tired of hearing the same old thing delivered in the same old inaccessible, rhetoric-clouded way. A new twist on the old language about storytelling. Something that cuts across all genres and categories, from novels and screenplays to memoirs, articles, and even essays.

I understand guys like Dean Koontz and David Morrell and Stephen King doing it. My guess is (and here's the cynic in me) that it was their publisher's idea, hoping to cash in on the abundant name equity of those authors. Having read a bunch of these books myself, never once have I found a writing book or workshop that cuts to the core issues of the craft in a completely clear and accessible way (maybe it can't be done, maybe writing will always remain an elusive avocation) and that actually delivers a development *model* and process based on accepted criteria for effective storytelling.

Or, more clearly stated: a writing book that shows storytellers what to write, where to put it, and why it works there without any of it being remotely formulaic.

Elusive or not, that's not asking too much.

Most writing books are aesthetically driven.

The trouble is, in their execution stories are every bit as engineering driven as they are artistic in nature. And *that* particular context of learning gets next to no coverage in the oeuvre of writing instruction.

Writing teachers of all types will eagerly tell you what needs to be done—"*your story needs heart … we need to experience the journey of the hero … you need pacing and crisp prose*"—but few offer anything about *how* you get it done and in what order it needs to happen, step by excruciating step. Mostly their instruction is about theories and aesthetic sensibilities, all valid, while delivering less than precise advice. Even Stephen King, an author whom I respect, suggests in his book *On Writing* that once you stumble upon the seed of an idea, you should just sit down and start writing a story about it. That the first draft is for you and the subsequent drafts are for someone else.

Right. Just take off with it and see where it takes you. As if what you'd write for yourself is somehow less critical or not subject to the harsh light of analysis or the standards of solid storytelling that apply to everyone else. As if making stories up without a clue *how* to write them well will somehow satisfy your artistic jones.

Where *that* takes you is back to the drawing board.

But it doesn't have to be that way. Unless you are a master of the form, function, and criteria for successful storytelling—and King certainly is—this is a highly inefficient and, therefore, ineffective way to write your story. When it comes to storytelling, pain is optional. When it comes to *selling* your story, though, pain is inevitable … but that's another book altogether.

King's approach—known as organic writing or, in some circles, *pantsing* (for seat-of-the-pants storytelling)—may actually work for some, but that's only if a) you know what you're doing to the extent that you don't need to plan out your story; b) you somehow stumble upon the proper structural sequence and intuitively meet all the criteria for the various essential components; and c) you're willing to complete the inevitable rewrites that come with writing without a story plan. And yet, this is the default approach for nearly every new writer and a startling percentage of established ones, published and nonpublished alike. Some actually *brag* about writing draft after draft after draft, as if there is some nobility in stumbling around the blank page looking for your story.

Imagine a golf professional recommending that the way to the PGA Tour is to pick up a club and start swinging away wildly, hoping that somehow, someday, you'll find your groove (and the green) and be able to drive the ball three hundred yards to the middle of the fairway, without ever paying attention to the accepted mechanics of how to swing the club.

That's the make-it-up-as-you-go approach.

Don't forget that we're talking about the goal of becoming a *professional* golfer, because being published is absolutely entering the professional ranks of writers.

If you've tried writing this way, and if you remain unpublished—or worse, *unfinished*—you may already recognize this sad truth. Many writers continue to cling to their organic ways, however, claiming that they "just can't do it" any other way.

We all select our fates based on the paths we choose.

Here's why this is nothing short of insane.

Those *published* writers who, like King, *just start writing* their stories from an initial idea do so using an informed sensibility about, and working knowledge of, *story architecture*. They get it; the process is both intuitive and instinctive to them, in much the same way a seasoned surgeon no longer needs to consult *Gray's Anatomy* (the book, not the TV show) before slicing into an abdomen. They just *know*. The story pours out of their head in the right order, with specific structural milestones solidly in place from the first draft. They understand *what* those milestones are, where they go, and why. What they organically create aligns with those principles, and subsequent drafts are actually upgrades rather than damage control.

Newer writers who don't understand those fundamentals, and who try to write the same way? Not so much. It pours out of their head and basically spills all over the place.

Two words: a mess.

And it often gets even worse from there, because those same writers who don't *get it* intuitively usually don't even recognize it as a mess. They slap some postage on it and ship the manuscript off to an editor's slush pile somewhere.

Let me be clear: I'm not unequivocally stating that you must outline your stories ahead of time or in great detail. That's not the point, though in most cases it *is* a good idea. Frankly, the more you understand about the principles of story structure, the more prone you'll be to do it this way. When you do, you'll be applying the most powerful tool in storytelling from square one, instead of at draft number five.

How you write is totally your call.

But how your publishable story aligns with the Six Core Competencies of storytelling isn't your call, any more than you get to invent a new way to swing a golf club or take out a spleen. However you create your work, if you want to sell it, eventually it *will* need to align with these principles. The sooner this happens in the process, the better.

Without the right knowledge, without mastering a formidable list of basics that is rarely talked about coherently, most of us end up with a dream that never materializes. The less story planning writers do before they begin the drafting process, the deeper hole they dig for themselves. Too often they don't even recognize the pit they're in, so when the rejection slips arrive they don't have a clue as to why.

I'll tell you why, and I haven't even read their manuscripts. They were rejected because one or more of the Six Core Competencies was executed at a level that failed to inspire the agent, editor, or producer to offer a contract. A failure, even a mediocre execution, in any *one* of the core competencies will almost certainly kill your chances. Just as a faulty wing—one of the core competencies of flight—will send an airplane spiraling into the ground.

But here's the good news: The knowledge of how to understand and apply the Six Core Competencies of successful storytelling *is* out there. In fact, it's right here in your hands.

What screenwriters know that too many novelists don't.

Interestingly, there are many books on screenwriting that do what most novel-writing books don't—they show us what to write, when to write it, what follows what, what should go where, and why, and tell us the criteria for ensuring that our creative choices are effective ones. In other words, *how to get it done.* A blueprint and a process for something that is often considered—especially by those who write organically—to be a craft that defies blueprinting.

I assure you, those writers are wrong. And after the pile of drafts required to get their story into publishable shape, you can be sure that the screenwriter hired to adapt it to the screen will go about the job quite differently. Because while organic writers are often loath to admit it, the very drafting process they advocate is nothing other than a process of searching for and blueprinting their story, one iteration at a time, until they arrive at a solid sequential structure for it. Using a draft to find the story is no different than using a stack of 3x5 cards or yellow sticky notes ... they're all just different forms of *story planning*.

So, this book is intended to apply those same storytelling principles of screenwriting—though carefully adapted, revised, and put into non-screenwriting language—for novelists and memoirists and anyone else who hasn't benefited from the rules of structure and principles of character development that apply to screenwriting. Rules, by the way, that actually set screenwriters *free* to create their stories efficiently, while we novelists wander a vast landscape of creative choices without a single road sign. This lack of form, function, and criteria is what makes writing and publishing a good novel so elusive.

Until now.

Why this book?
Because neither a killer idea nor a Shakespearean flair for words will get you published without a command of these six core principles of dramatic storytelling.

This book is for writers who have taken all the workshops and read all the how-to books (or, perhaps even more timely, for those who are on Day One of their writing journey), and still don't understand what's wrong with their writing, and why it doesn't attract an agent or sell to a publisher.

Don't get me wrong, writing a great story will still be hard, even if you do it in accordance with this model. This model won't write the novel for you. Consider our golf analogy: If you had the same expert instruction and training as a golf pro, chances are you'd still find yourself, at best, vying for the club championship instead of a tour card.

Such is the quest for greatness, regardless of the game.

This book is the culmination of over twenty years of developing and teaching writing workshops, and writing novels and screenplays. The model presented here—*The Six Core Competencies of Successful Writing*—is completely of my own creation, yet it is based on the sum total of everything we know about what makes stories work.

You may have heard some of this before if you've spent any time at all studying the craft of storytelling. The truth is the truth; I didn't invent it. But

I bet you haven't had it presented, organized, and put into a context, even a language, that suddenly makes the process quite this clear and accessible.

That's why I wrote this book. Thousands have taken my writing workshops, and while some people pick at a few nits—ardent seat-of-the-pants writers don't give up their mantle easily—and more than a few arrive with grave doubts, most attendees leave as excited believers, a bit shocked to learn there really is a blueprint for a story, and that it rarely materially changes. Even if you only apply a fraction of this—and you'll end up doing it your own way anyhow—I guarantee you'll be more efficient and effective as a storyteller. Many times people have told me—and this is the highest praise I can imagine hearing after a workshop—that this is the clearest and most empowering thing they've ever heard about writing, in some cases after up to thirty years of workshops. They ask me, "Why the hell hasn't anyone put it together like this? Why don't you write this stuff as a book?"

Having regularly heard such validation, and having applied the Six Core Competencies myself, I began to believe that there was something of value here for writers who are looking to quantify, analyze, calculate, and blueprint the writing muse—to plan their stories using proven principles, or at least write them organically from an informed context of that understanding—and do it without the slightest compromise to their creativity or to the delight in making up stories.

I loathe formulaic writing as much as the next guy.

What you're about to learn isn't formulaic. And if it is, well, you can break the news to decades of mystery, thriller, romance, and adventure stories that didn't seem to think so. Is designing and building an office tower formulaic? Is flying an airplane formulaic? Is doing open-heart surgery formulaic? If they are, it's what makes them *work*. I prefer to think of these things as *process and criteria-driven skills*—or core competencies. And in this sense storytelling at a publishable level is no different.

Here's another analogy. Human beings bring only a handful of facial features to the blueprint of how we look—two eyes, two eyebrows, a nose, a mouth, a pair of cheekbones, and two ears, all pasted onto a somewhat ovular-to-round face. That particular blueprint doesn't often vary much, either. Interestingly enough, this is about the same number of essential storytelling parts and milestones that each and every story needs to showcase in order to be successful.

Now, consider this: With only these eleven variables to work with, ask yourself how often you see two people who look *exactly* alike. In a crowd of ten thousand faces, you would be able to differentiate each and every one of them, other than a set of twins or two in attendance.

Where we humans are concerned, the miracle of originality resides in the Creator, who applies an engineering-driven process—eleven variables—to an artistic outcome.

Where *art* is concerned, there is something to be learned from that.

We get to play God with our stories.

And just like the Big Author in the Sky, we have a finite set of tools to work with, and an expectation, a format, as to how they are assembled. If nature can deliver billions upon billions of versions of an eleven-element blueprint with hardly any duplication, we storytellers shouldn't begin to label this same level of story blueprinting as a formulaic undertaking.

A story is only formulaic if you allow it to be. It has nothing to do with abiding by the principles of solid storytelling and the handful of elements, parts, and milestones that comprise it.

Do you even know what they are? You'd be shocked at the number of writers who have been laboring at this for decades who don't. Give me a few hours of your time with this book, and you will.

After years of reading and critiquing unpublished and rejected manuscripts from aspiring writers, I began to see patterns. Those patterns, or the lack of them, aligned perfectly with the standards defined within the Six Core Competencies model, which validated this approach as a viable process for writing a novel, screenplay, play, short story, memoir, article, or essay.

Let the journey begin.

Open your mind and park your doubt (and your organically driven cynicism) until you find yourself in the thick of this journey, which not only shows you how to approach the craft of storytelling, but why organic, nonstructured approaches are chaotic, inefficient, and ineffective.

And even if you continue to prefer to write by the seat of your pants, you'll benefit from having a criteria-based checklist of elements to shoot for as you go.

There is no getting around this truth. Successful stories written in an organic fashion end up covering the *exact* same ground, meeting precisely the same criteria and eliciting the same enthusiastic reader response, as do successful books written from a story *plan*. Because both end up aligning with the principles of the Six Core Competencies.

And the ones that don't—story plan or not—end up in a drawer somewhere.

The Six Core Competencies approach starts with the criteria and the architecture of storytelling—the *engineering* and *design* of a story—and uses it as the basis for narrative. Organic writing starts with narrative and an idea—not necessarily in that order—and uses them as a process to discover and apply (or stumble upon) the criteria and the architecture.

Either way, you can get there … *if and when* you bring the Six Core Competencies to the task. And not a moment before.

Even if you call them something else.

One more thing before we launch.

You should know that my first published novel, *Darkness Bound*, sold to a major New York publisher on the very first submission, with virtually no changes or rewrites required, and that it went on to be a *USA Today* bestseller. How? Certainly not because I'm the next Stephen King, a fact history has proven to be true. Rather, because it was designed and written according to the principles of the Six Core Competencies. And, because of the efficiency they imparted to the process, it took only eight weeks to write.

The same was true to a slightly more liberal extent with my four other published novels. The longest rewrite to the polished first drafts I submitted to any of those editors, at their behest, took less than an hour to implement. One of them, *Bait and Switch*, was named by *Publishers Weekly* as the lead entry on their *Best Books of 2004—Mass Market* list, after a starred review and an Editor's Choice nod.

Formulaic? I don't think so. Easy? Not on your life. Just *doable*, with the right set of principles and tools.

PART ONE

WHAT ARE THE SIX CORE COMPETENCIES ...
AND WHY SHOULD I CARE?

1

THE POWER OF A FRESH
STORYTELLING MODEL

You can go your whole career as a writer without someone asking you to define the essence of *story*. What it means. What it *is*. What it isn't. For many writers this is a good thing. Because their answer just might come up short. Your first goal as a writer is to not be counted among this group.

You absolutely need to know, at the very core of your being, what a story is and what it isn't. And everything in between.

There are many ways to define *story*. Story is character. Story is conflict. Story is narrative tension. Story is thematic resonance. Story is plot.

Trouble is, all of these are partially correct, while none of them, when viewed as isolated definitions, are *completely* correct. Even if you combine a few of them, they still fall short of expressing the *essence* of a great story. Without that essence, what you have is a kitchen table full of ingredients waiting for a recipe that allows them to become a delicious sum in excess of their individual parts. That turns your story into a literary feast.

Even the most delicious of ingredients require blending and cooking—stirring, whipping, baking, boiling, frying, and sometimes marinating—before they qualify as edible, much less delectable. So it is with the building blocks of stories, as well.

Many writers just sit down and write without a recipe. A story may or may not emerge, and that lucky writer may or may not be cognizant of the presence of the various structural elements and storytelling presence—the recipe—required.

Some writers give these issues due diligence through some form of *story planning*, be it notes on a cocktail napkin or yellow sticky notes on a wall, or through a full-blown outline. Some even do it in their heads.

Either way, it's all just a search for a story that springs from the seed of an initial idea. And in that search, whether we realize it or not, or even if we care to admit it or not, our success depends on those dramatic principles, a set of story elements, the presence of smooth functionality, and an effective process, all of which melts together into a literary stew that defines the core essence of *story*.

What seems to be lacking—until now, at least—is a defined process that embraces all the requisite elements and underlying principles of a good story. A development model that is as much a functioning set of tools as it is the context from which we write.

Just as an engineer relies on an architecturally sound blueprint to build a structure that will bear weight and resist the elements—a vision and a plan based on proven physics and structural dynamics—writers can benefit from approaching the craft of storytelling armed with a keen command of the literary equivalent. It's unthinkable that an engineer and an architect would meet at the construction site one day and just start digging holes and pouring concrete. Even with a shared vision or an artist's rendering of the end product, it just wouldn't work. In addition to a detailed blueprint, in the real world both parties bring a contextual awareness of an informed planning process based on an in-depth understanding of the physics and principles that reside at the core of their craft.

But like an architect's vision that yields an engineer's blueprint, the resulting product may or may not always be everyone's cup of tea, even if it's structurally sound. That's the *art* of it. Standing up against a stiff wind is one thing, making the cover of *Architectural Digest* is quite another.

Writing is no different. We build our stories on a foundation of structurally sound principles. But from there we depend on something less definable and teachable to elevate our work. To raise it to something that publishers will buy and readers will consume and embrace. What the writer creates from these principles and the development model that puts them into play is no less aesthetically challenging or artfully endowed than the work of a writer who, perhaps because of ignorance or the overt rejection of such a tool chest, labors over a manuscript for years in search of the very same fundamental literary physics.

In other words, we can work hard or we can work smart. Hopefully both. A killer story development model doesn't take the hard work out of writing, but in any case it infuses the process with a heavy dose of *smart*.

THE PHYSICS OF STORYTELLING

There are many theories and principles floating around in the vast oeuvre of writing instruction. The list of things a writer needs to understand and execute is long and complex, but that list can be grouped into six separate yet dependent categories. And in doing so the fog that shrouds the storytelling challenge begins to lift.

I call them the *Six Core Competencies*. When applied to the story development process, you end up with an approach that is based on nothing short of what is, in essence, *story engineering*.

It works for writers for the very same reasons it works for the folks who build stadiums and skyscrapers. It's based on natural law. On time-tested, proven truths. For builders, that's physics. For writers, that's the Six Core Competencies. In no way does using these compromise the experience of the writer or the value of the end product. The Six Core Competencies create a story development model that leaves nothing out of the writing equation, except perhaps the need for an abundant number of drafts.

Execute them all at a professional level and you may find yourself in the hunt for a publishing contract. The model can't infuse your work with artful genius—that continues to defy quantification or definitive criteria—but it will get you into the game and make you competitive with authors who are already publishing. Demonstrating your command of the Six Core Competencies is your ante in to the world of publishing. From there, like a tryout for a major league team crowded with other hopefuls who are in full command of the basics of their game, you need to bring something magic that sets you apart from the crowd.

Leave out one of these Six Core Competencies, or execute any one at a less-than-professional level, and you will be sent back to the playground.

With this model in hand, at least you'll know what to shoot for. And, what is expected of you by those who represent and publish your work.

A STORY DEVELOPMENT MODEL

The Six Core Competencies comprise the first storytelling *model* I have seen that brings all of the necessary components and skill sets of successful storytelling under one approach. That drives toward the core essence of *story* in a comprehensive and methodical way, over and above simply being a collection of *things* that a writer must know. This development model provides checklists and criteria for any story.

Here's the truth: With some isolated, and therefore irrelevant, exceptions, *every* published novel or produced screenplay delivers on *each* of the Six Core Competencies described in this model, at least to some degree. Even if the author doesn't recognize it, or happened to back into them after multiple drafts. And even then, the *really* successful ones take them to a level of integration that defies definition. That becomes *artful*.

Which leads us to another truth: Leave one out, or execute one poorly, and you won't sell your story.

THE SEARCH FOR STORY

Since the very first story was set to parchment, writers have used the *drafting* process—creating version after version of their story, adding to it and revising it as they go—to discover and explore these same Six Core Competencies. Intuitively they know they aren't done until they've covered these bases, even if the bases themselves reside outside of their awareness and understanding. They just keep writing until it feels right, which puts the entire proposition at risk. Because too often these writers don't even know what it feels like. If they don't intuitively grasp them, or if they are in denial, or if they abandon the story before they're all in place, they never really find the story at all. At least not to the degree necessary to make it work.

Imagine the power and efficiency of understanding the necessary components and skill sets *ahead of time*. I'm not talking about story planning, per se, but rather arriving at the keyboard *armed* with the awareness and understanding of the principles required to empower your story to greatness.

Why do some prolific writers—think Stephen King or Arthur C. Clarke or Nora Roberts—seem to spill stories out of their heads that embrace the Six Core Competencies in such a way that their revision process is all about *adding* value and polish and nuance, rather than fixing major holes and out-of-rhythm narrative exposition? The answer is that they *get it*. They inherently, at the very core of their talent, understand the natural laws of a well-told story, and the Six Core Competencies that come to bear on the process of putting them onto the page.

Sadly, this is not the case for the majority of writers, who aren't even aware of the standards they need to reach. They settle for less than the requisite six.

But all that is about to change. At least for you.

In fact, it could be argued that *talent* is nothing more than the degree to which an author understands and applies these Six Core Competencies to their storytelling. Because prose with the lyrical magic of Shakespeare is not required to get published. You merely need to be clear, crisp, and clever at the right moments, with a general overall competence and professionalism. What *is* required, though, is a storytelling acumen that, whether cause or effect, reflects the principles and criteria of the Six Core Competencies.

This model results in *empowered* storytelling, rather than exploratory or even blind storytelling. Whether you spill them directly out of your head or plan for them before you begin to write, the Six Core Competencies manifest two direct and immediate benefits: better stories and better early drafts of those stories.

Reason enough to invite them into your process.

2
THE SIX CORE COMPETENCIES—
A 10,000-FOOT VIEW

It's time for you to crack open your new tool chest of writing clarity. Inside await the Six Core Competencies, each with its own list of moving parts, checklists, and criteria.

You may be wondering why it's taking so long to announce what they are. You may have even thumbed forward in this book to find them, which is fine. But it's just as important to understand the relational context of these tools as it is to have a first encounter with them. Like a child visiting the cockpit of an airplane, or an observer watching a surgery through an operating room gallery window, the tools hold little meaning until one understands their inherent value, the problems they prevent, the creative power they wield, their irreplaceable nature, the risks of using one improperly, and the potential for mastering them once this vast and critical context is understood.

So, before we roll them out, allow yourself the advantage of a little more insight into that context.

A STORY VIEWED AS A LIVING, BREATHING THING

A story has many moods. It has good days and bad days. It must be nurtured and cared for lest it deteriorate. And it has a personality and an essence that defines how it is perceived. Just like human beings. In fact, comparing a well-told story to a healthy human being becomes an effective analogy to better understand the interdependency of the parts and the delicate balance of chemistry and biomechanics that allow the body—and a story—to move, to thrive, and to grow.

Imagine a body without a heart. Or a set of lungs. Or a brain. Without these functioning organs, the human body is unable to survive. They are essential to life, as are the liver, the cardiovascular system, and the complex network of digestive mechanisms. The failure of any one of these vital organs—in lieu of a transplant, which is perhaps analogous to a *rewrite* in this case—ends life itself. Other body parts can be lost or be rendered dysfunctional without ending the viability of life, but such a life is altered and usually compromised in some way when that is the case.

So it is with our stories. There are certain elements that are essential for the story to work. They are not remotely negotiable. When those elements don't function well, the story suffers. It becomes dysfunctional. There are other literary elements that contribute toward the well being of a story, and while they aren't always essential to continued life, they do contribute toward a story that is fully alive and able to exist without compromise.

Like people, some stories run at full speed, others just sit there and suck up oxygen. Now, in the spirit of this very physical analogy, think of getting published as getting drafted by a pro sports team or earning your tour card on the PGA. To play at that level you need all your body parts, alive and well and strong. Merely breathing, consuming air and food—just doing the basics of staying alive—won't get you to the professional level.

Our stories are no different. You can't write mediocre stories. If you seek to publish, you need them to be strong, well muscled, quick on their literary feet, and highly skilled at the games they seek to play. Your stories need to be competitive with other stories that bring those same qualities to the tryout.

Sure, mediocre stories are still published all the time. Notice, however, that such stories almost always have a famous name on the cover, which speaks to the existence of a different expectation and marketing paradigm for established authors, one that is neither fair nor avoidable.

Some writers don't understand that certain basic elements of a story are *essential*, as is the relationship between them—just as the heart and lungs and blood work together toward the operation of the body. So they create stories that, in the name of either art or ignorance, shortchange those life-giving parts and end up facing a steady stream of rejection slips. A writer may be among the most eloquent narrative stylists since John Updike, but if he doesn't have a solid command of the essential elements of storytelling, he won't publish anything.

Which essential elements are commonly shortchanged?

Stories without drama or conflict. Stories with nobody to root for. Stories with no ambiance or sense of place. Stories with lousy pacing. Stories with no heart, no soul, no meaning, and no purpose. Derivative, been-there-done-that stories. Those writers don't understand that there is a list of essential, fundamental organs that bestows life upon a story. And like a would-be surgeon who has no training whatsoever in the essential functions and skills of the craft, a core level of understanding, and a hands-on level of competent implementation, there is little chance for the patient's survival.

The Six Core Competencies deliver that basic level of understanding to writers seeking to bring their stories to life. When applied in context to a full understanding of how the parts relate to one another, they become the contents of a powerful writing tool chest that not only opens the door to future publication but is essential to it.

What the Six Core Competencies can't do is bestow life itself.

It is theoretically possible to assemble all the parts of the human body, all properly installed and connected—think Frankenstein's monster—yet there will be no life until something *magic* happens. Or, if you don't believe in magic, some combination of electrochemical energy and luck that defies science. A spark of life is always required, and we have yet to discover the formula for that when it comes to storytelling.

That said, we do know that this literary spark, an injection of heart and soul and meaning into our stories, doesn't happen in a vacuum. It happens—and *only* happens—when the Six Core Competencies (by whatever name) are solidly understood and implemented within the body of the story in an inspired manner.

Your story won't work without them. This is nonnegotiable.

A Tale of Two Writers.

One understands and utilizes this model, one doesn't.

The one who doesn't may start out with a great story idea, even a great character. But without the context and content of the Six Core Competencies to apply to her storytelling process, she may not understand that she needs to *set up* the stakes of the story before the primary antagonistic force kicks in. She may not understand the nature and need for a setup at all, resulting in a story in which the reader has too little invested. She may get through two hundred pages of the manuscript before she realizes that her character has no backstory and no inner landscape, and therefore no potential character arc, that the pacing is irregular and too often too slow, and that she's forgotten all about subplot, much less subtext and, therefore, the very essence of any thematic resonance.

It all seemed so easy when she was reading the novels of her favorite authors. Authors that demonstrate no more linguistic dexterity than she does. This is a writer who is winging it, writing intuitively, and after those first two hundred pages she faces one of two challenges—she realizes that her story is broken and that she needs to start over, or at least revamp it; or she does not realize the sad state of things and presses onward with a story that is already doomed.

Now, the writer who brings the Six Core Competencies and their criteria to the process avoids all these problems. Not that the work becomes easy, but the path and the requisite standards become clear. Whether this writer uses an outline or constructs the story as he goes, what ends up on the page is already in alignment with the basic principles, allowing his future drafts to be for the purpose of adding value rather than putting out fires.

WHICH CORE COMPETENCY COMES FIRST?

To answer that one, you need to understand that the Six Core Competencies break down into two categories:

- the four basic *elements* of the story,
- the two narrative *skills* required to effectively implement them.

At first glance this may seem absurdly simplistic. But remember, the Six Core Competencies are like six categories of aligned pieces of the storytelling puzzle. Within each is a longer list of specific things to consider, and then each of those specific things has its own qualitative criteria and checklists that ensure you've considered them properly. There is nothing about storytelling that doesn't clearly and cleanly fall into one of these six categories.

Think of the game of baseball for a moment, which can be described in a similar manner. There is the realm of hitting, which has numerous principles and skills that the player needs to master. Then there's pitching, which has more specific options and skills, all of them different than those that apply to hitting. Then there is fielding, broken down by position, and base running and all the other strategic options available in specific situations, both offensively and defensively. There are five buckets of elements and skills you need to master in baseball to play the game at a high level—hitting, fielding, running, throwing, pitching. Omit any one of them, or be weak in any of them—for example, you can hit but your grandmother can field better than you—and you won't turn pro, period.

So it is with storytelling. Only in our case there are six.

3

DEFINING THE SIX CORE
COMPETENCIES

There's really nothing new under the sun when it comes to writing. But there is a multitude of ways to approach it, to define it, and then learn it. The search for understanding is simply a need to wrap your head around it all.

The Six Core Competencies of Successful Storytelling is a developmental model that allows you to do just that. It separates the major categorical elements of storytelling into discreet, easily understood buckets of information and criteria, all of which are then poured out as a rich, seamless story that actually works.

Consider a chef preparing a gourmet dish as an apt analogy for writing a story. First, the chef acquires all the ingredients called for in the recipe. There are basic principles to follow (eggs Benedict, for example, doesn't fly without eggs, ham, an English muffin, and hollandaise sauce); still, there is room for the chef to play with the recipe to make it his own creation. But never does the chef consider violating the basics—you can't serve the egg hard-boiled, for example. The chef understands all this as he assembles the ingredients, and knows there is a time and place to pour those ingredients together. The egg boils separately as the ham fries and the sauce is mixed, with the English muffin waiting under the broiler.

Separate functions all, waiting to become a sum in excess of their parts. At a certain point, and in a certain way, all of these ingredients are combined and garnished to become the dish in question. And yet, lest the chef get too irresponsibly frisky, eggs Benedict always starts with eggs. The cook doesn't begin the process intending to whip up some spaghetti and take a creative detour toward eggs Benedict while the sauce boils. To some degree, the only the thing the chef can mess with here are the spices.

Writing a story is very much the same thing.

There is no element, no aspect of the storytelling process, that doesn't belong in one of the six buckets of Six Core Competencies. Genre is a subset of concept. Setting is a subset of scene execution. Backstory is a subset of character. Subplot is a subset of structure, and unfolds in context to concept. And so on.

Like that eggs Benedict recipe, notice how each of the story ingredients—concept, character, theme, and structure—despite how separately they may have been developed, are poured forth from their categorical mixing bowls to become one. For the story to work they must relate to and appear in context to each other, regardless of which bucket they once called home. Theme and plot relate to character arc. As does structure. Concept relates to theme in that concept sets the stage for the theme to announce itself. And so on, again.

The value in separating the core competencies into separate buckets is that we can then clearly understand the definition and criteria for each, which are unique and therefore demanding of fully differentiated understanding, as well as how each relates to the others. If you approach storytelling without this separation of disciplines, the process you end up pursuing is like trying to define layered and esoteric essences and experiences such as chaos or love.

Unless you're a poet at heart, good luck with that.

One of the reasons writers get confused about the separate core competencies is that, within a story that works—and as consumers, that's what we spend our time reading so we don't see a lot of works in progress from other writers—the lines between these skill sets blur. As a story development model, the Six Core Competencies is a checklist that *must* be addressed and completed before a story will work. The checklist begins with the highest level criteria: Are all four of the essential categorical elements of the story in play? Are all four strong and compelling? It not, the story won't compete at a professional level. And of course, if you don't execute them with both of the two requisite implement skill sets, the same outcome will ensue.

From there the long list of criteria gets more specific.

Every *successful* story meets those criteria to some extent, even if the author had no idea she was manipulating six different skill sets and flavors of creativity. And that's fine, as long as it gets onto the page. Which it certainly can. It's possible to learn how to play the piano by ear or to fly a plane by feel, but it's a lot harder to keep from crashing. If you want to learn how to tell a story, and tell it well, and if you've been frustrated with getting your head around the process, then I encourage you to give this creative paradigm and its process a try.

WHY THIS MODEL EXCITES WRITERS

Many writers, especially those who have struggled with storytelling or with understanding their rejection slips, tend to recognize the value of the Six Core Competencies approach very quickly. Even before they try it. Why?

Because it offers hope and clarity. It illuminates a path, a strategy, an expectation, and a recipe for dramatic success. It answers the most basic and frustrating of questions: *How do I know what to write, and where do I put it in my story?* The Six Core Competencies model makes those answers accessible, and does it without smacking of formulaic writing, any more than a recipe smacks of formulaic cooking.

Often it is those writers who have been banging their organic-oriented head against the storytelling wall for decades that become the most ardent supporters of this approach after they've tried it for themselves. Because at last they are free to apply their vast creativity within a structure that works, rather than one they believe they are allowed to make up on their own.

The Six Core Competencies do not define or offer a formula. Rather, they define *structure* driven by *criteria* for the elements that comprise it.

To attempt to write a story any other way is to seek to reinvent the storytelling wheel. And that's just not gonna happen. At least if you expect to publish.

You could write a book about *each* of the core competencies.

In fact, virtually every book about writing—other than the "how-I-did-it" books like Stephen King's *On Writing*—is, in fact, just that. But only when you consider them in context to each other do you have something that can liberate you from frustration, at least over the course of a workshop agenda.

Even if you're the most organic and nonlinear-thinking of writers, there's something in this model that can help you.

Here then, at the most introductory level of definition, and in no particular order, are the Six Core Competencies of Successful Storytelling:

1. CONCEPT—The idea or seed that evolves into a platform for a story. Best and most empowering when expressed as a "what if?" question. The answer leads to further "what if?" questions in a branching and descending hierarchy, and the collective whole of those choices and answers becomes your story.

2. CHARACTER—Don't leave home without one. Every story needs a hero. We don't need to like him (contrary to what your high school composition teacher told you), but we do need to root for him.

3. THEME—Yes, it's like putting smoke into a bottle, but it can be done. Not to be confused with concept, theme is what your story is illuminating about real life.

4. STRUCTURE—What comes first, what comes next, and so forth … and why. And no, you can't just make it up for yourself. There are expectations and standards here. Knowing what they are is the first step toward getting published.

5. SCENE EXECUTION—You can know the game, but if you can't play it well you can't win. A story is a series of scenes with some connective tissue in place. And there are principles and guidelines to make them work.

6. WRITING VOICE—The coat of paint, or if you prefer, the suit of clothes, that delivers the story to the reader. The biggest risk here is letting your writing voice get in the way. Less is more. Sparingly clever or sparsely eloquent is even better.

That's it. There's nothing else under the writing sun, because anything you can think of that pertains to developing and writing a story aligns under one of these categories. Notice that the first four are "elemental" while the last two are "execution-driven" skill sets. You need to master all six of these to write a publishable story. If one is weak, the story won't succeed as well as it could, and it'll probably earn you a rejection slip. If one is missing altogether, the rejection slip is a done deal.

The bar is high. But now you have a ladder.

4

LAUNCHING THE
STORYTELLING PROCESS

WHICH CORE COMPETENCY COMES FIRST?

It doesn't matter. Like those essential organs in the human body, they all have to be present and functioning well before the story can breathe on its own. That said, by definition one of them always *does* come first in the process. The genesis of the story, the very first spark of thought that leads to another thought that ends up being a story, always emerges from one of the four elemental core competencies—concept, character, theme, or, less often, structure. It doesn't matter which, because the other three elements must be added to the mix—and, just like the original idea, *developed*—before the story can work.

Just as many stories begin with a character idea as they do with a conceptual idea. Someone you'd like to write about, or perhaps the profile of a hero or villain. At this point, this initial moment of conception, your character has absolutely nothing in place for her to do, she is nothing more than an image and short bio in your head. Think Sherlock Holmes—chances are Arthur Conan Doyle conceived him before the idea for a caper hatched in his mind.

Just as many stories begin life as a flash of a conceptual notion, sometimes in the form of a compelling "what if?" proposition. Could be that Clive Cussler wondered what it would be like to raise the *Titanic* from the ocean floor before even a glimmer of Dirk Pitt existed in his mind. Could be the other way around, too—and that's the point. Fact is, *Raise the Titanic!* was

Cussler's third Dirk Pitt book, which means character came first. But with a killer concept like that one, it's easy to assume otherwise.

And it doesn't matter what we assume relative to the work of other writers, it usually begins with one or the other. But you're not done—you can't even really start—until they're *all* there. Which element came first isn't the issue. You can start with any of them.

Sometimes a story begins with a thematic intention, a writer who wants to spin a tale that illuminates a certain issue or arena (a culture, place, or environment—think *The Lovely Bones*, *The Firm*, and the film *Top Gun*) without the slightest notion about a story or a hero. When you add concept and character to theme, you have the makings of a story, and not until.

A lot of people would believe that Dan Brown's *The Da Vinci Code* began with a concept. An idea. A compelling "what if?" proposition. Why? Because the "what if?" questions in that story are so compelling ... he must have started there, right? If that was the case—and it isn't—Brown would then add his hero to the mix, imbue it all with a rich thematic landscape and a sequential structure, the sum of which would then comprise the four requisite elements. Then he simply executed the two requisite skill sets and cashed in on what would prove to be a $300 million author payday.

And yet, like the Cussler example, this isn't how it happened. *The Da Vinci Code* was the second in a series of Robert Langdon novels, the first being *Angels & Demons*. Which means that the *original* seed of *The Da Vinci Code* wasn't a concept, but a character. The only thing that carries forward from the initial story *was* that hero, Langdon, and perhaps an agenda with Catholicism. Brown had to add the three other requisite elements—concept, theme, and structure— to that first piece of the storytelling puzzle. He had to give Langdon a *story*, and fast, or he had no sequel.

That process defines what we all face when we hatch a story. We get an idea from one of the four elements of the core competencies—to be real, though, it almost always comes from the first three: concept, character, or theme—and then we must add the other three elements to it.

That's the very definition of story development.

Shortchange any one of them and the story will fail. It doesn't matter which came first because at the end of the day they're all there, and working together.

Of course, it's highly possible that Brown had been nursing the conceptual and thematic aspects of *The Da Vinci Code* long before he wrote either book, but they didn't coalesce into the story that became the best-selling modern novel ever until they were added to the initiating element, which was the hero himself.

Here's the big mistake too many writers make.

They get that initial idea, and then they start writing a story about it. Without giving the other three essential elements much, if any, consideration. Or without finishing the development of all three. They wait for it to come to them—they *expect* it to—in the drafting process. Organic writers who develop their stories using multiple drafts are, in fact, searching for and fleshing out the other three elements as they go, along with the initial idea itself. Story planners go deep into all four elements *ahead* of time, creating a linear structure and then rendering their first draft as much an exercise in structural execution as it is a search for character and theme.

Either way, the story won't work until there is presence, balance, and power among all four. And unless you know this, unless you practice this, you are at the mercy of your storytelling intuition, and little else. And because so few of us are, in fact, at Stephen King's level in that regard, we should ignore his advice and steep ourselves in this knowledge before, during, and after the writing itself.

WHERE DOES A STORY IDEA COME FROM?

This is one of the most common questions writers are asked. It could be a dream that causes you to bolt upright in the night. It could be a random thought at the most unexpected of moments. It could be a notion that has haunted you for decades.

But always, it will be derived from one and only one of the four essential elements of a story—concept, character, theme, or sequential structure. The trick is to recognize which of the elements you have in hand, and to understand that the next task is to add the other three to the mix. *Before* you begin writing a draft. Often the second element galvanizes almost immediately. You may bolt upright in the middle of the night with a burning desire to write a novel about being unemployed, and within seconds you envision your hero. The proximity between the arrivals of these two ideas may seem as if they happened simultaneously, but one element came first and spawned the other. And I can tell you, coming up with the third and fourth elements and honing the first two will involve plenty more thought and creative sweat equity.

When this seemingly simultaneous flash of creativity occurs it is actually a good sign. When one of the elements is so rich with possibilities that one or more of the other elements instantly announces itself, you know you have a potentially powerful story on your hands. Just don't make the mistake of shortcutting the development of the others by seizing that moment to begin your manuscript. That would be like starting to cook the eggs Benedict without having any butter for the hollandaise sauce.

I like to say that we are gifted with that first initial seed of a story, and from a place we don't completely control or understand. The other three are up to us. They must be conjured, contoured, and fitted together into a seamless whole. We get to play God with our story from that point forward.

And therein resides the hard work of storytelling. Because, if you're playing God, you need to get it right.

THE THEORY BEHIND THE MODEL

It may surprise you at this point to learn that there is no prescribed writing *process* associated with the Six Core Competencies model. The model is far more focused on *what* you need to know and need to implement than *how* you do so.

In other words, you can still write your book any way you please. If you do it from an informed perspective on the Six Core Competencies, your process will ultimately be effective and, for the most part, efficient. If you don't, no matter how you proceed, it will be neither effective nor efficient, especially in your early drafts. Because, in that case, your drafts become a means of discovery, nothing more, until all the elements are solidly in place.

Which means you can be either a story planner or an organic writer who makes things up as you go along. Either way, if you understand and apply this model, you will succeed in writing a draft that covers all the requisite bases.

The *art* part is still up to you.

That said, a certain inevitability kicks in: The more you know about the Six Core Competencies, especially story structure, the more prone you will be to consider the various milestones and parts that comprise the ultimate sequence of your story *ahead* of time. In other words, this model may just turn you into a story planner who jots notes and outlines, even if that seems like the most unlikely of outcomes at this point.

Knowledge does that to a person. When you know what needs to be done, it makes sense to plan for it before you leave the garage.

It's like a pilot who, upon first learning to fly, has no idea there is such a thing as radar. He can operate the airplane just fine, but once in the sky he depends on his eyes, instruments, and gut feelings to keep from running into another flying object and to arrive at his destination before the fuel runs out. Then one day he discovers—go with me here—the Six Core Competencies of Radar and Navigational Flight Planning. Suddenly a whole new world of efficiency and safety opens up to him, and contrary to the chatter from the old guys in the pilot's lounge, it doesn't compromise his joy of flying in the least. In fact, it assures him that he will survive, and he will get from point A to point B with fuel to spare because he now knows how to file a flight plan.

No matter which approach you take, including a hybrid writing process that considers the major milestones of your story while leaving you free to explore what happens between them—this, by the way, being a very popular developmental process, especially for former *pantsers*, or those who write by the seat of their pants—you are engaging in the very same process.

No matter how you proceed, you are always searching for your story. Developing it. Considering options, making choices. Optimizing dramatic tension and pace. Giving your characters the best path toward adventure, growth, and redemption.

So, whether you're a plotter or a pantser, a planner or a plodder, at the end of the writing day we are all in the same boat. We are all just searching for our story. The essence of the Six Core Competencies developmental model contends that the more you know about the criteria and application of the elements that will be on the page when you're done, the more effective and efficient that process will be.

PART TWO

THE FIRST CORE COMPETENCY—
CONCEPT

5

CONCEPT—DEFINED

Earlier we addressed the issue of defining *story*. While that may seem a bit like defining food for a room full of wannabe chefs, it is the lack of a full and *enlightened*—that being the key word here—definition that holds many writers back. You'd be shocked at how many writers, even some who have been attending workshops for years and have written many novels and screenplays along the way, continue to turn in manuscripts that aren't actually *stories* at all. Instead they are character sketches or episodic expositions that don't exhibit the minimum criteria that would turn them into a *story*.

Story may seem obvious and intuitive. But it's not.

The same is true of *concept*.

Defining *concept* is tricky because, in the lexicon of the writing world, it is both overused and misused, and therefore, often misunderstood. The confusion stems from the fact that *concept* is, sometimes subtly, a different essence than an *idea* or even a *premise*. And it is very different from *theme*, which is a common source of confusion on this issue.

All three terms—idea, concept, and premise—have become generic and interchangeable. And while that may be harmless in a casual conversation, it becomes problematic for writers seeking to understand the most basic core realm of their story.

WHAT A CONCEPT IS *NOT*

Your story's *concept* is one of the Six Core Competencies, and therefore an element that is nonnegotiable. It doesn't have to be *high* concept, but there does need to be a concept in play. If you accept that concept is not the same thing as an *idea*, and if all you begin with is an idea rather than a concept, you are setting yourself up for failure.

A non-story example: An *idea* is to travel to Florida. A *concept* is to travel by car and stop at all the national parks along the way. A *premise* is to take your estranged father with you and mend fences while on the road.

Now let's put that notion in literary terms, looking at the initial seed of a story. An *idea* would be to write a story about raising the *Titanic* from the bottom on the sea. A great idea. A *concept* would be to suggest that there are secrets still hidden there that certain forces would kill to keep concealed. A *premise* would be to create an archetypical hero who is hired to do this job and in doing so saves his country from potential attack.

With apologies to Clive Cussler, that's what *Raise the Titanic!* could have been, proposed here solely to help differentiate the different realms and contexts of these three terms. Clive did just fine with that story without my help, so let's move on.

Idea vs. concept vs. premise. They are the same, but different—critically different when you are planning and writing your story.

It *could* be said that a concept is actually an idea by another name. But this is like saying that a piece of bread and the world's most delicious brochette are the same thing. Bread, yes. But brochette is bread on steroids, bread dressed to kill, which is precisely how one should contrast the essence of a concept vs. that of a mere idea. A concept is an idea that has been *evolved* to the point where a story becomes possible. A concept becomes a platform, a stage, upon which a story may unfold.

A concept, it could be said—and it should be viewed this way—is something that asks a question. The answer to the question is your story.

The idea to write a story about ballet dancers is *not* a concept. It is just an idea. But when you add a forward-thinking realm to that idea, and do it in the form of a question—*what if a ballet dancer loses her leg at the knee but perseveres against great prejudice to become a professional dancer?*—you have evolved the idea into the realm of conceptualization.

The initial idea always becomes a subset of the concept. It remains at its heart, but the concept is so much more than the idea alone.

Notice in this example how the expanded idea (concept) is already a snapshot of a story. How it asks a question that suggests an answer. The answer *is* the story. An idea that asks no question and presents no dramatic stage is not a story. It is not yet a concept until it does.

Notice, too, how the concept is not the plot itself, only a window into it. It cannot be a plot until conflict is introduced and defined, and certain sequential milestones are set in place. If your idea is to create a certain character, that doesn't become a concept until you give that character something to do, something to achieve or survive.

An idea can also be thematic intention—such as, *I want to write a story about infidelity. I want to write a story about addiction recovery. I want to write a story about corporate greed.* These are all *themes*. There is not a concept among them ... yet.

An idea can suggest or envision a character. *I want to write a story about a fighter pilot. I want to write a story about a cheating husband. I want to write a story about a dishonest lawyer.* None of these are themes, though theme quickly springs to mind. And none of them are concepts ... yet.

An idea can even spring from a linear structure. *I want to write a story about the 1980 U.S. Olympic hockey team. I want to write a story about someone who recovers from cancer.* Again, no theme yet, no character yet, and no concept. At least not yet.

An idea can spring forth from any of the four elements of story—concept, character, theme, story structure—as defined by the Six Core Competencies. Which is to say, an idea can be a concept, a character, a theme, or a sequence of events. Until one or more of the elements from the core competencies is added to it, though, it is none of those things.

CONCEPT AS A DELIVERY STRATEGY

A story about the 1980 U.S. Olympic hockey team and their gold medal may seem to defy the notion of a concept, because it is what it is, you can't mess with the truth. But you can—and should—land upon a conceptual *delivery* strategy to show us that truth, and it doesn't always have to do with plot. The moment you tell that story through the eyes of a single player—the goalie, for example, or maybe the coach—then you have evolved the idea into the realm of concept. *What if we tell the story of the 1980 U.S. Olympic hockey team through the eyes of the goalie who became the spirit and face of that team, making the journey more personal and visceral, as opposed to journalistic?*

Now you have a *story* to tell (it became the 2004 hit movie *Miracle*, starring Kurt Russell). You didn't at that initial *idea* stage.

In the movie industry, studio executives have ideas. *Let's do a film about a haunted house. Let's do a film about a submarine.* The list is endless and highly redundant. In almost every case, though, they hire a writer to evolve their idea into a story. And it begins by taking the idea to a *conceptual* level.

In *The Lovely Bones*, a terrific and hugely successful novel, Alice Sebold's concept has as much to do with her delivery strategy as it does the story's plot. Her *idea* was to tell us a story that shows us what heaven is like. Her *concept* was to create a narrator for the story who was already in heaven, narrating the tale directly from heaven, and then turning it into a murder mystery. Notice how the original idea, at that stage, didn't have that level of depth, and therefore it wasn't a platform for a story at all—a concept—until it did.

Sebold's concept, then, could be expressed as a question that demands an answer: *What if a murder victim can't rest in heaven because her crime remains unsolved, and chooses to get involved to help her loved ones gain closure?*

Now *that's* a story. One that sold over ten million copies, by the way.

CONCEPT VS. IDEA VS. PREMISE VS. THEME

Let's continue with *The Lovely Bones* to clarify how concept is its own essential core competency, while idea, premise, and theme are different elements altogether. An idea is always a subset of concept. A concept is a subset of premise. But neither the idea nor the premise becomes a story without a qualifying concept.

Once you turn an idea into a compelling "what if?" proposition, you have something that throws the door open to a story. You have a *concept*. Could you still call that concept an "idea," in a non-literary sense? You could—just as you can call a stealth fighter an airplane, or brain surgery an operation. But a concept is so much more than an idea. When you refer to an "idea" in this generic sense, you're just using the word as a noun rather than a more precise writing term. That's good enough for elevator talk, but not sufficiently enlightened to help you face the blank page.

A premise is a concept that has brought *character* into the mix. As such, it could be said that a premise is, in fact, an expanded concept. *"What if the narrator of a story spoke to us from heaven about her own murder?"* That's a concept. *"What if a fourteen-year-old girl cannot rest in heaven, and realizes that her family cannot rest on earth, because her murder remains unsolved, so she intervenes to help uncover the truth and bring peace to those who loved her, thus allowing her to move on?"* That's a premise, because of the hero's quest it defines. A matter of degree, perhaps, but one the author must understand.

Theme is a completely separate can of worms. We'll devote a whole section of this book to theme, as it is one of the Six Core Competencies and therefore essential. For now, though, as we seek to contrast it from *concept*, understand that theme is the essence of what a story *means*, rather than a descriptor of plot or character. What does the story of the raising of the *Titanic mean* to you? What does it illuminate about real life, about the world? What does it make you think about and feel? If there are answers to those questions, you are talking about *theme*, not concept.

Your initial idea *can* come from the realm of theme. When John Irving wanted to create a story about abortion, he did just that. His original thematic idea for *The Cider House Rules* expanded into a concept about an orphanage, a young doctor, and an incestuous father-daughter relationship. But not until he evolved it so that it served as a dramatic stage did it become a *concept*.

Some might consider these labeling issues moot. But as the creator of your stories, you need to have a handle on the different realms of understanding you must bring to your story, and if you can't differentiate them, you can't get there efficiently, or even effectively. If you write from an idea that is not yet a concept, your drafts will suffer for it until you do. If you write without a concept at all—some do, you've just never heard of them—settling for a linear flow of episodic narratives, your drafts will fail until you do. If you begin writing with *only* a theme in mind, believing that your theme *is* your concept (by definition, it's not), you'll end up with an essay or an editorial more than you will a story, and your attempt to retrofit plot and character into such a development strategy will likely turn out to be quite a mess.

Once again, the Six Core Competencies model keeps you focused on what must be discovered during the development process, however you go about it. When you accept that an idea is yet not a concept, and that a compelling concept *is* required, you are much further down the story development road than you would be otherwise.

And if your idea came to you in the form of a legitimate concept—it happens—your next task is to test it by seeing how smoothly it connects you to the other requisite elements.

6
THE CRITERIA
FOR CONCEPT

The first criteria to apply to your concept is to make sure you're not confusing it with a simple *idea*—which may actually reside in one of the other core competency buckets—or your story's *theme*. An *idea* for your story isn't enough. And a *theme* isn't a concept at all. If that still sounds less than precise, go back to the previous chapter and get up to speed on how concept differs from idea, premise, and theme. Because it is essential that you grasp this notion.

Once you do, from there the criteria for an effective concept become fairly straightforward.

IS THE CONCEPT FRESH AND ORIGINAL?

On one level this is obvious. You don't want to submit a novel with a concept that has someone discovering secret messages in the paintings of van Gogh, or a story about raising the *Lusitania* from the bottom of the sea.

But what about genre? How do you bring something new at the conceptual level to a murder mystery? To a romance? You do it by going *deeper* into the conceptual realm with a view toward setting the dramatic stage for an unfolding story that isn't as predicable as your chosen genre might suggest.

Clive Cussler had the idea to write a deep-sea adventure. Just an idea. Only when he cooked up the notion that he could raise the *Titanic* did that idea evolve into a concept, one that meets all of the criteria we are about to discuss. It was an adventure thriller, but one that readers hadn't seen before.

To declare that you are going to write a certain *kind* of story is only an idea. Take a murder mystery, for example. Even if you dress it up a bit—the victim was a lawyer, the evidence points to his wife—it's still just an idea. It should promise more.

But let's try for something deeper, with yet another mystery idea. Let's have the detective set out to solve a cold case, based on new evidence that has come to his attention. To say that this crime went unsolved is still just an idea, there's nothing remotely conceptual in play yet. But to address a twenty-year-old cold case already written off as solved, and then discover that the Los Angeles police department covered up evidence and framed an easy target lest they be exposed for pre-Rodney King racial profiling and violence … that's a killer *concept*. Michael Connelly's novel *The Closers* took that idea and made it a bestseller.

Same basic idea, but taken deeper and rendered both compelling and thematic.

In citing that example, it's also good to recognize why Connelly's concept is so powerful. Because it embraces a thematic realm that readers are sensitive to and well aware of, even referencing a known incident in history (Rodney King's beating at the hands of police officers, all of it caught on tape). In solving the crime along with the hero, the reader is asked to address and feel the thematic human implications of the case, rather than just put two and two together. This is why Connelly is consistently at the head of the class of mystery writers; his stories are rich not only with concept but with themes that arise from them.

Nelson DeMille did the same thing with his concept for *Night Fall*. His concept took a real event—the 1996 TWA Flight 800 disaster—and created a speculative plot-driven story, starring a hero he'd already established in an earlier novel and based on known conspiracy theory.

The more specificity you can bring to your story's concept, and the more compelling an edge you can bring to it, the richer the resultant dramatic sequence will be. But it doesn't have to reinvent the dramatic wheel, either. In Charles Frazier's novel *Cold Mountain*, for example, the concept involved a Civil War soldier trying to make his way home after surviving the war. That's not exactly *The Lovely Bones* in the originality department, but it was a number one bestseller because of the rich characterization and themes, delivered with stellar storytelling from a solid narrative voice. It simply *worked*.

A concept, for better or worse, always needs to be in play. Which means it always needs to be more than merely an *idea*. The more compelling and original it is, the better. But concept is only one of the Six Core Competencies, which means that whatever it may lack in edge, the other core competencies need to step up to compensate for the shortfall.

As with *Cold Mountain* and many other bestsellers that don't seem all that wildly conceptual, sometimes brilliant execution is the best concept of all.

If it's not particularly fresh and original, does your concept at least present an opportunity to impart a new spin on a familiar theme or premise?

This is really a question of how far you drill down into your story. The enlightened writer knows that when the concept isn't particularly edgy or fresh, it needs to evolve to a place where there is at least *something* about the notion that brings an element of compelling freshness, unpredictability, and curiosity to it.

The best genre stories do just that, while still coming straight from the wheelhouse of whatever it is about its genre that keeps people coming back.

Take the TV series *Murder, She Wrote*. On one level the concept doesn't seem all that compelling—a nice little old lady is solving murders nobody else seems to be able to solve. Clever. Sounds fun. What is fresh about it, though, is the fact that she should be retired, she should be off knitting somewhere, but instead she's doing what is normally done by cynical middle-aged gumshoes with dark pasts.

It doesn't take much to bring a differentiating edge to an otherwise vanilla concept. When that morsel of freshness is something the reader can relate to, you get extra points from an acquisitions editor, and from your readers.

Is your concept compelling?

You could argue that being compelling is just a combination of being fresh ahd original with a new spin, but it can and should exceed the sum of those two criteria. It isn't enough that your character and your theme be compelling ... you need to give your hero a motivated situation and an intriguing goal or problem to conquer.

It's perfectly okay to want to write a story about your grandmother growing up on a farm in Iowa. The specificity of that idea—and that's all it is at this point—begins to elevate it toward the realm of *concept*, but there's nothing all that compelling about it in a commercial sense. The writer might even agree, quickly citing a strategy to make the story compelling as it unfolds on the page, as we meet the character and fall in love with her, root for her, live that fascinating childhood with her.

Once again, execution is the great equalizer here.

Fair enough. But ... if it can't be expressed up front at a conceptual level, the writer will be hard pressed to make it compelling on the page, as well. Her draft will become a search for that compelling essence. But if the writer already knows what it is about the story that will *become* a compelling force, by definition there *is* something conceptual already in the mix. It should be isolated, explored, and then stated as a concept that bears some degree of compelling energy.

Does the concept set the stage for an unfolding dramatic story?

It's interesting to note how the criteria for a solid concept build on each other, constantly elevating, branching, and even descending (the contraction here is deliberate and meaningful) to something even more powerful and compelling. We usually begin with an idea that isn't yet a concept. We hammer on it to infuse it with freshness, we imbue it with compelling energy, and suddenly the idea is something much more layered and promising than it was in its more simplistic infancy.

Here's an example of an initial concept that can be embellished in either direction, ascending *and* descending. Let's say Clive Cussler began with the concept about a story that deals with the raising of a long-lost ship from the ocean floor. That's all he has at this initial point, he hasn't identified his ship yet. Then, bolting upright in the middle of the night, he has the notion to make his ship none other than the *Titanic*. That's a higher level concept, or an *ascending* value-add. Then, let's say he comes up with the idea of someone wanting to keep the secrets of the *Titanic* from being discovered. A force that will oppose him. That's a lateral or a *descending* value-add that drills down into the actual story line.

Your initial concept, based on an inspiring idea, may or may not reside at the highest level of conceptual potential. You can go up or down from there as you see fit. In fact, you absolutely should.

All of this is driving the concept toward the setting of a dramatic stage upon which your story will unfold. Right here, at this point in the development process, is where it becomes critical that the writer understand what *story* is, at its most elemental level: After a hook and a setup the hero begins a quest, the pursuit of a need or a solution, from which springs a specific goal (survival, revenge, happiness, health, peace, wealth, justice, etc.), and then must square off with and ultimately conquer (or not) obstacles—this being the most critical element of storytelling: *conflict*. You then toss in a few inner demons as well as some exterior antagonistic forces, giving the hero something to battle and outwit and conquer as he strives to reach his goal.

A good concept makes all that easy to buy into.

Your grandmother's childhood in Iowa? If that's all the concept promises, it's missing a quest and a goal. It's missing the implication of conflict, and thus is void of any real compelling energy.

But you can almost always fix a vanilla concept by going deeper and taking risks. And if you can't, the Six Core Competencies model has just saved you from wasting a year of your life writing a manuscript that won't ever work, because even if your concept is a bit milquetoast, the others can save your story.

What if your hero, your grandmother, wanted to be a doctor? What if, in those mid-century times, this was an unheard of goal for a young woman, and to complicate matters she had no money or means? What if, after being denied access to her dream, she engages in self-study to the point of discovering a medical breakthrough on her own, something that perhaps will save one of her family members, which gets the attention of the powers that be, who are still conflicted about allowing her into med school on scholarship? What if there are misogynist bigots and jealous foes who want to stop her, who want to steal her idea, or even wish her harm? What if she must choose between her family and her betrothed (subplot) in order to move forward with her dream?

Suddenly, with those ascending and descending add-ons to your original idea, that vanilla concept is triple chocolate thunder with extra sprinkles. It's still a story about your grandmother growing up in Iowa—and if it's a true story, your challenge is to isolate whatever edge makes the story compelling to you, and then elevate it to a level that it will become interesting to a reader who doesn't know you or your grandmother—but now, stated at a conceptual level that has benefited from a deep drill down to a richer level, it's actually a concept that will work.

Knowing the narrative goal in your storytelling is everything. It is the most powerful gift you can bestow upon your story, and yourself. Your *concept*, clearly and compellingly stated, is the first step in your journey toward knowing and then pursuing that goal.

Does the concept lend itself to the other three essential elements of storytelling?

When I was in college I wrote a paper for my creative writing class. I had what I thought was a killer concept—a guy knows his wife is having an affair, so he goes to the hotel where they are having a tryst to confront them, sneaks in the kitchen entrance and climbs the stairs—they're painting that day, so the floor numbers are covered in primer—counts the floors until he reaches their floor, which he learned about by eavesdropping on a phone call (this being before e-mail and texting), busts open the door and shoots the two entangled occupants with a shotgun before they can roll out of bed. They never knew what hit them.

Except, my hero forgot one thing: Hotels don't have a thirteenth floor. So when he was counting floors to get to room 1501, he actually arrived at room 1601. He broke into the wrong room and shot the wrong couple. Who, as it turned out, were on their honeymoon.

Oh, the M. Night Shyamalanian ironic horror of it all.

My professor announced to the class that there was one story he wanted read aloud. I knew it was me, it was *that* good. And so I proudly stood up and read my seven-page masterpiece. When I was done my face glowed with pride of authorship.

That was right before the professor eviscerated me in front of the whole class. My story was a gimmick. It had no meaning. It had no value. It stretched credibility. It was over-the-top. It completely and totally sucked, regardless of my fancy prose and what I thought was a nifty little concept.

A clever trick does not a concept make.

I've never forgotten that day or that feedback. Our stories aren't about our prose, and they aren't about our concepts, either. At least in a vacuum. If the concept doesn't naturally align with a journey for great characters and deliver a thematic punch along the way, one that makes people resonate with their own humanity, it isn't a good concept after all.

That's the criteria. It isn't just about cleverness and a trick ending. It isn't about an idea. It's about setting the stage for something bigger and better.

A few years ago I took Robert McKee's famous storytelling workshop, in which he used M. Night Shyamalan's *The Sixth Sense* as an example of a really lousy story. No matter that it did $600 million at the box office. It was an example of a concept that didn't connect to either character or theme. What if a dead guy doesn't know he's dead, and we see the afterworld from his point of view? The problem was, we never knew why. There weren't any stakes. And we didn't really root for him because until the end we had no idea what was going on. It was all about a sleight-of-hand ending. Literary junk food. Shyamalan's descending career spiral bears evidence to the longevity of such a storytelling strategy—each film based on a trick concept like that did less and less at the box office.

His concepts not linking to character and theme is why that's so.

Can the concept be expressed as a succinct "what if?" question?

This could be the most important of the criteria, for two reasons.

First, if the concept is rich and compelling to any degree, phrasing it as a "what if?" question will not only be possible, it will be clarifying and empowering. Because a good question demands an answer. And the answer is your story.

The other reason is that when you pose one "what if?" question, it immediately leads you to another. And then another. And so on, until a string of "what if?" questions emerges that begins to expand and define the story itself, in both an ascending and descending direction. For the writer this becomes an extraordinarily powerful story development tool, one you can apply to exploring and deciding upon every major story milestone in your sequential structure, and in each and every scene if you choose to take it that far.

Did Dan Brown seek to challenge the veracity of the Christian religion at square one of the development of *The Da Vinci Code*? Perhaps not—he's not returning my calls, so we can't be sure. That said, we *can* use his story as a great example of the power of "what if?" applied to storytelling. Let's say Brown began with this conceptual question: *What if Leonardo da Vinci implanted clues to his views on Christianity and the veracity of scripture within his painting of* The Last Supper? That alone meets all the criteria—it's original, it's compelling, it sets a whopper of a dramatic stage, and it certainly does open a can of "what if?" worms moving forward.

If indeed it *was* the starting point, which isn't a given. That's the beautiful thing about the "what if?" model—when you're done, when the story is deep and rich and connected, it may be tough to tell exactly where it all began. Because the concept went in all directions from that starting point—*up* to higher conceptual ground ... *forward* into the details of the story ... and *deeper* into the nuances of character and theme launched by it.

There are dozens of compelling "what if?" questions attached to *The Da Vinci Code*. Notice how the first few are at a high conceptual level, and then, in a descending hierarchy, they begin to illuminate the structural milestones of the story itself.

- What if Christ didn't die on the cross after all? What if the entire Christian religion is a contrivance and a deeply held secret resulting in a conspiracy?

- What if there is a highly secret group of men whose life mission is to preserve that secret? What if they are willing to kill to protect it?

- What if there are other secrets? What if the fabled Holy Grail is, in fact, the womb of Mary Magdalene, bearing the child of Jesus? What if that child survived, and the lineage continues to this day, meaning the ancestors of Christ are walking among us?

- What if Leonardo da Vinci was a member of yet another secret group that knows this to be true? What if da Vinci gave us clues to this fact in his paintings, especially *The Last Supper*?

- What if the museum curator at the Louvre is killed because of what he knows? What if he leaves clues about the hidden messages, and about those behind his murder, written in his own blood?

- What if members of a secret group of priests are being killed in an effort to expose the truth behind the church's two-thousand-year-old conspiracy of deceit?

- What if the hero of our story is called in to decipher the curator's cryptic messages, and finds himself accused of his murder?

- What if the woman who is helping him is not who or what she seems to be? What if she is connected to the truth in a way that is more significant than anyone knows?

- What if someone known to the hero seems to be helping him, but has manipulated him to apply his skills toward his own dark means, and intends to kill him once he has proof of the underlying truth?

On and on this list of "what if?" questions goes, to an extent that you could write one for virtually every scene and every story point in the novel.

APPLYING CRITERIA TO YOUR STORY

With the understanding that the inherent "what if?" questions that drive story development end up at some point in a hierarchy, your first job is to simply jump into this sequence and see where it leads in either direction.

Do "what if?" questions arise that take the story to a higher conceptual level? Do others drill deeper into it?

This is among the most powerful tools in all of the storytelling process. But like any good thing, there comes a point where you can get too much of it—"what if?" questions can be contradictory, creating forks in the storytelling road, options that at a glance look equally compelling—thus forcing you to make decisions about the story that, in turn, cause you to discard other options.

It is the quality and inspired creative wisdom of those decisions that will dictate the success of your stories. Your only road map toward that success, besides your intuition and learning curve, is the criteria associated with each of the Six Core Competencies of successful storytelling.

Remember, at *some* point in the development process you must create a concept for your story. The genesis of your story, your original spark of an idea, may define a character or focus on a theme, maybe even a sequence of events. Just don't make the mistake of stopping there, or starting to write a draft from there. Take the time to develop and evolve a compelling concept, and use the "what if?" process to explore and enrich it.

You may find that your original idea was even better than you originally thought.

Or, if after significant bleeding from the forehead you just can't make it work, you may realize there really isn't a story there, after all.

Better, in either case, to discover this before you've written an entire draft.

7

HOW DO YOU KNOW IF YOUR
CONCEPT IS GOOD ENOUGH?

E ven when your concept meets the criteria listed in the previous chapter for this core competency, it may or may not be compelling *enough*. Until you submit your work to an agent or a publisher, the jury that delivers this verdict consists of one member—you. As writers we are on our own to make that call, even when we solicit opinion to inform that decision.

We can sweat the details and the processes and the mechanics of writing until we're blue in the carpel tunnel, but if the core idea itself is lacking in some way—or perhaps even more confounding, simply mediocre—all may be lost before the ship sets sail. And in this less than precise profession perhaps more than any other, we may not know it until we're done.

There is an inherent risk in desiring to publish. It involves trying, perhaps only subconsciously, to write what we *believe* will sell. To imitate authors who are already selling. To follow trends. To be commercial.

This is always a bad choice if it's what drives you. The commercial viability of your story should be a variable, something you calculate and gauge, rather than something you allow to define the work. At the end of the day this is still art.

A commercial aesthetic is what drives those painters whose work lines the wall of the mall poster store instead of the downtown galleries. Yet, both sets of artists do their work according to a shared set of *fundamentals* and to expected processes. The line that separates it all is vague and slim. That line is what we call *art*, and the ability to manipulate it without crossing it is what we call *talent*.

WHO ARE YOU AS A WRITER?

Too often our motivations to write a story don't align with our choice of story idea. That is the hidden trap that awaits us as storytellers. We pick the wrong story, and for the wrong reasons. To avoid doing that, we need to understand who we are as writers. Specifically, *why* we are writers.

It's like a studio musician compared to a composer. One doesn't necessarily beget the other. You can succeed in either realm, and sometimes in both.

In writing novels and screenplays, as well as memoirs and essays, we are always called upon to be composers. In fact, we need only be adequate musicians if our compositions touch the heart and mind. In choosing *what* to compose, we must understand *why we desire* to compose that which we end up creating. That understanding will lead us to the right conceptual choices.

My wife keeps urging me to write romances. Why? Because I'm a romantic guy, at least in her eyes. And, romances defy trends and sell like crazy. More authors publish romances than any other genre of fiction. So why don't I go there? Because it's not who I am as a writer. If I chose to write a romance, I wouldn't bring who I am as a writer—even though that may be who I am as a person—to my selected concept. I would be guessing, selling out, trying to forecast what might sell within this niche.

A better choice is always to write the kind of book you enjoy reading. The kind of book that allows who you are to surface and to touch others. That sensibility leads us to the best choices when it comes to landing on the right concepts for our stories.

How do you *know*?

When you finally land on an idea, and when you then evolve that idea into a concept, when it intrigues you or perhaps possesses you, how can you be sure it is worthy of the time and monumental effort required to evolve it into a complete novel or screenplay? How can you know that others will agree that *this* is a great idea? Who is to say what *is* a great idea, and what isn't?

Can a less-than-great idea *become* a great story? If so, how?

Fact is, we never really *know*.

There is no way to get to the point of knowing. You must evolve and trust your instinct on this issue—your art, your aesthetic judgment, your identity as a writer—and doing *that* is the great mystery and forehead-bleeding challenge of writing.

Trust me, this is what separates the successful from the throngs of the otherwise equally talented. The successful have a knack for picking the *right* ideas.

Certainly there are abundant examples to be cited of story ideas that had at least three enthusiastic backers: the writer, an agent, and the acquiring editor or publisher. As long as those three parties to the publishing equation *believe* in the story, it *can* get into print. But it begins with you, the writer. Once *you* believe in your story, your job then is to find one agent and then one acquisitions editor who share that belief.

It isn't just the dumpsters full of rejected manuscripts that comprise the body of work that fails to find an agent or a publisher because the idea isn't of sufficient power. All those titles you've never heard of on that bookstore shelf, the ones that won't be around in a few months? Them, too. Those writers *thought* they knew.

Chances are those writers submitted an adequate execution of a mediocre idea. They either chose *wrong*, or they missed something. They were trying to be commercial, to fit in, to play to the market. They would have been better off writing from a place of passion and vision. Even if they feel they are alone on that planet when they do.

Only when you are published and branded within a niche should you worry about how your concept fits in with the marketplace. Not that you should ignore that variable, but don't allow it to drive your creative choices.

So again … how do you *know?*

Nobody has that definitive answer. Including the editors from major publishing houses that pass on titles such as the first Harry Potter (rejected nine times), Stephen King's *Carrie* (rejected thirty times), and *Gone With the Wind* (rejected thirty-eight times) as a daily matter of course. They don't *know*, either. All of us—authors and editors alike—are doing the best we can, using what we have at our disposal to increase our chances of guessing correctly.

The Six Core Competencies help you execute your ideas and passions to the best of your ability. But even they can't allow you to *know*.

There is, however, a way to dramatically reduce your chances of being wrong. It involves writing from the heart, writing with passion, writing from a place of hope and confidence. And, writing from a set of principles that lead to a plan.

If you, the author, don't believe in it, nobody else will, either.

Ask yourself—why am I a writer?

Where am I on this journey? That question alone can lead you to the right story concept and the right elements that ensue from it. It really can.

I have read many unpublished manuscripts, and I have marveled at what some writers believe to be compelling stories. This is why I beat the drum of the Six Core Competencies, because each and every one of them needs to be executed at a professional level. *Concept* is no less and no more subject to that truth. A bland, less than compelling concept, one that is forced and contrived, even when it meets the criteria competently executed, will not result in a story that will enable you to find an agent or a publisher, unless—because not all successful stories are highly conceptual—you can find a way to empower the other core competencies toward exceptional excellence.

Trouble is, one writer/agent/editor/reader's *bland* is another's *Cold Mountain*. Which is why we never *really* know. The best you can do is to choose the right story for *yourself*, and for the right *reasons*. And then, execute the hell out of it.

There are very powerful and personal questions that reside at the heart of this issue.

Why are you writing this particular story?

Is it because you need a block of stone upon which to carve? Is it because you've been to a writing workshop and you now have all these tools and all this pent-up desire to write *something*? So you sit down and dream something up, something you believe you can whip into a solid story by applying those tools?

Will any story do, as long as you get to exercise your skills as a storyteller? Or is there a burning need deep within you to explore and express something specific?

Big difference. A career-defining difference.

PUTTING THE "HIGH" IN YOUR HIGH CONCEPT STORY IDEA

In the lexicon of writing we often encounter the term *high concept*. We are left to interpret and sometimes intuit the meaning, and in doing so we naturally land on stories such as *The Da Vinci Code*, *The Lovely Bones*, and even *Avatar*. Which leaves character-driven stories to the realm of low concept, which is not a term we hear in that same lexicon.

Before one judges a story idea as *high* vs. *low* concept, one must consider the *genre*. Because what's high in one genre is vanilla milquetoast white-bread generic in another.

An analogy might help make this point. Let's go to golf, and let's use Tiger Woods to make this point clear.

Golf is a fairly nonathletic game. It's more like shooting pool or darts than, say, wrestling or rugby. Just a notch above croquette and lawn darts on the athleticism scale. If you've seen the potbellies and less than muscular arms on some of the leading players, you realize you haven't seen such girth in professional sports since Mickey Lolich pitched for the Detroit Tigers. Within this rather nonathletic game of golf, there is really only one obvious *athlete* in the bunch—Tiger Woods.

Look closely at the pictures. The guy is the real deal in a physical, athletic sense.

So, among golfers, Tiger Woods is *high concept*. Same game, different level of athleticism. He stands out, he gets attention, and he outperforms his peers. But ... if Tiger Woods walked onto a tennis court or a basketball court, or a baseball field or football field or rugby field, he wouldn't stand out. Not in the least. He wouldn't be high concept at all, even if his skills were deemed sufficient (just like other golfers with beer bellies the size of throw pillows bring sufficient skills, if not quite athleticism, to their sport).

Which is to say, what is *high* concept in a cozy mystery, a police procedural or a love story *isn't* high concept, by comparison, in a thriller or science fiction epic. The same can be said for writing in shorter forms—the elevation of the concept depends on the ultimate venue. What's high concept in *Rolling Stone* may not make the cut at *The Washington Post*.

And this truth sets you free.

Because within your chosen genre, you need only define *high* concept in context to the expectations of *your* game, rather than what is more obviously considered to be high concept elsewhere.

In the movie *(500) Days of Summer*, a love story, the concept could be described on one level as really nothing more than *boy meets girl, boy falls for girl, girl rejects boy*. Not *high* concept at all, if that's all you took from it. But see it again. Look deeper. That story is a romance. And within the romance genre, including romantic comedies, what constitutes high concept is *different* than what defines high concept in a spy thriller, or many other genres. (*500) Days* does, in fact, deliver a high concept story idea because it tells the story in a nonlinear fashion and inserts surreal and comic elements in ways that the average romance or even romantic comedy does not.

Same with the novel *The Lovely Bones*. A character-driven murder mystery. And yet, as with the previous example, the writer's choice of voice, point of view, and perspective was conceptual rather than predictable, and both choices elevated those works to critical and commercial success. Once again the delivery strategy is the compelling concept, coupled with a narrative voice that elevates the audience experience to an unexpectedly delightful level. That alone makes it *high* concept.

In a thriller, two people falling in love is not high concept, it's a subplot. In this crowded genre you have a different standard where concept is concerned. It is the originality, the inherent suspense and narrative edge—an inherent fear, fascination, or curiosity—of the evolved idea that makes it compelling.

High concept is not character focused or character driven. Rather, it suggests a dramatic scenario or device—be it clever, unexpected, unseen, terrifying, or just plain brilliant—that becomes the landscape upon which characters will reveal themselves.

YOU ALWAYS HAVE THE POWER TO ELEVATE YOUR CONCEPT

A cozy mystery *can* be high concept, as can a romance. It's just that the high concept bar isn't all that high in these genres in comparison to others. Just add something fresh and unexpected at the conceptual level, something an agent will say she's never seen before, something that brands your story as bigger and different than the crowd. Your success here hinges more on the juice of your plot exposition and the appeal of your hero than it does on the height of your concept.

Established genre authors don't need high concept; their name alone sells their books. But to stand out among a pile of manuscripts that, like yours, are well written and well populated with compelling characters, you need a genre-appropriate concept that glows in the dark.

The wattage of that bulb is yours to decide. Let genre be your guide, and then elevate your imagination, and your concept, to a higher place.

AN EXERCISE

- Write down the initial idea for your story.

- Evaluate that idea as a concept. Is it one? If not, apply the criteria for a great concept and elevate your idea toward the realm of a compelling concept.

- Now evaluate your concept again relative to the criteria of originality. Is it original and fresh? Or does it at least bring a new perspective or spin to a familiar story line? Does it set the stage for a dramatic story to unfold? Is it compelling?

- If your concept is precisely what you want yet isn't what anyone would call original or compelling, what is your plan for the other core competencies that will compensate for it and elevate your story to a level that is original and compelling?

- If you haven't done it yet, write your concept in the form of a "what if?" question.

- Does that question compel an answer? Is there a story there?

- Is there a higher level of conceptual "what if?" question waiting to be asked?

- Write as many follow-up "what if?" questions as you can that are inspired by either your highest level "what if?" question, or your original one.

- If you've already outlined or written your story, write a "what if?" question for each major story point, including the inciting incident.

- Does your concept stand the test of time? Are you as excited about it a week after creating it as you were when you first solidified it in your mind?

- If you can't come up with a succinct "what if?" question that defines your concept, consider that your story is not yet ready to write. It may be too complex, too vague and undefined, or at the other end of the spectrum, it may be lacking in dramatic potential.

PART THREE

THE SECOND CORE COMPETENCY—
CHARACTER

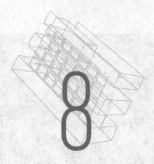

8

THE FUNDAMENTAL ESSENCE
OF CHARACTER

There's very little about writing that's more common, boringly predomi-
nant, and patently *obvious* than the vast oeuvre of advice on characterization. Our characters need to be rich, deep, and compelling, and miles
distanced from stereotype. Okay, we *get* that.

Still, *character* stumps and challenges us.

Some writing gurus beat the character drum to the exclusion of all else.
They'll tell you that story *is* character. That plot is nothing more than giving
your characters something to do. That theme is nothing more than allowing
your readers to observe your characters dealing with the consequences of
their decisions, thus mirroring and commenting on reality itself.

Maybe. Then again, saying that character *is* story is insufficient enough
to be labeled as inaccurate and incomplete. Character is certainly an essential *element* of a story—in fact, it's one of the Six Core Competencies of
successful storytelling—but when you are trying to wrap your head around
the entire requisite skill set of storytelling, it is not the whole enchilada.

THE SEVEN KEY CHARACTERIZATION VARIABLES

Think of these as realms, as areas of potential character illumination. Here
they are, in no particular order:

- **Surface affectations and personality**—What the world sees and
  perceives about a character, including quirks, ticks, habits, and
  visual presentation.

- **Backstory**—All that happened in the character's life before the story begins that conspires to make him who he is now.
- **Character arc**—How the character learns lessons and grows (changes) over the course of the story, how she evolves and conquers her most confounding issues.
- **Inner demons and conflicts**—The nature of the issues that hold a character back and define his outlook, beliefs, decisions, and actions. Fear of meeting new people, for example, is a demon that definitely compromises one's life experience.
- **Worldview**—An adopted belief system and moral compass; the manifested *outcome* of backstory and inner demons.
- **Goals and motivations**—What drives a character's decisions and actions, and the belief that the benefits of those decisions and actions outweigh any costs or compromises.
- **Decisions, actions, and behaviors**—The ultimate decisions and actions that are the sum of all of the above.

Everything about your characters depends on this final variable, and the degree to which the character's decisions, actions, and behaviors have meaning and impact depends on how well you've manipulated the first six variables before, during, and after the moment of decision or action.

That list alone is an invaluable tool for any writer. There are abundant workshops and books covering each of the variables, but fewer are the models and approaches that integrate and break them down, or even identify them *all*.

People aren't that simple. Everything we think, say, and do is a product of the sum of these factors. If you want your story to be driven by deep, rich, and compelling characters, you need to blend these elements into the narrative.

THE ESSENCE OF STORY

Try to define the *essence of a story* in one word. Many words are required to describe it well, but try to think of the single most powerful, critical word if you could choose only one.

Did you choose the word *character*? Many do. Those who don't often choose the word *plot*. Plot and character. That just about says it. Some claim that character *is* plot and plot *is* character, which, if you look at it closely, becomes an example of grad school psychobabble. But neither is the one word that will define it best, and thus empower you the most. Neither defines the one thing that separates a *story* from something that isn't a story.

There is one word that says it better.

That word is *conflict*. Something that opposes the goal you've given to your protagonist. Without that opposition, the story becomes more like a diary, there is no sense of dramatic tension, and ultimately, no reason for the reader to make an emotional investment. Without conflict, the character is not required to summon courage or to conquer his own demons. Without conflict life is easy, and that's not the stuff of a compelling story. Conflict is therefore necessary in terms of character and theme, as well as plot—it defines plot—and on several levels.

It's important to understand how conflict imparts context to your story, because you can focus on character and plot and still not have really nailed the one thing that makes a story a story.

Character is one of the four essential story elements (among the Six Core Competencies), and the absence of any one of them renders a story incomplete and ineffective. No concept, no theme, no structure—even with a great character—no story.

Character *is* important. Critically so. Only by fusing a deep, foundational understanding of character with your equally deep grasp of the other five requisite core competencies—concept, theme, structure, scene execution, and writing voice—will you put yourself in a position to publish your work.

The key word here is *fuse*. As in, *integrate*. Character is the catalyst that empowers *everything* else in your story. Characters experience theme. Characters act out along a linear structure. Characters live out the plot and the antagonistic forces that make plot possible.

WHAT'S LACKING IN THE CONVENTIONAL WISDOM OF CHARACTER

In the March 2009 issue of *The Writer*, the lead article was entitled, "Breathe Life Into Your Characters." At this point you may be saying, sure, sounds great, who wouldn't want that? You may also be saying, as I did, "Been there, read that."

The Six Core Competencies model will help you recognize most of what this and other how-to articles about characterization pass off as core information but is actually little more than frosting. Because you can breathe life into something that is still boring, illogical, less than compelling, and less than heroic ... those characters are just lively while they're at it.

A great character in a lousy story doesn't cut it. You need more than *lively* characters. You need depth and substance. You need relevance, a basic connection to the reader that is as real as it is compelling and entertaining. You need bona fide heroes, arch villains, complex players on an intricate dramatic stage.

Not to mention, you need to give them something interesting to *do*—a great story landscape upon which they can strut their stuff. One that challenges their inner demons, paves a rocky path toward their goal, and mirrors reality in a way that touches readers.

That particular article, like many of that ilk, goes on to explain things like giving the characters a life of their own (whatever *that* means) ... showing your character's *feelings* (as opposed to what?) ... giving them meaningful goals (without which there is no story, so thanks for this little gem of obviousness) ... imbuing them with idiosyncrasies and habits (this is a huge pitfall if that's *all* you do) ... complicate them with inconsistencies (Humanity 101, which can quickly lead to stereotyping) ... thinking up some cool names (please ... it actually *said* that) and allowing them to have relationships with others (one word: *duh*).

Wow.

You deserve better. You deserve a foundational understanding of character and a set of tools, criteria, and checklists that will help you develop rich and compelling characters.

THE CONTEXT OF CHARACTER

Ever notice that when actors talk about their work, they rarely mention the *plot* of the stories that frame their roles? And the only *conflict* they seem to care about is that which haunts their character's psyche? Even when the interviewer's question is *about* the story at hand, they much prefer to focus on the challenge of portraying their *character*—who that fictional person is on the inside, how they relate to the character personally, getting to know that fictional person, lending the character depth and complexity and shading and nuance. They talk about the need to *understand* and invest themselves in that character, about doing research and inhabiting their world, all before they can don the wardrobe and apply that make-up identity for an audience.

Which can all come off as a bit hilarious when the fictional character in question is the hero in a comic-book-to-high-budget-Hollywood-blockbuster. When Heath Ledger portrayed the Joker in *The Dark Knight*, you'd think it was Sir Laurence Olivier breathing nuanced life into Hamlet.

Actors talk almost exclusively about character because character is their craft, their bread and butter. They leave the storytelling to the writer and the director, and if you could hear *those folks* talk about it, the soundtrack would be quite different. You'd hear them talk about the *exposition* of a story—probably without using that word—in context to both character and theme. In other words, plot and conflict.

Why? Because ...

CHARACTER IS NOT STORY

More than one writing guru and established writer has described the essence of storytelling as character-focused, just like those actors we see being interviewed on *Entertainment Tonight*. But that's like saying the essence of baseball is pitching, the essence of music is singing, the essence of medicine is diagnosis, and the essence of cooking is salt and pepper. It's not wrong, it's just not *right enough*. Because there is so much more to consider.

Successful storytelling depends on the blending of four very different yet connected elements, executed through two primary skill sets that are even more connected—again, the Six Core Competencies. Character is one of those four elements, but it is not by any means the whole ballgame.

Character does not exist in a vacuum. It must be developed and put on display in context to and in relationship with the other core competencies. Realizing that becomes empowering for writers seeking to wrap their head around the entire writing enchilada. When viewed in this subordinated context, character becomes a powerful storytelling *tool*.

THE MISSION OF CHARACTER

Character is too often framed as a standard or a goal, rather than broken down into component parts, which are then organized and made available as a developmental resource for writers. Since high school we have been told we must populate our stories with compelling, well-rounded characters. A character that is *likable*. Then, in the name of teaching us how to do that, we are shown film clips and pointed toward books featuring characters that exemplify such standards.

In effect, the call to action becomes as simplistic as … just do *that*. Write your characters *that* way. Make them mysterious, deep, conflicted, tormented, duplicitous, even downright Machiavellian. Give them backstories and weaknesses and vulnerabilities and agendas. Spice them up with personalities and quirks. All good advice. All spot-on appropriate and valid. But this is like a baseball coach showing a video of Nolan Ryan in his prime and telling his pitchers to *just do what he does*.

So the real question about character development isn't *what*, but *how*. How do we imbue a character with all those qualities of depth and complexity?

If the baseball coach is asked that parallel question after watching Ryan throw another no-hitter, and if his answer is "practice, practice, practice" … well, that's just not good enough. Nor is the same advice good enough for writers.

It's not wrong, it's just not sufficiently empowering. Unfortunately, when it comes to character development, that's pretty much what we hear. We get the list of target qualities, we are shown examples, and we are told to practice.

A better approach is to define and categorize the *components* of character so that each aspect of creation can be examined and approached separately.

GOING DEEP

One of the goals is to avoid characters that are stereotypical, archetypical, too familiar, shallow, or otherwise less than compelling. If we accept that a character is the sum of his choices and behaviors, defined by his past and compelled by his motivations and goals, we understand that no single thing—a trait, a memory, a dream—defines the big, multidimensional picture of a character. Rather, a richly drawn character is the sum of many variables.

Think of the separate variables that comprise a fully rounded character as dials on the character-development machine. Each goes from 1 to 10. With seven knobs on the control panel—the seven realms of characterization introduced earlier—there are no less than ten million totally unique settings for any character you can dream up.

And that's just an analogous example. Fact is, each of those dials has an infinite number of available settings, ranging from dead or comatose to divine perfection and ensuing cultural immortality.

If we view the component parts of character as variables, we can then gauge the level of weight and freshness we should apply—the settings on those dials—to the folks who populate our stories, and in context to the nature of the story we are writing.

The good news is that there aren't all that many realms to choose from. As mentioned earlier, there are seven major categories of character possibility, though you can break them down into any number of subgroups and combine them in any number of ways. Virtually anything and everything you can bring to a character can be assigned to one of these seven categories. And yet the categories overlap. When combined with the various levels and options within each of these building block characters, the result is a list of options that numbers in the tens of millions.

With so many available choices, no two characters should ever be alike. Just like people in real life—which are also easily assigned to categories, within which awaits an unfathomable wealth of twists and turns—are as unique as snowflakes.

Your job as a writer is to make it snow.

THE THREE DIMENSIONS
OF CHARACTER

Somewhere along the writing road you've surely heard a character described as *one-dimensional*. Maybe in a review, maybe from someone who's just seen a movie or finished reading a novel. Or worse, maybe from an agent to whom you've submitted your work.

The implication here is, of course, that there are other dimensions to explore as you develop your characters. But what are they? Why don't we ever hear characters described as *two*-dimensional? What's that extra dimension about, anyhow? What does it even *mean*? And why are the only *obvious* three-dimensional characters out there lately appearing on a movie screen or marching in a Disneyland parade?

The term *one-dimensional* in relation to fictional characters means flat, stereotypical, and predictable, a character with all the depth and complexity of a walk-on from an episode of *Seinfeld*. Or, your sister's ex-husband … that one's your call.

THE DEEPER DIMENSIONS OF CHARACTER

Given the implication that we should strive to write *multidimensional* characters, especially heroes and villains, it behooves us to understand what those other dimensions are all about.

As with story structure, you could just set out to intuitively slap together a little intuitive character depth—in effect, the *pantsing* approach (as in, *seat of the pants*) to character development. Maybe you get it right, maybe you don't. And if you do, maybe it's a coincidence, or maybe your intuition is keenly developed to the point where you and Stephen King don't need any story planning, it all emerges from your head ... perfectly.

Good luck with that.

Such is the risk of pantsing in *any* area of story development. If you don't know what you're shooting for, if you just make stuff up as you go without much if any aforethought, it probably won't work. In fact, unless you're at King's level, it definitely won't work. At least until you write another draft. And another one after that.

And if *that* happens, you actually are engaging in a form of story planning after all. The kind that takes months or even years, and doesn't come with standards, milestones, and comparative benchmarks that let you know when you're done.

Good luck with that, too.

Or you could, by design, imbue your characters with three very separate and compelling layers—*dimensions*, in this context—that are carefully crafted to bring your story alive with resonant emotional depth.

Real life unfolds in 3-D.

So should the people who populate your stories.

These three-dimensional realms stand alone as unique, yet they always overlap. Human beings are the sum of all three of the dimensions described here. What the world sees, even if it's a smoke screen for dark and deeply hidden secrets, is an amalgamation of their best and worst essences. Sometimes it's those dark and deeply hidden secrets that make your characters especially compelling. The reasons for the need to hide those secrets become part of the puzzle your story must unravel.

In the previous chapter we introduced seven primary categories, or realms, of character development variables. Be clear, though, these are not dimension-specific. In other words, all seven can exist within, or at least impact, *each* of the three dimensions of character.

Which, in effect, turns those seven realms into twenty-one distinct possibilities, each with an infinite degree of possible depth and variation.

Think of those seven realms as spices.

Then think of the three dimensions of character as courses in a meal. A salad has certain spices, the appetizer has certain spices, the soup has certain spices ... and we aren't even up to the main course yet. Some of those spices can be identical, while others are specific to the dish into which they are sprinkled.

Character analysis invites *over*-thinking it all. So let's keep it simple. As a writer you should always be thinking about one of two things relative to your characters—the variables you apply, and a sense of clarity about which of the dimensions those variables exemplify.

It is the relationship between these two things that becomes the writer's playground.

Let's look at an example to see how a single variable—let's choose worldview—can manifest from with each of the three dimensions. Someone might take on the persona of a highly religious person to an extent this defines him for others (a first-dimension manifestation). That choice, that mask, might stem from the fact that this person is married to a sincerely and deeply committed religious person (a second-dimension source of this facet of character) in order to make the marriage work. But in private, perhaps when traveling on business, he sleeps around with whomever is available (a third-dimension issue stemming from the choices he makes when it could go either way) in direct contrast to how he is perceived.

To better wrap your head around this concept, let's look closer at the three dimensions and see how they can reside within a single character simultaneously. In fact, to make your characters deep, complex, and compelling, they should do that.

THE FIRST DIMENSION OF CHARACTER— SURFACE TRAITS, QUIRKS, AND HABITS

Think of this as the *exterior* landscape of your characters. Their personality. What the world sees and assigns meaning to. Or not. Sometimes the meaning assigned by an observer of these surface quirks is quite contrary to the character's intention. Imagine a forty-eight-year-old out-of-shape guy wearing a Tapout ball cap ... sideways. It says a lot. And what it says is probably not what the poor wannabe thinks it says.

This first dimension shows the way a character looks and acts ... her hair, her make-up, the kind of car she drives, her wardrobe preferences, where she hangs out, her musical tastes, her taste in food, certain attitudes and prejudices, and so forth. It is largely a combination of two things: how she sees herself, and how she desires to be seen. Sometimes those factors contradict each other, which is, in itself, a product of the second dimension, which we'll get to in a moment.

For example, someone going out of his way to make sure everybody notices he is a wine snob is a first-dimension moment of characterization. Whether it's valid or not isn't the issue. What is the issue, in terms of pegging which of the three dimensions we're seeing in play, is what the character strives to wear as a mask, an outward identity. Something everybody does to some degree, which means it isn't always bad or deceitful, just human.

Just to be clear, let's quickly and temporarily jump ahead to the other dimensions of character to establish contrast between them. What is the difference between these surface choices (the first dimension) and those other two realms?

- In the *first* dimension of character (which includes the list above), what you show the reader about your character simply *exists*. You leave it to the reader to assign meaning. If a character chooses to drive a fifteen-year-old Corvette with torn leather seats, the reader may or may not assign meaning to this choice. Because it may or may not mean anything at all. And the second you do show the reader what's behind these first-dimension tidbits of characterization, you've just crossed over into the second dimension.

- In the *second* dimension of character, the reader learns the *reason* for choices and behaviors that define outward perception, or the effort to control it, which may or may not align with any meaning the reader has assigned to it on her own. Here in the second dimension, the writer strives to expose the backstory, agenda, and meaning behind those first-dimension issues of characterization. In our example, the Corvette may have been a gift from the character's father, and he can't part with it for sentimental reasons. Which, in turn, may or may not indicate a can of worms where his paternal relationship is concerned. Then again, it may be the effort of a schoolboy outcast who always wanted to be cool, still believing that driving a Corvette, even an old beater, labels him as such. His choice is driven straight out of his backstory, and thus we've just deepened a first-dimension morsel of character (the Corvette) with a second-dimension layer.

- **In the *third* dimension** of character, all of the choices made at the first-dimension level become subordinated to more important choices and behaviors made when greater weight and consequences are at stake. If the character has to wreck his Corvette in order to avoid hitting a dog, for example, in spite of what it means to him, this is a third-dimension variable because it indicates the heart and soul, if not the moral compass, of the character. First-dimension and second-dimension indicators, which tempt us to assign meaning, don't always align with third-dimension choices. Also, third-dimension choices in that latter part of a story become the primary means of demonstrating character growth, known as *character arc*. In the previous example about the cheating spouse, the moment adultery occurs is a choice that defines his deepest, truest character, which is precisely what the third dimension delivers to the reader. In this example, the reader sees this guy from three perspectives, each of them one of the three dimensions of character.

What you see may or may not be what you get.

Back at the first dimension of character, surface choices (quirks, tics, and mannerisms) aren't always valid indicators of meaning, or of intention, and therefore of *true* character. It may all just be a smoke screen, a cover up, a mask or a comfort zone. Or it could even be a cultural thing—not all people with tattoos are hip, tough, or troubled, they may simply like the design—but without another reader-visible dimension to explain such choices, the reader will never know. If you, the writer, don't show the reader a deeper dimension, you leave it to the reader to assign meaning and attach value. And because how the reader feels about your character is perhaps the most powerful variable in writing a story, you shouldn't leave that outcome to chance.

You are surrounded by first-dimension character choices each and every time you go out in public. You make them yourself simply by virtue of selecting how you dress that day. Writers who pause to notice the first-dimension realm of the real world, and who strive to analyze whether the intended message matches the actual perception, or if there is even any intended meaning at all, are engaging in a form of practice and research that will serve them well in their storytelling.

Which is to say, even when we stop typing and leave the house, we remain writers.

How deep do we take this?

Peripheral characters in our stories are usually one-dimensional, as they should be. In fact, it's a mistake to delve too deeply into peripheral characters merely for the sake of adding depth. You can always tell a new writer who has just emerged from a character workshop by the depth with which she has tried to characterize the pizza delivery guy.

Not good. Focus on developing your hero and villain and any other major players, and let the bit players come and go. We really don't need to know what it was about the pizza delivery guy's childhood that made him take up food service as a career.

That said, even your peripheral characters, if given stereotypical quirks and tics, come off as clichés. The inherent opportunity when writing a peripheral walk-on character is to make her interesting at a glance, something other than a cliché, in the few moments the reader has with her. Or, if a cliché fits the moment, to make that choice instead. The best use of a peripheral character is to show the reader how a more important character relates to her or perceives her first-dimension efforts to brand herself.

If , for example, the pizza guy is wearing a Yankees cap while living in Boston, this may indicate suicidal or at least antisocial tendencies. Just showing us the hat is enough. But you can do more with this, if it fits. If your hero notices, or even comments on the hat, you may be seizing the opportunity to deliver another morsel of characterization for that major player, thanks to the walk-on's first-dimension quirk.

Rule of thumb: Never extend the time a peripheral role player occupies in a story for the sake of deepening *his* character. Use a natural and appropriate amount of time to give him a quick and interesting edge. Such characters serve a purpose relative to *plot* exposition and, in some cases, contributing to the characterization of a major player. Other than that, if you have a walk-on, allow him to walk off quietly.

As for your primary heroes and villains, you need to go deeper. Even then, one of the greatest risks in crafting a great character is to go *too* deep for reasons that don't enhance the story or the reading experience. In other words, depth for the sake of depth is not a good thing.

No matter what your high school creative writing teacher told you.

Quirkiness for the sake of quirkiness is a fool's game.

The grouchy lieutenant in the local police precinct who never smiles and is always spilling coffee on his cheap shirt? That's a one-dimensional character. The slimy politician preaching values on the evening news before stopping by a brothel on his way home? That's a one-dimensional character. The hooker he spends time with, the one with a proverbial heart of gold? One-dimensional.

At least until there is something more to comprehend about the reasons *why* these characters are as they are and how those variables conspire to either hide their true nature or otherwise fuel their actions and decisions.

Why? Because the reader doesn't know what, if anything, is behind those behaviors, or those quirks. If the character is a hero or a villain, we *need* to know.

The moment a major character acts like one of those examples above, you are obliged to take the reader into the second dimension to bridge the gap between their first- and third-dimension decisions. This is the essence of going deep when it comes to characterization.

This issue is often a great trap of newer writers, who infuse their characters with all manner of quirks and kinks and little tics designed to make them cool, weird, or compelling. But if those quirks and kinks are *all* you offer the reader in the hope that the reader will fill in all the blanks, chances are you've created a one-dimensional character.

And if the quirks are *too* quirky, it's actually *worse* than a cliché.

A recent movie preview showed a series of quick cuts that included a young man and his romantic interest on a dinner date. The girl ordered dessert *before* the meal, claiming, "That's just what I do." Unless the writer shows us why, and unless the reason makes sense or somehow contributes to the actual story, this becomes a classic example of quirkiness for the sake of quirkiness, which usually facilitates a reviewer verdict of shallow clunkiness. Then again, if that quirk is but a facet of a more complex set of choices, perhaps it can be justified as useful.

In any case, avoid such gratuitous details of characterization at all costs. Which means, make them ungratuitious and meaningful.

In Tony Scott's movie *Top Gun*, the hero, Maverick, has a penchant for bucking authority. For buzzing the aircraft carrier control tower. For making bad decisions, including chasing down the hot flight instructor for after-hours karaoke.

Until we know why these choices are in evidence, and what will become of them, they remain first-dimension issues of character.

THE SECOND DIMENSION OF CHARACTER— BACKSTORY AND INNER DEMONS

If the first dimension is what you *see*, is the second dimension what you *get*?

Not yet. The second dimension explains *why* you see what you see in the first dimension. What you *get*, in context to this model, is still precisely what the character *wants* you to get, and little else.

Only in the third dimension do we actually see through the first-dimension façade and trappings and the second-dimension excuses to truly understand a character ... or, by the end of the story, *what you get*.

Example: You create a character who has just been hired for a new job. So he puts on the face of the ideal applicant, smiling, glad-handing, sharp dresser, team player, can-do attitude. All first-dimension stuff.

What's the second dimension in this example? He's doing all this because he's been fired four times. For a bad attitude, being a lousy teammate, acting with dishonesty ... all of it borne of the fact that he has authority issues stemming from his childhood.

Now comes the complex interface between that second-dimension explanation and the first-dimension quirks. Just because someone has childhood issues, even issues that drive him to bad choices and behaviors, and thus, a contrived façade to cover them up, doesn't necessarily mean that this is who he is at the heart of his character. Then again, it might.

With only these two dimensions in evidence, you either assign meaning to the first (he's a really nice, cool guy) or to the second (he's actually an unemployable schmuck who's faking it). When it counts, which guy will show up?

We don't really know until a third dimension of character emerges. In other words, his true character emerges, eventually, through his choices when there is something at stake.

Glimpse the inner landscape of the human experience.

In the second-dimension realm we get a glimpse, maybe even a clear look, at the *inner* landscape of a character. Regardless of how you've dressed him up with first-dimension exterior personality.

Where the character came from, the scars and memories and dashed dreams that have left him with resentments, fears, habits, weaknesses, and inclinations that connect to why he is as he appears to be. These are all second-dimension forces that prompt and motivate and explain first-dimension choices of identity, even when those quirks are a complete smoke screen.

The painfully shy person who is actually a hoot once you get to know her? That's a can of first- and second-dimension worms engaged in a complex dance of human suffering, fear, and psychological scars. Cast into the web of a plot, the dance takes on a rhythm and an escalating pace until the character can no longer hide who she really is, or perhaps forces her to choose who she will become.

Such are the dynamics of effective storytelling.

Glimpsing an inner landscape allows the reader to *understand*, which is the key to eliciting *empathy*. Empathy is the great empowerer of stories—the more empathy the reader *feels*, the more he will invest himself in the reading experience. And when that happens, the story can't help but be successful. It's precisely how some stories with seemingly unspectacular plots end up being legendary success stories.

In *Top Gun*, we don't like Maverick when he's putting his teammates in danger while showing off from the cockpit of an F-14. He's a hotshot, a prima donna. He's wall-to-wall attitude, but it's all just compensation for deeper issues that allow us to understand and empathize, and eventually root for him.

When we finally get a glimpse of what's behind all that attitude—his father's military failure and his own need to get out from under that shadow—not only do we better understand his humanity, we may *feel* it in a way that hits close to home. Suddenly he's viewed differently, even if you still don't like him. Because chances are you now *empathize* with him. You cut him some slack.

And maybe, just maybe, you're hooked, because you know he's going to have to overcome his weaknesses in order to reach his goals, and perhaps save the day.

Think about the books you love and the characters that star in them. The reason you love these stories has as much or more to do with the character than the plot, and the reason *that's* true is because you *feel* for the character, you *get* him, you empathize, you invest yourself *emotionally* in the reading experience. But without the plot, the character has no stage upon which to show the reader both the character's surface and true self. The combination of the two core competencies defines the reader's experience.

Back to those books you love. You rooted. You cried. You chewed your nails. You loved. You felt loss and you shared joy. You experienced fear and hope. You felt the consequences of this character's success and redemption.

You *cared*. Because you related to, and empathized with, the hero.

The most fertile ground for the cultivation of this reader response is the *inner* landscape of your primary characters. The very things that have, over time, come together to cause the character to make those surface first-dimension choices, like them or not.

Quirks or no quirks, the second dimension is the real stuff of storytelling, because it sows the seeds of reader empathy.

But you're not done yet. There's a third dimension you must add to bring it all home. Because even the best and most understood of intentions do not a hero or villain make.

Decisions, actions, and behaviors *do*.

THE THIRD DIMENSION OF CHARACTER— ACTION, BEHAVIOR, AND WORLDVIEW

Who that person *really* is, at his core, is the stuff that resides at the heart of the third dimension of character. In a pinch, when it counts, when there are consequences, which character traits will emerge? The first-dimension phony? The scarred second-dimension loser? Or someone else?

If it's someone else, as demonstrated by a third dimension of character, that's called *character arc*—the hero conquers inner demons to show himself as someone else, someone who has conquered inner demons to make better, even courageous decisions. Or perhaps he is simply showing us his *true self* when all the trappings of his façade and the drama of his past have been cast aside. That someone else is actually his *true* character.

Or not. Maybe he simply makes better choices in the context of your story as a means of salvation, or maybe he was just having a good day. He might even revert to his old second-dimension-driven first-dimension ways once he's saved the day, like a drug dealer called upon to save a child from his murderous peers. He's a hero in context to that challenge, to that defining moment, yet remains a drug dealer at heart, albeit one with some semblance of a social conscience.

In other words, a deeply drawn character, a complex character, a three-dimensional character.

There are few rules in the process of character development. But there are tools, options, and choices, which are defined and empowered by an understanding of these three dimensions of character.

A hero takes a stand, accepts risk, makes decisions, boldly (or not) dives in and executes. Even if he has issues. Even if on the outside he seems unlikable, or unlikely to emerge as a legitimate hero. He does it. He overcomes. He conquers fear. He defeats his inner demons and rises above himself and his exterior obstacles to do what must be done. And when he does, he is demonstrating *third*-dimension character depth.

Villains have feelings, too.

A villain, on the other hand, rationalizes behavior and is insensitive to, or refuses to accept responsibility for, the associated costs and violations of accepted social standards. Or at least those that inconvenience him. Even if he does have a sense of right and wrong—itself a nice touch of complexity in a hero—he makes selfish and insensitive choices when there are stakes on the line, sometimes kidding himself (and believing it) that losses and darkness are acceptable in lieu of a greater good. Which, in most cases for a villain, in his mind pertains to his wealth, status, or earthly pleasures.

Great villains have complex second-dimension character issues that are the raw material for their moral compass and worldview. Within their personal psychology these issues license them, if not motivate them, to make the decisions that they do. Without a glimpse of that second dimension, we are left with little more than a moustache-twirling comic book bad guy.

In the novels of Dennis Lehane, the line between good guys and bad guys is often vague or a moving target. But on either side of the moral fence, we always get a clear glimpse of a backstory that lends clarity and empathy in context to the resulting set of character motivators. Lehane was once a social worker, and while we don't really know if his own life experience included the childhood darkness that permeates almost all of his work, it perhaps explains his ability to take the reader deep into the minds of his characters to render them some combination of real, complex, and compelling.

True character, or the person *behind* the mask—in this sense defined as moral substance, or lack thereof—while perhaps explained through backstory, is not *defined* by backstory or inner demons, extreme as they may be, until the character decides or does something. Those decisions and actions expose the third-dimension character that, in turn, demonstrates both true inner character and character arc.

Writers almost always draw on their own lives when crafting their characters. At some point in your life you may have been angry enough to kill someone, or at least punch someone's lights out. But you didn't. Why? Because of your *character*. That decision defines you.

Now, imagine that you had yielded to that impulse. Same backstory, same inner turmoil and agenda, same inciting series of events, same emotions … but a different decision, leading to a much altered outcome. One with a different set of consequences, and thus, a different *story*. That decision would have defined you, too.

As you wrestle with these dimensional aspects of characterization, remember that the goal isn't always to demonstrate virtue, either for your heroes or your villains. Virtue is an option.

The three dimensions give you options, and options are the tools of character depth.

Here's a character example.

Consider former president Bill Clinton. Who was this guy, and what was his *true* character?

This example quickly illustrates the different facets of *character*, how in one area you can be a sterling example of achievement and virtue, and in another, not so much.

Was Bill Clinton brilliant? Off the charts. Was he handsome and charismatic? No argument there. Did he care deeply about his country? Absolutely. Was he a good friend, teammate, and husband? We're not so sure, based on a few of his demonstrated third-dimension character choices.

His first-dimension traits screamed of class, intelligence, style, and a strong but charming personality.

His second-dimension character remains challenging, because we still don't know much about his psychology and the background that shaped it, other than he is clearly hesitant to accept responsibility for all of his actions until nailed to the wall, and that he has trouble remaining in the background while his wife's career ascends. In real life such mysteries often remain unsolved, but in our fiction we benefit from a deeper glimpse at the backstories and inner demons that result in both first- and third-dimension characterization.

Judge the man as you may, clearly his third-dimension character ended up on the stage of public scrutiny. It says volumes about who he is, what his priorities are, and how he responds under pressure with great stakes, including his reputation, at risk.

Note that none of that has anything to do with the first-dimension issues of how he wears his hair and cracks wise comments with an endearing southern drawl. Nor do the second-dimension excuses come to bear on the aftermath, just as someone who doesn't know the law escapes prosecution because of a second-dimension excuse.

It's the third dimension that ultimately defines character, for better or worse. Everything else is just a foreshadowing, a smoke screen, or an explanation.

THE ART OF INTEGRATING THE
THREE DIMENSIONS OF CHARACTER

While it is clear that the first two dimensions may or may not dictate the third, that doesn't render them frivolous. In fact, they are key to the crafting of *layered* characters. Real life is a showcase for all three dimensions of characterization, so our stories should do no less.

These three dimensions are your tools as an author, to use layer by layer to create the most compelling, complex, frightening, endearing, and empathetic character you can. Too many writers settle for the first dimension only. Even more writers focus on the second dimension to the exclusion of the third.

Even more fail to *integrate* these realms convincingly and compellingly.

That process of integration is the *art* of storytelling. And there's no manual for it beyond a grasp of these fundamental principles. Just as twenty pitchers show up in spring training with an equal grasp of the fundamental skills and technique, only five get a spot in the starting rotation, and only one, if that, makes the all-star team.

Success in any artful pursuit remains, to some degree, an unquantifiable or even definable mystery.

But be clear: Your work as a storyteller intending to sell your work is not done until your hero and your villain are fully fleshed out in *all three* realms.

Do that, and do it well—which means, the relationship between the three dimensions makes believable and compelling sense—and you'll never hear that criticism of *one-dimensional* or *shallow* leveled at your characters again.

10
CHARACTER UNMASKED

Sometimes the more you know about a person, the harder he or she is to like. Great first impression, but it's all veneer and bluster. In true John Edwards meets Jesse James fashion, we have only to look for the exposure of the true character—the *third* dimension of character—of some of our more promiscuous and smug politicians and celebrities to see how consequences collide with appearances.

Any character, politician or regular Joe, is the sum of their actions and decisions, as motivated and colored by their worldview and moral compass, and perhaps demonstrated or masked by their outward-facing first-dimension persona.

For example, consider a fellow who has been cheating on his wife off and on for decades. Nobody at work knows this. Everybody in a room full of friends *may* know about it—except, perhaps, his wife—but they don't talk about it. Which says something about *their* character if they know about it and pretend they don't.

About that wife—people may not only *like* her, but because of their secret knowledge about her philandering husband, they may also *empathize* with her. The only person in the room who doesn't realize *that* is the cheating bastard himself.

Then again, perhaps those people would also empathize with the husband if they truly knew what a nagging, judgmental shrew his wife really is behind the closed doors of their life together.

Let's say this guy is funny and often charming, the first one with an amusing story and an entertaining way to tell it. He's warm, he's glib, and he hides his agenda well. Doesn't want to ruffle feathers. His creed: Let's just have a good time, preferably with me getting all the attention, and get this evening over with without an incident that will embarrass me. If you're my friend, you've got my back.

He's also natty, well groomed, wears his hair with a touch of youthful edge, drives a luxury car. These are all first-dimension attempts to present and define himself to the world in a certain way, one that confuses the truth about his true character. What we see on the outside with this guy isn't by any means who he is at his core, when it counts.

At his core, despite the sunny personality, he's a selfish, cowardly shadow of a real man.

TRUE AND HIDDEN NATURES: TOOLS OF AN ENLIGHTENED WRITER

Appearances are one thing. But if you got this guy on a shrink's couch, he'd straighten your hair with dark stories of his past in an attempt to explain and justify his present weaknesses, choices, and preferences.

How he was raised and what transpired behind the closed doors of his childhood home may be part of his *explanation*, but they aren't his *true* character either. Not everybody is ruined by their past. Certainly, from a literary point of view, all that stuff plays a role in understanding how he thinks and what he does. But they are not *who* he is. Nor does it justify decisions that bring about negative consequences, both for himself and others. The past is never who we are, yet it is always a factor in who we have become.

His *true* character is the sum of his choices and behaviors, defined by the moral boundaries they cross, the risks they take, and the consequences they bring. Part of our true character is our ability to overcome that which compromises the character of others faced with similar second-dimension experiences.

A nice guy, sure. Funny, absolutely. Leading a tough life with a bitchy woman, perhaps. But his true *character*, his moral code ... it is what it is. And in this case, it's pretty low.

Such is the stuff of our stories at *all* of those levels. And sometimes, low character makes for good reading. At least it does in fiction. The characters in our stories have secrets to hide, tales to tell, excuses to offer, façades and illusions to maintain. All of them linking to and stemming from the *second* dimension of characterization.

But in fiction—unlike a cocktail party where the guy in the earlier example is sucking all the air out of the room—it's not that simple to turn away from the truth. Perhaps in the first part of a story you can fool a reader into believing someone is a certain way, but sooner or later you need to expose the character for who and what he really is, good or bad.

If you don't, your major characters will be one-dimensional. It takes more than a smokin' and jokin' good time protagonist to hook a reader.

So what does hook a reader in terms of character?

Certainly our heroes and villains, even our bit-players, should be complex and less than perfect. But in fiction, the art of crafting a compelling character isn't his *likability*. Not even close.

Whoever told you that *likability* is the critical variable was probably your high school creative writing teacher. *We need to like our protagonist* echoes through the early halls of the writing journey, often distorting what the evolved writer needs to really understand. But just look at some of the protagonists in movies. Unlikable heroes are as likely as not.

Maybe we like them, maybe we don't. That's not the issue. That's much too simplistic these days. Gordon Gekko in the film *Wall Street* is a fascinating and compelling character who isn't remotely likable. In Dennis Lehane's bestseller *Shutter Island*, the protagonist was anything but likable. He was, quite literally, a basket case. Same with Lehane's hero in the bestseller *Mystic River*.

But like them or not, when it comes to a protagonist, the reader *must* root for him. We must accompany him on his emotional journey. Even if he's a scumbag before and after the story. And we can't root for him until we *empathize* with him.

When it comes to *antagonists*, we must understand what it is they desire, and perhaps—in a well-crafted story—*why* they operate as they do to get it.

Remember, the essence of storytelling demands that we place our main characters on a path. A quest with something at stake, with something to do, to achieve, to learn, and to change. That goes for heroes, antiheroes, *and* villains, by the way. And, that we have placed obstacles—some external, some from within their deepest psyches—to make the journey challenging and interesting. Not so much for them, but for us—the readers.

Make the reader empathize with the character.

The trick, then, becomes the balancing of character imperfections that might otherwise put us off with the *empathy* we need to muster for our hero as she proceeds on her quest. If your hero battles alcohol addiction, for example, show us she has the strength and will to overcome it to the extent necessary to achieve her goal within the context of the story, and thus reap the positive consequences of her efforts.

Readers love a vulnerable hero who *recognizes* her own weaknesses and temptations, then conquers them in favor of a higher calling. She comes to realize that she's been on the wrong path, that she's sorry. And so she repents, she heeds a more noble calling, at least in the context and time frame of the story at hand. Or if not, at least she makes her final decisions from consciousness, rather than allowing her demons to drive her.

That, we can empathize with. We can get behind such a hero, root for her, even if it's temporary. Because we've all been there, we're all human.

Even if our characters aren't.

PLAYING BALL WITH YOUR CHARACTERS

In the first decade of the new millennium, the game of baseball experienced a series of character assassinations for players who had either been accused of using steroids or caught red-handed doing so. Some of those players continued to deny involvement, even in the face of significant evidence that included the testimony of those who shot the stuff into their butt. Others copped to it right away.

Two of the latter, Andy Pettitte and Jason Giambi (both New York Yankees at the time), actually emerged from the scandal as admittedly guilty, but also with the forgiveness of the public. And to some extent, precisely *because* of how they handled it, an even stronger fan base. Their readiness to accept responsibility says much about their true character, even more, perhaps, than the fact of their guilt, which was in the past. But because of their choices at the moment of truth—because of their *true character* as men—their careers continued, their endorsement deals survived, and the public still roots for them.

Why? Because we *empathize* with them while *respecting* their behavior in the face of this challenge. We respect their honesty and willingness to accept responsibility. To not insult us with dishonesty.

That's character. They are the good guys in this story.

The others? The ones who looked investigators in the eye and lied through their teeth, who refused to answer, who appeared before Senate committees wearing suits that could not accommodate their chemically augmented musculature? Their careers and Hall of Fame hopes spiraled into the toilet along with their respect.

That's character, too.

On both sides of this example you'll notice that the first-dimension icons of character remain rigidly in place. Mark McGwire likely still drives the same ridiculously expensive German car, still treats interviewers like dirt, and still deals with the fact that his bodybuilder brother served a prison sentence for dealing illegal steroids—all first- and second-dimension issues of character.

But the third-dimension choices—the ones demonstrating his true character—are the ones that define his future. Despite the fact he went back to baseball as a humble hitting coach, those decisions are what will keep him out of the Hall of Fame, which he would have otherwise entered on the first ballot. Those decisions define his public perception in a way that Andy Pettitte and Jason Giambi avoided, also because of *their* third-dimension character choices.

Barry Bonds couldn't stand it that McGwire set the home run record instead of him. So, he (allegedly) juiced up to the point where he could apply his already considerable gifts and strength to secure the record for himself, and to this day continues to deny any awareness that he was cheating.

Again, character on display. The real world is a clinic for writers who pay attention and break down what they see around them into first-, second-, and third-dimension issues of characterization.

In terms of storytelling, it is the writer's manipulation of *reader empathy*, rather than the nature of someone's faults and gold stars, that results in effective character dynamics, ones that infuse a story with stakes and vicarious emotion.

Which are absolutely *required* to get a story published.

11

THE HUMAN NATURE
OF CHARACTER

Most writers didn't major in human psychology in college. Which is a shame, really, because that's one of the most important aspects of writing great stories. Our heroes and villains need to behave according to the known principles of human behavior, which may not be something you instinctively understand.

One way to grasp the rudimentary basics of how and why people do what they do is to watch *Dr. Phil*. Really. Or *Oprah*. Or, if you'd rather read about it, grab the latest pop psychology bestseller and take some notes. Or better yet, attend one of those seminars on how to get your life together. Because each of these self-imposed experiences will show you why people—characters—think what they think and do the things they do. And if it's valid psychology in real life, it'll be valid psychology in your stories, too.

Read Thomas Harris's *The Silence of the Lambs* and pay attention to the psychology. Both Hannibal Lecter and "Buffalo Bill" are classic studies in human psychology of a very dark variety. Stephen King's stuff, too, is mastery of human psychology at its best and worst. It isn't as simple as having an alcoholic, disapproving father and a psychotic mother wielding a wire hanger or bringing a knife into the shower. The backstories that inform our worldview and burden us with *issues* are rarely straightforward or obvious, and yet they are almost always the genesis of your main character's story arc.

When you can wrap your head around basic human psychology, recognize that you are working with issues of second-dimension characterization in the process. What you need to understand about human behavior can be reduced into several real-world buckets, into which you can dump all the details you want.

People are driven by resentment.

Someone pisses you off. You may have forgiven him for it, but unless you've dealt with the issue, chances are you harbor some resentment toward him. Maybe for years.

We *resist* that which we *resent*. You will resist being completely kind and open with someone you resent, for whatever reason, at least until he does something to take away your resentment. Such as apologize. You will resist his ideas, his contributions, his very presence. This can manifest in subtle and insidious little ways, or it can come right out of your mouth. Or, it can never manifest at all, but it's there in your head, festering like a slow cancer.

We resent that the president of Goodwill Industries made $800,000 a year. (That's a true story, by the way.) So we resist giving our next garage full of junk to them, calling St. Vincent de Paul instead. A classic resentment-resistance dynamic, for which we lose not a minute of sleep.

You resent getting dumped by your old boyfriend. So you resist sending him a Christmas card every year, even though he sends one to you, which you burn without opening. Instead of thinking it's sweet, it actually makes you angry or sad. Which only serves to deepen your resentment.

In the TV series *Men of a Certain Age*, all three of the main characters are driven by resentment. One resents his ex-professional basketball player father's judgmental, disapproving harshness. Another resents his wife and his own behavior after losing her. And the other resents the fact that he's too old to continue to be fulfilled by his bachelor lifestyle. The program is about nothing other than these men and their behaviors, all of which are fueled by their resentments.

THE HEALING POWER—AND
DRIVING FORCE—OF REVENGE

We also tend to look for ways to exact *revenge* against those people and things we resent. You resent your wife for spending too much money when she goes shopping. So, as revenge, you splurge on fishing equipment even though you know she's not happy about it. *Especially* because she's not happy about it.

Welcome to the common modern adult marriage. Good or bad, it runs on very human psychology. You may not exhibit any signs of resistance or revenge at all, even though your resentment festers. Your resentment may manifest in your life as a cardiac event, which in a story is a reasonable and classic application of this dynamic.

The consequences of resentment and revenge manifest as third-dimension decisions and behavior, motivated by second dimension issues. The first-dimension window dressing that covers it all may go in either direction, either announcing it to the world or hiding it completely. For example, you run into a former lover who cheated on you, but you forgave and forgot, and then she cheated on you again, marrying your best friend. Tough stuff, easily resented and eagerly avenged. Now let's say you run into that lover at a class reunion. The wounds have never healed, and when you see her, your blood instantly boils. But she's thrown you a curveball—she's visibly pregnant. And, she's still happily married to the former best friend with whom she cheated while you were together.

So, what do you do? It's third-dimension time, because it doesn't matter how cool you look or act (first dimension), it doesn't matter why all this happened (second dimension), what matters is what you'll do right now, in this moment. Be polite? Be distant? Ignore them both? Forgive them? Try to humiliate them? Act like nothing ever happened? Make a scene, storm out? Or perhaps, wish them well with a warm hug … and *mean* it. Whatever you do, this is a third-dimension moment, and it defines your character.

As a writer crafting such a scene, you should have a keen handle on all three dimensions—how your hero tries to appear before the wheels come off (first dimension), an understanding of why his emotions are teetering on the edge of a cliff the moment his ex-lover walks in (second-dimension), and the ultimate choice of behavior (third dimension).

Notice how the second dimension doesn't dictate the hero's choice, but rather it illuminates the hero's *motivations*. Second dimension psychology is what it is—it happened, it hurt, it's never healed. So now, in this moment of pain and pressure, whatever the hero does defines him precisely because of these second-dimension issues. The reader wouldn't be able to assign character meaning to the hero's actions and decisions—does he take the high road or does he ass-out?—without an understanding of that second-dimension characterization.

We don't always carry our resentments and thirst for revenge on our first-dimension sleeves, and it doesn't manifest as a choice of haircut or car. Such first-dimension statements are born more of a desire to be *perceived* a certain way, rather than the need to act upon our inner forces or backstory experiences. And again, that desire can manifest in either direction—exposure or concealment.

All three dimensions conspire to create character. Yet they may still exist as discreet and motivationally separate drives.

Try this, if you dare.
Make a list of all the things in your life, both close and at arm's length, that you *resent*. Then notice how that resentment influences your attitudes, behaviors, and decisions toward those people or things. Pay attention to how each entry makes you *feel*. And then, in turn, how it may influence how you *act*.

Welcome to being human. Resentment drives us daily. Hopefully not exclusively.

The point is that you, as a creator of characters, have choices to make in this regard. An understanding of this resentment-resistance-revenge dynamic is a valid model upon which to base your character's decisions and actions.

And in the writing game, validity matters.

Characters are sometimes defined by their backstory.
And sometimes they are who they are *in spite* of their backstory. Which direction this goes is yours to decide, and the decision is based on what best fits the nature and tonality of your story and the players you are casting to play these roles. This is something you can make up in the

moment it arrives on the page (pantsing), but it requires careful planning in context to the larger arc of the story.

Whether conscious or subconscious, in submission to or defiance of, our behavior is connected to our roots, our personal history. Which in many cases is just dripping with issues of resentment, and in many more cases is virtually defined by the values and behaviors of the people who raised us.

If you don't think this is true, ask yourself why doctors have children who become doctors more than truck drivers have children who become doctors. You can generalize this even further—professionals have children who go into professional-level work more than blue collar workers have children who become professionals.

On the downside, statistics show that children of abused parents are more likely to become abusive parents. Same with children of alcoholics, though in a much more common and complex cycle of rationalization.

Some of us model our behavior after our parents. Some of us do the opposite. The consequences of both have huge implications. And in either case, what you see on the page has second-dimension context to it.

It's all backstory.

The hero in *Top Gun* comes to mind. Everything that character does in the first half of the story, before his character arc begins to manifest, connects to a backstory of a father who failed as a military officer. We didn't have to know that, but the writer made sure we did so we might empathize with behaviors that might otherwise simply be offensive.

For our heroes, empathy is at the core of second-dimension character issues.

The objective is to understand the backstory of your character to the extent that it logically and *validly* explains who he is as an adult in your story. This, in effect, adds a middle layer (second dimension) of characterization that not only explains first-dimension characterization, but also lays the groundwork for third-dimension behaviors that deliver a satisfying character arc.

People are also often driven by their worldview.

One's *worldview* is a set of collective values, politics, preferences, and beliefs, as expressed through attitudes, prejudices, habits, and choices. One's worldview is usually the product of backstory and culture—most characters who are terrorists, for example, were brought up to be terrorists, either via parenting or their culture—though these elements can shift as the character grows and evolves through different experiences and periods in his life.

For example, a preacher's daughter goes to school at the University of Southern California, and all of a sudden she's a beer-swilling cheerleader dating a drug dealer. Or, she becomes the first female associate minister at a stuffy old southern church. Same backstory, different outcomes.

All of which, by the way, is based on a set of second-dimension variables you completely control as an author.

In real life, not so much.

12

CREATING BACKSTORY

In fall 2009, a football player at the University of Oregon made national news—and YouTube—by punching out a Boise State player after losing the opening game of the season. It was an immediate hit (pun intended) on the Boise State stadium's jumbotron, then on the news as it was dissected every which way by sportscasters, and finally in the court of public opinion. None of it pretty.

The player was suspended for the season. Massive approval ensued in the press and among the general public. The school had saved its waning reputation. The new coach saved his job. The critics saved face. And in the process the player lost his dream, and possibly a shot at an NFL career.

Great story, eh? Know what makes it even better? Something called the *backstory*. The events and dynamics that preceded the event itself exerting influence on the players in this little athletic soap opera.

Because there was a lot that went into the dynamics of that dark moment. Just as there is a lot that goes into the dynamics of the key moments in *your* stories.

The loss of that player's cool was third-dimension character—true character—exposing itself. As were the decisions that were made *after* the fact, by the coach and by the player. The reasons behind it all, though—the backstory—were second-dimension issues of characterization. And while they didn't get that much play in the press, they would be essential if this true story were part of your novel.

In the heated moment it went down, the punch was a combination of first- and third-dimension issues driving a third-dimension decision/action.

The way the player danced and backpedaled with a recycled Mike Tyson shuffle after the cheap shot was thrown was a first-dimension quirk. It meant nothing … unless you *think* it did. And that's the point. But the punch itself was all third dimension, an expression of character that had nothing at all to do with impressing anyone, it was all about who that guy was at his core.

Which, interestingly enough, was precisely the opposite of what critics of the decision to suspend, and later the coach himself, cited as a counterpoint. That view held that the moment did not represent the true character of the young athlete at all, that he was merely caught up in the moment. Which begs the question—if that were true, would every player on the Oregon roster have done the same thing?

In our fiction it is our job to give our characters such moments to react to. The decisions and actions they take in those moments are absolutely expressions of their true character, arising from the third dimension of character depth. Throwing a punch isn't a first-dimension affectation. The second-dimension background of the young man is what it is, and in the moment when it counted he reverted to his truer nature.

Here's the backstory of this example:

First of all, the player came from a culture of conflict—the mean streets of the inner city—with childhood, scholastic, and domestic backgrounds that positioned football as his ticket out. His *hope*. Prior to the incident he was a budding star, a tale of triumph over adversity. The next day he was done.

Remember—write this down, it's critical—nothing fuels a story quite like *hope*.

Then there was the hype leading up to the game itself, in which the player popped off right and left in the press about how Oregon would "whoop on" this opponent, all this being first-dimension trash talk leading toward what he hoped would be revenge against a loss to these same guys the previous year.

Then the coach wrote it all off as part of football being an aggressive game played by aggressive young men, all but sanctioning the trash talk and thus fueling the bad blood between the two teams and schools. At this point nobody on the Oregon side was being accused of having high character, and nobody on the Boise State was saying anything at all.

Then there was the kid who received the cheap shot to the jaw, a defensive tackle the size of a small bus, who after his team pummeled Oregon in convincing fashion, confronted the guilty player with taunting words and an unfriendly tap on the shoulder pads. One can almost write *that* dialogue from where you sit. He reportedly had a history—a backstory—of mouthing off, and would be receiving a *talking-to* for his role. Also a first-dimension issue of characterization, leading to third-dimension consequences.

All of this is *backstory*. What went down before, and behind, the actual event.

From there it gets worse. The Oregon coach had second thoughts about the season suspension of his star running back and decided to bring the offending player back to the team, albeit with certain academic and citizenship criteria and conditions, which were never disclosed. This apparent change of heart was in direct contradiction to his proud and prompt disciplinary action the day after the incident, for which he had accepted gracious praise.

Enough human psychology to fuel a season of soap operas with a bubbling stew of first-, second- and third-dimension characterization.

Backstory is the stuff of second-dimension characterization. It can explain and rationalize both first-dimension affectations and third-dimension choices and behaviors, and it can stand in contrast to either, in which case it adds an interesting layer of complexity to it all.

Either way, great stories always cover this base.

BACKSTORY AS A STORYTELLING TOOL

In the previous chapter we discussed how the actions of your characters need to have psychological validity and, at the very least, a visible connection to some behavioral explanation (second dimension) with roots in the past. Backstory is how you make that happen.

Some writers actually write out a backstory for their major characters, often at great length. The objective of this exercise is to create a linkage between their actions within the story and the psychological roots that fueled it.

If you're pantsing your story, you'll have to retrofit a backstory that makes sense in a subsequent draft. But just like everything else about storytelling, you can choose to play this element in detail, and with proper context.

Either way, if you don't get it right, you'll find yourself with a one-dimensional hero.

THE ICEBERG PRINCIPLE

There is, however, a risk if you choose to craft a detailed backstory ahead of time. By writing out and investing a lot of energy in a backstory, you'll be tempted to use *too much* of it.

The trick is to show just enough backstory that the reader can intuit where the character is coming from, rather than spelling it out. Flashback scenes solely for the purpose of explaining backstory are rarely a good idea. You should be more artful and subtle in delivering backstory as part of the narrative flow.

Then again, if backstory is a major element of the story—as it is, for example, in both *Mystic River* and *Shutter Island* by Dennis Lehane—you can certainly weave them into the narrative as you see fit.

Here's the primary guideline, called the "iceberg principle": Show about only 10 percent of your character's backstory. Literally. A glimpse, leading to an ongoing context. Show enough to allow the reader to glean and make assumptions about what remains behind the curtain of time, yet continues to influence the character's worldview, attitudes, decisions, and actions.

RECOGNIZING BACKSTORY WHEN YOU READ IT

As it is with many elements of storytelling, the best way to get a feel for execution is to look for and acknowledge it when you see it in other stories. Pretty much every novel you read and movie you see will have a strategic backstory in play. Your job as a writer-in-progress, or even a crusty old pro, is to notice how it's done and reflect what you've learned in to your own manuscript.

In the TV drama *Castle*, the backstory involves the occupation of the hero and his playboy ways. He's a famous novelist with a talent for women and an aversion to commitment. That explains his role and his attitude as he works alongside a gorgeous police detective doing her best to remain immune to his undeniable charms, not to mention his investigative sensibilities.

In the hit show *House*, the lead character brings a backstory of drug addiction (to quell the pain of a major leg problem) and relationship failure to every episode. This licenses his continued pill popping and interpersonal abuse, which juxtaposes with his diagnostic genius to create a deep and fascinating hero who does his best to masquerade as an antihero. Each week the program offers delicious subtext as the characters openly discuss their efforts to manipulate and mess with each other—a tasty stew of first-, second- and third-dimension characterization that has become a perennial Emmy nominee.

In the movie *Avatar*, the hero's backstory is literally visible: He's disabled from his military service, and the brother of a highly trained guinea pig about to participate in a massively technical scientific experience. The coincidence of identical DNA, which is necessary for the plot to work, results in the hero taking his brother's place, and his lack of experience—direct from the backstory—is the primary catalyst in his relationships and his experiences.

With a light and deft touch that understands that backstory is a contextual tool, rather than part of the real-time storytelling sequence, the writer is equipped to infuse characters with believability and accessibility, which are essential to reader empathy.

BACKSTORY IN SERIES NOVELS

If you're writing a series, backstory is even more critical. In fact, the influence of backstory is the primary thing—in addition to the character and her ongoing growth—that carries over from book to book. Each novel should stand alone in terms of a book-specific plot, with full resolution delivered. But the backstory-inspired story line remains unsolved, though each entry should move that level of the story forward concurrent with the complete resolution of the more immediate plotline.

Harry Potter is a great example of this. Harry's past is the driving force of the ongoing tension in the series, as Harry gets ever closer to finding a way to thwart the plans of the dark wizard who murdered his parents and, once discovered, maneuvers himself into position to exact revenge in the name of justice.

The first book in such a series is where the backstory naturally gets the most play and focus. What you establish there—which may comprise the book-specific plotline in this first volume—becomes a less-direct focus in subsequent books, though enough revisiting is required to acquaint new readers with the driving context that continues to exert a powerful influence.

We see this everywhere on television, where we are used to watching episodic series. In the old classic *The Fugitive*, backstory permeated every scene, yet each episode sees Dr. Richard Kimble presented with a new adventure and a new problem to solve.

Novelists can learn much from television with regard to how to connect episodes of a series, and the focus of that learning curve is always backstory.

13
INTERIOR VS.
EXTERIOR CONFLICT

Earlier I suggested that the one single word that best describes story is *conflict*. While some like to argue the point—there are abundant writers who will argue virtually *any* point—it remains irrefutable that conflict *is* essential to good storytelling. Without it, all you have is a character vignette or a diary at best, episodic pabulum at worst.

In that sense, conflict refers to what *opposes* the hero in a quest to achieve whatever it is he needs to do, win, accomplish, avoid, find, achieve, realize, understand, or otherwise attain. That conflict makes its initial meaningful—literally, in this case, as it *imparts meaning*—appearance (though it may have been foreshadowed and even previewed earlier in the first part of the story) at the First Plot Point (see chapter twenty-two), also known as the *inciting incident*. After that moment the hero's journey in the story is launched.

Everything prior to the First Plot Point contributes to the setup of that turning point in the story. Even when it seems as if the story actually started earlier with the appearance of some antagonistic element, look again—we really didn't understand what it meant for the character, at least not to the level that the real First Plot Point either further defines that meaning or somehow changes it. What it changes *to* is the stuff of the rest of the story.

These are all plotting issues, which we'll cover in detail later in Part Five. But it has a direct bearing on the issue of characterization. Because that, too, needs to have been set up in the pages that appear prior to the First Plot Point.

The mission of the First Box of your story (see chapter twenty-two) is to setup two things: the plot *and* the character. It is at the First Plot Point where the two collide. In good stories, however, things aren't quite as simple as that sounds.

Because in good stories heroes are *complex*, they're conflicted, they're multidimensional. Sometimes they aren't even all that *likable*—which, as we've seen, is a less critical criteria for a protagonist than the need to *empathize* with what the hero needs to accomplish and is going through in the process.

In the first part of your story, prior to the First Plot Point, you need to show us the first dimension of character for the hero, and possibly the antagonist as well. You also need to hint at second-dimension character issues before the First Plot Point hits, because we need some basis for what we'll see the character doing in the way of response to it.

Third-dimension characterization is tricky at this point, but vital.

Because, at this point, the decisions and actions are those that show us a character who has *yet* to change, to evolve. In terms of *character arc*, what the character does in the first part of the story probably won't be the same flavor of action or decision that will manifest in the last part.

Let's look at an example. We may not *like* a character that gets drunk on a camping trip. But, even though he's acting stupid, we can certainly empathize when a hungry bear targets him as its next meal.

In the first part of such a story, a third-dimension decision on the part of the hero might be to drop to his knees and pray. A coward, someone who freezes under pressure. In the closing of the story, though, his response might be to grab a thick stick and fight for his life, because all that freezing hasn't gotten him anywhere. Both are third-dimension actions, driven by second-dimension factors.

That example illustrates a powerful point—your story can actually shift the character's second-dimension psychology. The character learns, he finally understands, he casts away old limiting beliefs and inner demons, resulting in different and better third-dimension decisions and actions later in the story.

Usually the inner complexity that arises from front-end second-dimension issues of characterization gets in the hero's way. It becomes, in effect, yet another obstacle as he strives to overcome whatever external barriers you've diabolically put in his path.

That guy running from the bear, for example. He's drunk, by his own doing, which complicates things greatly. Because the bear is *not* drunk.

Some stories, especially in what, for lack of a better term, are described as character-driven novels and screenplays (*Top Gun* again), are almost completely about inner demons. The overcoming of second-dimension backstories is precisely what the story is really about.

When this is done well, *Top Gun* notwithstanding, it's called *literature*.

THE TWO LEVELS OF CONFLICT IN EVERY GREAT STORY

Every great story presents two levels of conflict for the reader's pleasure: one, an *external* obstacle to the hero's quest, and two, an *internal* demon that hinders the character's ability to make the best possible decisions under pressure. An inner drive, weakness, belief system, or kink that makes him weak, that tempts, diverts, and seduces, that blinds him to the truth, that summons skewed values and warps his ability to see more clearly.

Examples of second-dimension psychology include deeply held religious beliefs (say, prompting one to turn the other cheek to a hungry bear), a parental hatred stemming from abuse or some other resentment, the distrust of authority, or some clinical issue such as fear of heights, claustrophobia, agoraphobia, and a long list of other phobias. Each of these issues could easily get in the way when the hero is called upon to make a crucial decision.

The hero in *Top Gun* once again comes to mind. His thing is assing-out as a vehicle of rebellion, making foolish decisions that put him and his wingman in peril. He does all this because he needs to overcome the stigma of his father's military failures, to appear fearless and bold, to stand out in a crowd, to be a cowboy in a world that runs on discipline.

Of course, by the end of the story he conquers this need and summons his inner hero, finally becoming the man his father never was.

Dexter is a genius example.

Perhaps the mother of all inner demons (perhaps a risky analogy there) is the TV series *Dexter* (and the series of novels by Jeff Lindsay that inspired it). The hero is—if this isn't an inner demon we should all take up pottery instead of writing—a serial killer. A bona fide, gets-off-on-killing-people psychopath who happens to be influenced by a backstory that includes a father who channels his son's thirst for death into a more productive outlet—the ritualistic murder of only those who *deserve* it.

This program is a clinic on characterization, because all of the requisite elements—backstory, inner demons, valid human psychology, worldview, and a dark basement full of quirks that include duct tape and the collection of blood on microscope slides—are in full view. They're fascinating in and of themselves.

Yet when pitted against scumbag victims who truly do deserve the very worst serial-killer appetites Dexter has in him, we somehow manage to summon enough empathy and understanding to find ourselves actually rooting for him.

Genius.

If Dexter's inner demon (he refers to it as his *dark passenger*) were allowed to remain in control, or even run untethered, the story would be less satisfying than if he found a way to grow out of it, to overcome that which was in his way. This overcoming of the inner conflict—or in Dexter's case, the *managing* of it—comes prior to and is thus enabling of the hero's ability to conquer any exterior obstacles that come his way.

Here's another way of putting it: The overcoming of an inner conflict is shown *prior to* the final showdown with the antagonistic force, and thus becomes an *enabling* factor with respect to the hero's ability to do what needs to be done to end the story.

Dexter's need to kill, and the criteria by which he does it, are all second-dimension issues of characterization. The second-dimension issues that motivate it are a MacGuffin—a catalytic plot element that keeps showing up, in Dexter's case via the ghostly appearance of his mentoring dead father—that always escapes our full grasp.

As for the third dimension, each week brings Dexter ever closer to embracing his own humanity, and his decisions reflect that emerging arc. His true character remains enigmatic—is he a killer or a hero? Can he possibly be both? And can we possibly actually root for a serial killer under any circumstances?

At the heart of what makes this work is yet another trick of human psychology, this time aimed at the viewer: We all love seeing evil people get their proper comeuppance. And we root for Dexter, dark as he is, as the delivery agent. At least he targets only victims even more heinous than himself.

Again ... genius.

How our heroes learn to overcome their own weaknesses and short-comings is the essence of storytelling within the realm of character. It is among the most critical missions that you, the author, have before you.

It is called *character arc*. And it isn't possible until you give your hero an inner demon—deeply rooted *issues*—to confront and, to whatever extent necessary, conquer.

14

CRAFTING A
CHARACTER ARC

We've been talking about inner demons, which we all possess, some of us more than others. A few we conquer as we get older, a few we don't, even with therapy. In which case we encounter divorce, career issues, and the constant ebb and flow of what we prefer to think of as life's ups and downs.

Most of the time the people we encounter don't know about or care about the backstory behind who we are and what we do. This, too, is real life. Which means that, for the most part, the only people in our lives who seek to understand the psychology behind our personalities and actions are our significant others, the occasional counselor or social worker, and, if things get really dark for us, the prison mental health counselor.

But the stories we write are not real life. Our stories can successfully exist at the darkest fringes of real life, as *Dexter* so poignantly demonstrates. So, while we can take our cues about inner demons from our own experiences, and from watching others wrestle with their own problems, we are also permitted to bring darkness and drama into what we write. And when we do, our readers need to know what's behind it all.

This very thing, this illumination of the backstory of character, is what separates multidimensional stories, stories with depth, from stories reviewed as flat and one-dimensional.

The interesting thing about inner demons—our *issues*—is the fact that the drama ensues not so much *from* them, but from our ability to *cope* with them. The inner demons of criminals and psychopaths are often not that much different than those afflicting the rest of us, they just deal with them in spectacular and often horrifying ways.

Which means we can apply a standard set of inner demons to just about any character. The fun, then, is showing how the character handles things.

And how he handles things is the stuff of *character arc*.

WHAT ARE THE COMMON INNER DEMONS?

Cowardice, selfishness, addiction, fear, conceit, arrogance, hatred, resentment, bias, lack of confidence, stupidity, genius, heritage, poverty, ignorance, sociopathic insensitivity, naiveté, a spotty moral compass, sexual deviance ... in general, any aspect of humanity that isn't in line with the expectations of others or the accepted ground rules of success within the boundaries of your story and the rules you've created for it.

In the movie *The Book of Eli*, the hero kills more people with his machete than Al Capone ever did over his entire career, and it's all perfectly acceptable. Why? Because of the ground rules of the story, which depicts a postapocalyptic society in which a kill-or-be-killed sensibility rules the day.

This protagonist is a study in three-dimensional characterization. He is outwardly calm and quiet, efficient with both his words and actions, and doggedly determined to get somewhere. His actions are all third dimensional in nature, since they illustrate precisely what his true character is from the very first scene. There isn't a moment of first-dimension window dressing attached to anything he does. Including—especially, if you know the ending—his sunglasses. Only at the end do we learn the full depth of the second-dimension forces driving those decisions—and the sunglasses—and it's powerful stuff. The movie ends up being completely all about those second-dimension, backstory-driven issues.

One of those second-dimension inner demons might just reside in your own closet. Or in the mental waiting room of a serial killer. As writers, we get to play God with how that goes down in the lives of our characters.

Great heroes do have inner demons.

So do great villains. We know our villains aren't perfect, but it's good to know that our heroes aren't perfect, either. If they were, they'd be boring. Villains may have once strived for perfection, or they at least act in the belief that what they are doing is justified or for the greater good. Or not. They might just enjoy hurting people with all the conscience of a sociopath, or worse, a psychopath.

Either way, your job as a writer is to allow the reader or viewer to come to understand what makes your character tick.

Character arc is *learning*.

It is gaining strength and insight. Acquiring that which is lacking. Shedding that which is hindering. Leaving the past behind. Forgiving. Making a better decision when it counts.

Villains seldom demonstrate a character arc, though it's not a hard-and-fast rule. Again, as God in this story, you get to dictate the fate of all you have created.

And when you have, and when it results in your character having grown or changed—not always the same thing—as a result of or in order to meet the challenges you've put before him, you've just infused character arc into your story.

Character arc is *consequence*.

The source and nature of inner demons are illustrated through backstory. This is originally presented in the opening part of the story, prior to the inciting incident, or what is (and will be when we get there) the First Plot Point. Those inner demons are shown to plague the hero through the middle body of the narrative, with the hero beginning to get the idea that he needs to fix something. Prior to that point, which usually happens after the midpoint of the story, we've seen an inner struggle with whatever is holding him back. (We'll cover this in more detail later when we discuss story structure in Part Five of this book.)

In the final section (or box) of the story our hero begins to make different and better choices—third-dimension choices—that demonstrate he is *getting* it, that he is no longer a slave to his inner demons, that at least for the moment at hand he can conquer his issues to do what must be done.

This is character arc, pure and simple.

It begins with the introduction of inner demons, and it concludes with showing how those inner demons have been conquered.

Examples of character arc: the meek become bold, the cowardly become courageous, the quiet become outspoken, the unforgiving decide to forgive, the resentful get over it, the clueless get a clue, the self-deceiving become self-aware, the dishonest come clean with themselves and others, the easily tempted become self-disciplined, the weak become strong, the unbelieving see the light, the oppressed get out from under the power of whatever oppresses them, victims become responsible for themselves, takers become givers, the insensitive develop a sensitivity chip, the naïve become fully aware, the bored become passionate, the cold become warm ... the list is the very essence of the human experience.

Your hero should *exit* the story enlightened, enriched, evolved, and enabled in comparison to how he *entered* the story. Maybe not completely, certainly not beyond credibility or belief, but enough to reach his goal. Enough to deliver the essence of your story's intended theme.

This learning cannot occur in a vacuum. It should be the result of dramatic trial and error, of action and consequence, literally of learning a lesson from the hero's experience *within* the story.

We've all heard it: *Show, don't tell.*

Character arc is the most critical element toward which you need to apply that principle. We must see and feel the character bettering his weaker self, rather than simply reading the news of it or have it spring from no logical, discernable source. He can't just wake one day and suddenly *get it*. (This is where some paranormal stories fall flat—the hero learns via a sixth sense, or a random realization from something bigger than himself, rather than from the pain and consequence of experience.)

In *Top Gun*, the hero learns to work within the system, to not leave his wingman when it counts and in doing so he gets the girl, saves the day and protects America from the bad guys, all without a hair out of place. I'm not remotely suggesting you emulate this story in terms of character development; it's not exactly hailed as a sterling example of the art of modern cinema. In fact, the story is pretty weak and thin ... the best part is all those cool fighter planes taking off from aircraft carriers.

But it does show us a few things. One of which is that some of the best learning comes from less-than-stellar examples, both in storytelling and in real life.

CHARACTER ARC AS SUBPLOT

Creating a story line that is subordinate to—but related to—the primary plotline, a background story that centers on the character's inner demons, is great fodder for a *subplot*. Because when subplot focuses on the hero's inner demons, it can also quickly become sub*text*. And subtext is a wonderful thing in storytelling.

That's two different sub sandwiches on the story menu, and as the chef, you need to grill them up *strategically*. Throw in theme (we'll cover that in more depth in the next section), which is also connected to the power or character arc, and you have a virtual literary buffet.

If the story is a thriller, for example, the subplot might concern the hero's ability to commit to something or someone in the face of the pressures of impending life or death. This lack of commitment or even a lack of courage becomes subtext that infuses the plot with higher drama, because we know the hero must conquer these inner demons in order to stand a chance against the real-world antagonistic forces you've put before him.

If the story is a romantic comedy or a serious adult relationship drama, the hero may have been so focused on her career that she's become awkward at personal relationships. The inherent risk of her making decisions from that context, both relative to the primary and subplots, becomes sub*text*. The same inner demon that prevents her from committing to another human being might also prevent her from committing to a course of action that could solve the primary problem presented in the main plot. Or better, when the primary plot *depends* on her connecting with someone in a way that calls for blind trust and loyalty.

If the story is already a love story, everything changes places—the inner realm of personal obstacles can become the primary source of the story's drama, while any exterior conflict is relegated to subplot, such as one of the parties getting transferred to the opposite coast to keep her career moving forward, and thus forcing a choice.

Or, one of the families in a love story might bring class prejudice to bear upon the budding relationships, thus becoming the primary conflict in the main plotline. In which case you've just clobbered us with subtext of a thematic nature that informs and influences the outward-facing drama.

The primary plot of *Titanic*, for example, was a love story that was forbidden because of social class distinctions, thus infusing the story with sub*text* concerning the class struggle that defined every relationship on board the doomed ship. The sinking ship itself was, because we all knew what would happen, reduced to the role of subplot—the primary tension there was wondering how cool the special effects would be when the ship went down.

You could argue that it was the other way around, but it doesn't matter. Both plotlines were saturated with subtext relating to social class.

Subtext usually is a second-dimension character issue. It burrows into deeply held belief systems and barriers that prompt emotional and psychological responses. Those responses are the catalyst for both first and third-dimension aspects of characterization, the former in the first half of the story, the latter toward the end, when the character conquers enough inner demons to do what must be done.

Subplot follows the same basic story architecture and flow as the primary plot.

A subplot is usually much simpler and less obvious than the primary story line. When it manifests in the form of limiting the character's choices and influencing behaviors, it eventually and successfully links to the main story line.

For example, a character's inner demon could easily influence her response to the arrival of the story's primary conflict at the First Plot Point (the inciting incident). In fact, it absolutely should. And when it does it becomes subtext fueling the primary story line.

For example, if someone is painfully shy, and the First Plot Point finds her suddenly promoted to a management position, her shyness informs her response to this new journey, and in a way that throws up yellow and red flags at every turn. The primary story line might hinge on her ability to save the company from ruin, or expose the larcenous ways of the boss. But whatever it is, it will be with subtext stemming from the fact that everything the hero must do is in context to that crippling shyness.

In this example, our hero should be well on her way to conquering that shyness (it's still subtext) right up until the story's Second Plot Point, which launches the final push toward the story's conclusion. She may need to confront the board of directors to expose the illegal agenda of the same upper management that promoted her, and it is the very fact of her shyness, in contrast to the egotistical bluster of her peers, that motivates the board to listen to her. Suddenly that inner demon isn't just subplot (which manifests, perhaps, as an awkwardly emerging love story). Now it's a major catalyst in the resolution of the primary story line. Will she be bold and take the risks necessary to do what must be done? The answer resides at the collision between subplot and primary plot, and in the shadow of subtext.

Or, sometimes the subplot can be completely separate. In that case, character arc needs to be demonstrated across *both* plotlines, the more behaviorally intertwined the better.

CHARACTER SUBTEXT AT WORK

In the hit TV show *Burn Notice*, Michael Weston is a intelligence agent who is constantly working to uncover who burned him—basically making him persona non grata within his profession—while addressing the plot-of-the-day (episode), which is always an empathy-inducing save-the-innocent scenario that gets wrapped up after fifty-eight minutes minus commercials, toward which he contributes his substantial spy skills toward the remedy.

The main plot is how Michael solves the case of the moment. The subplot is his love relationship with his trigger-happy sidekick, and whether the local police will stop him before he nails the bad guys using less than legal means. The sub*text* is his ongoing status as having been burned as a spy for some unnamed government agency, which at the end of the day is the primary plot of the series itself.

The latter is also a sub*plot*. Yes, subtext can become subplot, and vice versa.

Don't sweat this, just understand what the elements are and let it rip.

It's easy to conclude that you have many options here. A full-blown matrix of them, in fact, with three variables—plot, subplot, and subtext—all in simultaneous play. And all of it the raw material with which the writer creates the character arc.

Literary juggling at its finest and most challenging.

Writers who create organically (pantsers) really struggle with this. In fact, it is the undoing of many. Because these are complex issues that, when finally rendered effectively, don't readily show the layering that goes into them. And without planning, such layering is extremely difficult to stumble upon as you create draft after draft.

The reality of good storytelling at this advanced level will turn you into a beat-by-beat story planner sooner or later. The more you recognize the validity of this model, the more drawn you'll be to putting some planning time into your stories before you write them.

Subplot from a character perspective is a dramatic question that is answered over the course of the story: will they fall in love, will she get the job, will they be disinherited, will they live or die, will they have sex before the ship sinks, etc. The second-dimension realm issue about the inner demon of your hero is a good place to look for a prospective subplot during your story planning.

Sub*text* is the existence of some social, psychological, economic, or other situational pressure that defines and influences the characters, such as social class, politics, career factors, etc. A newly elected politician in Washington, for example, must navigate the chilly waters of political etiquette, expectations, and party lines in every aspect of her work—that's classic subtext in play.

Again, the second dimension of characterization—the psychology and backstory that defines the character—is almost always the richest source of subtext.

MORE SUBPLOT AT WORK

In *The Cider House Rules* by John Irving, the subplot is Homer's ability to hook up with Candy romantically. Will they or won't they? Stay tuned as the main plotline unfolds. The sub*text* of the story is the ever-present issue of right to life and abortion, and the pressures it puts on the characters.

In this case, subplot is character, subtext is theme. This is a familiar paradigm, one you should pay attention to and apply.

In *Top Gun*, the subplot is the hero's budding relationship with the ultra-hot flight instructor. Again, stay tuned, because hijinks ensue. The main plot—admittedly weak—is some conglomeration of whether the hero would wash out (this being the link between the main plot and the subtext) before he can save the day from an impending attack by bad guys.

The subtext of *Top Gun*, however, isn't really a question at all, but an influencing *pressure*: The hero lives under the dark shadow of a disgraced military father, nobody likes or respects him, and it pushes him toward irresponsibility and bravado to the point of risking his career and the lives of his teammates.

The writer's insight here is to understand the differences between plot, subplot, and subtext, and then master them—and more importantly, plan and work with them—from a character perspective. When you do, you have everything in place to make your hero's arc both bold and profound.

15
CHARACTER–
THE SUM OF THE PARTS

When a story works, the core competencies have come together, like spices in a great meal, to become something in excess of what they would otherwise be alone.

Rest assured, the creator of that best-selling story waiting for you on your nightstand reached clarity through one of three processes: She understood the elements and processes of story development, and knew how to craft and blend them ... she was intuitive enough as a storyteller to make them work without really knowing how or why ... or she got lucky.

I don't know about you, but I don't want to leave my storytelling to luck. And while I'm often intuitive as hell—that, by the way, is as much a product of experience as it is a *gift*—I sleep a lot better knowing there's a structure, a process, and a paradigm for storytelling that doesn't compromise the creative process.

Indeed, story planning *empowers* stories. And anyway, pantsing is just story planning—the *search* for the story— by another name.

One of the most critical focuses of any story planning process, an element that benefits from planning every bit as much as plot, is the creation of your characters.

Characterization is one of the Six Core Competencies that contribute to making the structural parts and milestones work.

Characterization is the vehicle that delivers theme.

Characterization is the window that allows a killer concept to expand and thrive.

Characters are the focus of scene creation and the lyrics of your writing voice.

And, perhaps to the surprise of many, character is also *structure*. Because a character arc depends on a prescribed four-part contextual sequence every bit as much as does plot.

CHARACTER AS STRUCTURE

Rather than think of story structure as four parts, each with different contexts and missions (a topic we will cover in Part Five on story structure), you can apply different labels for the same sequential stages that apply directly to a character arc.

Just as the four structural parts (which align perfectly with the three acts of a screenplay; the only difference is that Act Two of a screenplay breaks down into two halves for this development model) empower plot, the same four parts define context and mission for character development. Which is to say, you shouldn't apply a Part 4 context to your character in Part 2 of your story.

This character development model keeps you writing the right thing at the right time, just as its parallel plot sequence model does for dramatic exposition.

These subtly different part-specific perspectives define the mission of each of the four story parts, which are roughly described as quartiles (each approximately 25 percent of the story's ultimate length). With this new take on linear structure from a character-driven point of view, each of the four story parts now has two congruent missions—one from a expositional perspective, and one from a character-arc perspective.

Which is plenty of guidance for you, the storyteller. You now have a road map that you can use to plan your story, both in terms of plot and character. Even if you're making it up as go along.

Especially if you're making it up as you go along.

Let's see how this looks.

Remember, this is story structure with a new coat of paint and a new set of nametags. This perspective focuses on character context as well as plot exposition. When we get to story structure later in Part Five, you'll see how the two separate contexts fuse to make your story exceed the a sum of its two primary elements—character and plot.

In effect, this model fuses them into one. And it works because now you possess an understanding of backstory, the realm of inner character conflict, and the essence of character arc, which is essential chemistry to making this model work.

STAGE ONE CHARACTER CONTEXT

In the first part of your story, known as the setup, your hero is not yet fully exposed to the journey that you will unleash upon him. The antagonistic forces aren't yet fully involved, if at all. We're meeting your hero in his life before all this happens, seeing what he wants and what he does, and seeing who he is in all three dimensions (see chapter nine).

However this all shakes out, though, it can be said that here, in the first quarter of your story before the inciting First Plot Point arrives, your character is disconnected from his ultimate goal and destiny in some way. A curve ball, a change of course is right around the corner.

In this opening quartile stage we are exposed to the full range of first-dimension characterization issues, without much explanation as to what resides beneath those nuances, and get perhaps only a partial glimpse of the consequences that manifest in the hero's life.

For example, if the hero's first-dimension choices make other people stay away from him like he's a leper, we'd see that right here in the opening quarter of the story, fully exposed for us prior to the arrival of the First Plot Point.

Which, as you will soon learn, changes everything.

This is also where you first introduce backstory, which directly links to inner demons and the obvious first-dimension choices that compensate for them.

STAGE TWO CHARACTER CONTEXT

After the First Plot Point arrives to end the opening quartile (or slightly less) of your story, the hero faces a whole new or dramatically evolved set of problems, objectives, obstacles, and needs. A new *quest*. During this stage he is *responding* to this new situation, *reacting* to it, running from it, investigating it, challenging it, disbelieving it … but not really attacking the problem yet, at least in an informed manner.

It could be said that the hero is *exploring his options* here, *wandering*. This is where he makes mistakes that teach him lessons about what he's facing, what he must achieve, and what blocks his path. This is where his old patterns and inner demons—the starting point of his character arc—kick in to haunt and compromise his efforts.

A huge mistake by newer writers is to have the hero begin to solve the problem at this point, rather than allow the antagonist to have his way with the hero. But it's too early. The hero is still plagued and handicapped by his inner demons, in combination with not really understanding what he's up against in terms of an antagonist force (that he may or may not be aware of at this point). This is where we see the hero flail and fail, and in doing so our empathy and emotions begin to build in his support.

Something needs to change, and quickly, or he'll ultimately, not just in the near term, fail. In many stories, the hero might even die.

We continue to see the first-dimension characterization on display here, and we see more of the consequences and constraints they cause. Here, too, is where we begin to dig beneath the surface to understand the second-dimension explanation and rationale for those choices, what pain they mask, and what illusions the hero seeks to create. And usually, how that is actually a mask that the hero will have to cast aside in order to reach his new goal.

STAGE THREE CHARACTER CONTEXT

After all this wandering around without much of a clue, flailing against a foe that's bigger and better than him, that confuses and confounds him, it's time to give our hero some hope. That's the mission of this third stage:

to empower the hero to attack the problem through the application of his learning curve, which requires a new willingness and ability to rise above his inner demons, possibly for the first time in his life.

In the second quartile of the story, the hero was responding; now here in the third quartile he gets aggressive and proactive. He attacks. It may not work as well as he hopes—in fact, it shouldn't, not yet—but he's not going to fail without a fight. The training wheels come off and the hero is doing unabashed battle with his obstacles, both interior and exterior.

Here in the third stage of character development we see how the inner demons, all rooted in the second dimension of characterization, have been completely in the way of the character's success and salvation. Interestingly, the hero begins to realize it here, as well.

STAGE FOUR CHARACTER CONTEXT

As the song says, *and then a hero comes along*. And by hero, we're not referring so much to the role being played, but the decisions and actions that allow the protagonist, and perhaps others, to become worthy of that title.

Here in the concluding context of the fourth and final quartile of the book (which is Act Three in a screenplay), the hero is better equipped to square off with the antagonist and its inherent obstacles because he's learned his lessons well. He's changed, grown, evolved. He has courage where once he was cowardly. He engages where once he was isolated. He's conquered inner demons that had tempted and haunted and filled him with doubt and dread, and now he's prepared to apply that learning toward the implementation of heroic decisions and acts—even to the point of martyrdom—to save the day.

THE GOLDEN RULE OF HEROIC OUTCOME

The term *hero* is both literal and descriptive in storytelling. Heroes don't get rescued. They do the rescuing.

It is critical that the hero of your story turn out to be the primary catalyst in the story's conclusion. He can't sit back and just watch it happen, even if he played a role in setting it all up. He must be in the middle of it, the primary agent of change and action, the centerpiece of the action, the one pulling the trigger, saving the day, making the final decision, taking the big risk, doing the unthinkable.

One of the worst mistakes a storyteller can make is to put the hero in deep jeopardy and then have someone else rescue him.

There should be no luck whatsoever when it comes to the hero saving the day or reaching his goal. It should be the outcome of the character arc. It should be a demonstration and application of all that he has learned, all that he has overcome.

Just as bad as rescuing the hero in these final moments is the inserting of pure coincidence or luck in allowing him to survive or reach his goal. This is known as *deus ex machina*, which is Latin for "god from a machine," and it'll get your story rejected faster than misspelling the editor's name in your cover letter.

In the bestseller *Night Fall* by Nelson DeMille, the story ends with all the evidence that would allow the hero to expose the truth about the crash of TWA Flight 800 (a real-life tragedy), as put forth in the story's fictional conceit. But rather than allow the hero to become the catalyst in how it all ends, DeMille risks literary disaster (the big-name authors tend to get away with stuff like that, and in ways the rest of us can't) by arranging a meeting between the press and the folks who are responsible for the cover-up, with all the evidence and truth resting on the table between them. Except this meeting was scheduled for 9 A.M. in New York on September 11, 2001, in the north tower of the World Trade Center. DeMille might argue that the plot's dependence on a real-life event excuses this *deus ex machina* denouement, and who's to argue the point. But it does illustrate the use of coincidence as a story point, and it should be avoided at all costs by anyone who doesn't already have a *New York Times* bestseller under his belt.

In her book *The Hero Within: Six Archetypes We Live By*, author Carol S. Pearson labels these four stages of character status as *orphan*, *wanderer*, *warrior*, and *martyr*. While I like all these labels, I don't think the hero needs to die in the end; he just needs to be *willing* to.

You could also think of them as any number of other four-part descriptors: *clueless, scared, angry,* and *smart ... unaware, surprised, focused,* and *courageous ... ignorant, confused, focused,* and *heroic ... destined, responder, attacker,* and *savior.*

But always, the best way to describe your protagonist at the end is, in a word, *hero.*

Whatever, the names are less critical than understanding the nature and essence of each of these four contextual stages of character development, and how they empower the character arc and the emotional involvement of your readers.

THE QUESTIONS OF CHARACTER

There's been more stuff written about characterization than any other aspect of the storytelling craft. And yet it continues to elude a lot of writers because, unlike structure, there's no template or format for a great character.

But there *is* a checklist, in the form of questions you, as the author, should be well down the road toward answering before you begin writing your story:

- What is your character's backstory, the experiences that programmed how he thinks and feels and acts today?

- What is his inner demon, and how does it influence decisions and actions in the face of the outer demon you are about to throw at him?

- What does he resent?

- What is his drive to get revenge?

- How does he feel about himself, and what is the gap between that assessment and how others feel about him?

- What is your character's worldview?

- What is your character's moral compass?

- Is your character a giver or a taker in life?

- To what extent does your character adhere to gender roles and stereotypes? And if he doesn't fit cleanly into one, *how* is he different?

- What lessons has your character not yet learned in life?

- What lessons has he experienced but rejected or failed to learn?

- Who are his friends? Are they like-for-like, or either above or below him in intelligence?

- What is your character's social I.Q.? Is he awkward? Eager? Easy? Life of the party? Wallflower? Totally faking it?

- To what extent is your character either an introvert or an extrovert? How does this manifest in his life?

- What is your character's most secret yearning?

- What childhood dream never came true, and why?

- What is your character's religious or spiritual belief system?

- What is the worst thing your character has ever done?

- Does your character have secrets? Perhaps a secret life?

- What does your character's life partner, closest friends, and employer not know about him?

- When, how, and why does he hold back, procrastinate?

- What has held him back in life?

- How many people would come to his funeral? Why might someone decide not to attend?

- What is the most unlikely or the most contradictory aspect of your character?

- What are your character's first-dimension quirks, habits, and choices?

- Why are they in evidence, what are they saying or covering for?
- What is the backstory that leads to those choices?
- What are the psychological scars that affect your character's life, and how does this link to backstory?
- How strong is your character under pressure?
- What is your character's arc in your story? How does he change and grow over the course of the story? How does he apply that learning toward becoming the catalytic force that drives the denouement of the story?

Notice how these questions go a whole lot deeper than a few surface quirks and a great sense of humor. And how, when you go this deep, those surface quirks don't matter; you can use them as window dressing as you please rather than mistaking them for actual issues of characterization. When you can fill in all these blanks for both your hero and your villain, you'll naturally find yourself realizing them on the page in a way that has subtle depth and nuance.

Make sure you don't force this.

Keep this level of depth the exclusive province of your main hero and antagonist. We don't need to know all this about the guy driving the taxi or holding the door.

The more of these answers you understand before you write your story, the quicker your character will become realized. If you expect to discover these things *as* you write, know that you're in for one of two things: a series of drafts and revisions that keep filling in these blanks, or the abandonment of this level of depth altogether.

Always remember that, when all is said and done, organic storytelling is no different than story planning. Both are merely a means of searching for and deciding upon your story. Which means that, whether you like to admit it or not, *both* are forms of story planning.

At the end of the storytelling day, all the arguments about character begin to sound the same. Story is plot. Plot is character. Character is theme. Story is structure.

And process, no matter how you cut it, is story planning.

Yes, yes, yes, and yes.

The heat of your story melds concept, character, theme, and structure into one seamless flow of narrative goodness. Like a chef executing a recipe, or even making up a new dish out of her head, a great banquet of storytelling richness is never an accident.

Don't think for a moment that the cook had no clue *how* the meal would turn out. A real chef beholds the ingredients set out on the counter ... and where the masses see a bunch of groceries and raw food, she envisions a glorious, multifaceted *feast*, spiced to taste with her deft and artistic touch.

Bon appétit!

PART FOUR

THE THIRD CORE COMPETENCY—
THEME

16
DEFINING THEME

"H ave you ever put down a novel or walked out of a theater and thought to yourself, *what the hell was that about*?"

Probably not. Agents and editors and script readers experience that moment all the time, but the reading and moviegoing public is shielded from that response by virtue of the work these folks put into the finished product. A well-told story, the kind that gets published or made into a film, usually doesn't elicit such a response. As an intelligent reader or viewer you intuitively know what it was *about*, and usually on two levels: It was about the plot … and, in a different experiential context, it was about what the story *means*.

The latter is called *theme*. It is one of the Six Core Competencies of successful writing in general, and storytelling in particular. Because great stories, the kind that turn their authors into A-list brand names, have *both* realms in play.

For example, you probably read *The Da Vinci Code*. Based on the number of copies sold, pretty much everybody did. It was about a crime, a heinous murder of a museum curator who left a clue about his killer written in his own blood. It was a mystery that became a thriller when the hero found himself in the crosshairs of unseen bad guys.

In terms of what *The Da Vinci Code* was about, that was the *plot*.

But *The Da Vinci Code* was about so much more than its plot. It was about the veracity of the dominant religion of Western culture. It was about a speculated truth that had been, according to the story, swept under the rug of time. It was about the lengths people will go to in the name of what they believe.

On a *thematic* level, *this* was what the story was all about.

WRAPPING YOUR HEAD AROUND THEME

In my workshops people always ask about the difference between *theme* and *concept*. Which, once you understand it, is like asking about the difference between chopped spinach and filet mignon. They're two items on the menu of our stories, completely separate and quite necessary to a balanced diet. Either one, served alone, is merely a snack. Tasty, but not completely filling or nourishing.

We looked closely at *concept* in Part Two. Now let's look at theme, which is an entirely different animal.

To put it in its most simple terms, theme is what our story *means*. How it *relates* to reality and life in general. What it says about life and the infinite roster of issues, facets, challenges, and experiences it presents. Theme can be a broad topical arena, or it can be a specific stance on anything human beings experience in life.

It can be a principle or an inevitable stage of growing up. It can be subtle or it can be on the nose. It can be contextual, or it can be the centerpiece of the story. And because it can be all of these things, or seemingly none of them yet strangely moving, it is often confusing to writers who can't quite grasp what it means to the craft of storytelling.

Theme is the *relevance* of your story to life. To reality, as reflected in your fiction. Theme is love and hate, the folly of youth, the treachery of commerce, the minefield of marriage, the veracity of religion, heaven and hell, past and future, science vs. nature, betrayal, friendship, loyalty, Machiavellian agenda, wealth and poverty, mercy and courage and wisdom and greed and lust and laughter.

Theme is life itself, as manifested in our stories, as seen through our characters, and as experienced through our plots.

Theme is how you touch your readers.

You may intrigue and ensnare them through your clever plot—often the objective of whodunit mysteries—or you may relate to them through your characters, as often happens in romances, but theme is always how you reach their heart and ignite their intellect.

Theme is what makes you think, makes you *feel*. It is what compels readers to invest themselves in your story. It is what will make them remember it and treasure it. Which, at the end of the day, is the one single variable that determines how successful your stories will be.

Theme can get you published. Theme can make you rich and famous. Neither is likely to happen, even to a fraction of a degree, without it.

Granted, that's a tall order. Theme can be a can of literary worms, or it can arise from the ashes of your writing on its own. When we recognize a successful story as an entity that is more than the sum of its parts, *theme* is precisely what we are talking about. Because how a writer brings this level of empathy and compulsion to a story is the *art* of storytelling. It is an essence that defies process, yet benefits from one.

Which is why some writers—too many writers—don't sweat it. They leave theme to chance. And when that happens, you leave your reader's emotional response to chance, too.

Better to be proactive about your theme. To be in command of it, rather than it being in command of you and your story. Even if it's as subtle and between-the-lines as a politician kissing a baby.

Story and theme. Theme and story.

They're interchangeable, overlapping, and in successful novels and screenplays they are *both* in play.

Some writers, when they leave the writing workshop and sit down alone in front of the blank screen, don't give much thought to the inherent *themes* of their stories. Which may not work out so well.

These writers may know—they *should* know—what their story *means*, and they're taking it for granted that the reader will, as well. Rare is the serious writer who sits down to simply entertain or play a trick on the reader. The intention is almost always heavier. Even in a story such as the film *The Sixth Sense*, which screenwriting guru Robert McKee labels in his workshops as the icon of shallow, mercenary storytelling. Because the whole thing is just a trick, a joke with an unexpected punch line, and when you try to assign meaning to it you have to stretch by a mile to even come up with a viable candidate.

If a writer is an evolved thinker across the other five of the Six Core Competencies, then this *write-it-and-see-what-happens* approach to theme actually has a chance of working. Because when you have covered the bases of characterization within the context of dramatic exposition, theme tends to become inevitable. You can't write about life experience without *saying* something about life's experiences. When a story is strong enough, when a character is deep enough, and when the conceptual landscape is universal and accessible, theme happens.

Sometimes this works, sometimes not. The more you want your story to say something specific about life and the world in which it unfolds, the more you can't rely on this organic emergence of theme. You need to write the story from a narrative strategy—an *intention* will sometimes suffice—that will allow your theme to speak loud and proud.

Understanding what theme is may not be enough. You understand how an airplane gets off the ground, too, yet you couldn't fly one if someone handed you the controls. What writers need is a *working* knowledge of theme *implementation*.

So let's go there.

17
IMPLEMENTING THEME

As one of the Six Core Competencies, you'd think *theme* would be some complex monster of a literary theory, just like character or structure.

In execution, though, not so much. At least, not always. As I said in the previous chapter, if you have complete control over the character arc in particular, theme can sometimes take care of itself. You don't have to have an agenda to speak to the truth of life, you simply need to explore and illuminate through the experiences of your characters and the consequences of their choices.

Then again, you can turn your story into a soapbox, which you can mount to preach your truth to the world, too. The risk of that is to brush up against the fine line of propaganda, but frankly it happens all the time in published books and produced films.

Theme in any story is analogous to *health* in our daily lives—the abundance of it vs. the lack of it defines how well we function. A state of health—and theme—is always present, good or bad, valued or not. Bad health leads to a compromised life. A lack of theme leads to a compromised story.

And that's the point. The more you value and cultivate the themes in your stories, the better those stories will be. If you're pursuing mediocrity, go ahead and allow theme to take care of itself. Depending on the type of story you are writing and the nature and depth of your character arc, this may be a perfectly workable strategy.

Thing is, you've got to be *really* good to pull this off.

On the other hand, if you want your story to take a *position* on an issue, you need more than a character arc to pull it off. And, by the way, you have to be pretty good at this to make *that* work, as well.

Nobody ever said this theme thing would be easy.

A PRIMER ON THEME EXECUTION

Theme is a factor that separates the professional from the newbie, the gifted (which in this trade can be an *earned* title) from the earnest but plodding apprentice. Because the professional knows that the discussion about theme quickly divides into two realms—stories where theme emerges from character, and stories in which the character experience has been *crafted* to focus on and communicate a *specific* theme.

Let's look at two examples, one from each realm.

In *The Da Vinci Code*, there's no question Dan Brown was selling us a point of view. Even if he wasn't doing so on a personal level, his characters and the nature of the story certainly led to specific reader conclusions about the issues of religion and the church, and the veracity of the history that spawned both. Because of that thematic intention on the part of the author, everything about Brown's story plan and character arc was shaded and pointed toward an intended and rabidly controversial reader conclusion: that Christ didn't die on the cross, that he had a child with Mary Magdalene, and that the Catholic Church knew of this truth and buried it in favor of their own power and rosy future.

Cynical? Perhaps. Persuasive? Doubtful. Commercial? Astoundingly so. All because of those themes. Were there multiple themes in that story? Absolutely. Just as there are in virtually any story that vicariously puts the reader into the emotional experience of the character while challenging the reader's belief systems and values.

Consider, however, *The Cider House Rules* by John Irving. This story is clearly about an issue—right to life. Abortion. Orphanages. The consequences of choice. And yet, unlike Dan Brown, Irving didn't land on one side of the issue in his story, even if he had such a stance personally. Through his characters he illuminated both ends of the spectrum of opinion, showing us challenges and consequences in either direction. The reader is left to experience the emotion of both, and thus decide for herself if her opinion had shifted because of it. Irving cast a light on the dark sides of the issue, telling us more than we wanted to know about how this might feel if it happened to someone you know and love.

It would be accurate to say that Dan Brown was *selling* us a point of view on an issue, while Irving was *exploring* an issue. As a writer, you need to be clear and confident about which of those approaches you adopt for *your* story.

THEME AS CONCEPT

While it's true that theme and concept are very different yet essential and codependent story elements—and at the risk of scrambling your brain here—a concept can be inherently thematic. *The Da Vinci Code* qualifies on that count. Another story comes to mind that is the poster child for this phenomenon, though—the film *Indecent Proposal*. That movie caused more marital arguments on the way home from the cineplex than any before or after. Because it posed a question that, quite by intention, forced everyone who saw the movie to ask and answer for themselves: If you desperately needed a million dollars, and some rich and gloriously beautiful eccentric offered a million dollars for one intimate night with your spouse ... would you either do it or allow it? And if you did, what would the consequences of that decision be?

While not necessarily recommended as a focus of your concept, a great concept is always immediately thematic in terms of its story potential. Stories like *The Da Vinci Code* and *Indecent Proposal* are simply at one end of that scale.

THEME AS SECRET NARRATIVE WEAPON

More than a few writers find themselves frustrated in their belief they can *out-write* the big-name authors, and based on narrative style alone—which is but *one* of the Six Core Competencies—they might even be right. John Grisham, Michael Crichton, Michael Connelly, Dan Brown, Nora Roberts, Janet Evanovich ... nobody's holding their breath waiting for a Pulitzer nomination for these folks. But don't fool yourself. These and many other published writers have conquered the Six Core Competencies, with no lack of emphasis on theme. It is the power of how they implement theme, rather than narrative eloquence, that defines their success.

Without strong thematic *intentions*—key word there—what you have is a sitcom. Literary junk food. Some critics and reviewers regard anything that smacks of genre to be *junk* novels ... even if they actually *liked* the books. And while those stories, too, get published, often within deep genre niches such as romance, mystery, thriller, science fiction, and fantasy, mainstream success over time isn't likely for those authors, just as it wasn't for Shyamalan and his plot-trick screenplays. At least until they bring a little theme to the book launch party. It's not coincidence that the major players within those niches—Michael Connelly, Terry Brooks, Nora Roberts—*do* imbue their stories with strong and provocative thematic landscapes.

To ignore theme is to leave its role in the reader experience to chance. To plan for it and proactively care for it as you write is to imbue your stories with the stuff of success, the elusive magic pill agents and editors are looking for.

THE THEMATIC CONTINUUM

Picture a scale from zero to ten. A line in the form of a continuum. Zero is a story with absolutely no theme whatsoever (think *Seinfeld*), and a ten is outright propaganda, which isn't necessarily bad, just driven by agenda. Such novels would include the work of C.S. Lewis and L. Ron Hubbard, which made no bones about selling you on a worldview.

In the middle of that continuum is *exploration*. A story like *The Cider House Rules* by John Irving. A story that is rich with life experience and consequences, a story that challenges values and beliefs and has viable arguments on either side.

This is perhaps the safer place to be, and for the simple reason that you minimize the potential for polarization.

Then again, Dan Brown might tell you that polarization is a terrific business model as well as a story strategy.

Where your story falls on that continuum is always your choice. And if you don't choose, if you don't establish a target, your story will land somewhere on it on its own.

Seinfeld		C.S. Lewis
0 _____ EXPLORATION _____ 10		

HOW TO TEST YOUR STORY'S THEMATIC POWER

There is a surefire way to test your thematic command of a story. And it never fails. When someone asks, "What's your story about?" how do you answer?

Do you say, "It's about two guys who rob a bank on the way home from a sales meeting because they just got fired?" Or do you say, "It's about economic darkness and anxiety and the watering down of our moral compass in the face of those pressures?"

The first answer is not remotely thematic, even if strong themes are present, which they inherently are because you are writing about the human experience. The second is *totally* thematic, even if there is a compelling underlying story—indeed, *because* of it—that makes it come to life.

Neither answer is wrong. Both answers, in fact, are better than either response alone. It is also not wrong to choose one end of the continuum over the other—you pay no attention at all to what the story means, focusing instead on a realistic and deep exploration of the character experience ... or you want to sell a point of view.

It is your *first* impulse in answering that question—*what is your story about?*—that tells you how vivid your thematic intentions are, allowing you to bring the thematic realm to the forefront as required.

And once you know, once you commit to it, then your intention will help craft each and every scene you write. *Knowing*, which translates to proactive intention, is the great implementer of theme.

18

THEME AND
CHARACTER ARC

As we've said, you can write the hell out of your characters—literally if you choose, à la William Peter Blatty—and allow theme to take care of itself. If the middle road of the continuum is your goal, or if your focus is on genre appeal and the gratuitous and vicarious deliciousness of your ending, this might be the way to go.

If your hero learns a lesson or two over the course of your story, it stands to reason that the reader has been exposed to that very same lesson. That the meaning of it all is loud and clear.

Let's say you are writing a story in which your hero has been troubled by alcohol abuse. This stems from an inner demon of an addictive personality and a backstory involving parents who were both raving alcoholics. By the end of your story your hero needs to overcome this addiction to accomplish what must be done in order to reach his goal and save the day. By definition, then, you are challenged to create that arc, from alcoholic to recovering alcoholic, over the course of your story.

You may not have begun with the intention of writing about alcohol abuse as a theme. You may not have all that much to say about it, actually, it's just a killer concept that won't let you go. Either way, though, the moment you bring an issue into a character's experience, and especially when that issue is an inner demon, you are putting your thematic hat on, worn simultaneously with your characterization hat.

Eventually you'll be wearing six hats at once, but for now just picture the two.

The blended thematic/dramatic mission of a story is rarely about something as specific as a succinct message, such as *how to conquer alcoholism*. That level of intention is best left to a textbook in the how-to section. Instead, your story might be *about* a marriage that is being destroyed by alcoholism. The hero's quest is to save the marriage. His alcoholism is merely an obstacle in his way, springing from an inner demon that we come to understand and with which we empathize.

The outer conflict might be that his wife has filed for divorce and is already seeing someone else, so the clock is ticking. But *the* inner demon—the stuff of equally gripping drama in a well-told story—is the chokehold that alcohol has on the protagonist as he tries to win her back.

Smells a lot like *theme* already, doesn't it? You don't have to try to change the world, or even one life, at the center of your intentions. That said, if you are to create real and substantive characters within such an arena, you absolutely can't avoid showing the reader the consequences of decisions on either side of the coin.

The hero's conquering of his alcoholic urges is his *character arc*. It cannot unfold without provocation; he can't just wake up one day and swear off the booze. It must be a natural response—a choice—driven by the character's needs, experiences, and consequences. By his *learning* what works and what doesn't work within the context of the story you've placed him in.

Your story becomes the classroom where those lessons are taught. Not because they are put in bold, but because they are *shown*.

Somewhere along the line someone standing in front of a class or a workshop uttered the words "show, don't tell." This is what they were talking about.

TWO REALMS OF CHARACTER-DRIVEN THEME

As you engineer this dramatic unfolding, though, remember that there are two realms of character conflict: inner and outer. The inner conflict is the barrier that blocks the hero's path to successfully encountering the exterior conflict. You must move down both roads simultaneously, one conflict informing and influencing the other.

In some stories the inner journey is every bit as dramatic and powerful as the exterior confrontation and quest. This is the stuff of bestsellers and smash box office hits, and almost exclusively the province of so-called *literary* novels. Yet again, this is precisely the source of dramatic tension in the film *Top Gun*—Maverick's ability to survive his own destructive inner drives is the only source of conflict and drama in the entire story. Very little else happens, which is why this particular movie is not considered a model script, nor is it model literature. Just model box office.

In the mystery genre we often see it in play with the hero detective. There is almost always an inner demon in play, a flaw in the form of a memory or a temptation or an addiction, maybe even a police record or a divorce, that has scarred and defined the character's worldview, confidence, values, and courage. As the clues pile up, the hero must battle and conquer those dark interior forces before stepping up to the task of finding the truth and exacting justice. It's not a formula as much as an *archetype*, one based on the inner landscape and almost always the fertile ground of *theme* in this genre.

Approaching theme in this fashion lifts a huge burden from the writer's back. It's one thing to set out to be thematic, and it's another to write a great drama with loads of internal conflict to go along with a great exterior plot. Simply having the hero explore and experience an issue, and then conquer the inner forces that would otherwise defeat him, becomes the execution of theme.

Even if theme is your highest priority—and it certainly can be— that's the best way to handle it. Your best strategy is to blend it into your character arc. Too much theme is preachy, way too much is propaganda. Your passion for a point of view can easily spill into your omniscient narrative, or if in first person, into the consciousness of your character narrator, both to the detriment of the story.

Show, don't tell. Script, don't narrate. Just the right touch on this count is the stuff of a potential bestseller.

CHARACTER ARC IN *THE DA VINCI CODE* ... OR NOT

In Dan Brown's juggernaut, the hero's character arc is neither pronounced nor critical to the outcome. This is one of the primary reasons the story itself—sales not withstanding—has not been critically praised. Its source of success is its concept and rich multiple themes—both off-the-charts extraordinary and powerful—rather than characterization, plot, or writing voice.

This isn't always the case with a literary gold mine. Series heroes, such as James Bond, rarely exhibit much of a character arc over the span of several films or books. The author relies on the appeal of the character, leaving any issues of theme to the global consequences of Bond's ability to stop the evildoers before they can hit the DETONATE button. But notice how the creators of series characters lately have bucked this trend to infuse their heroes with an arc and their stories with theme. Batman, Spider-Man, and all manner of comic book icons now have movie backstories (the original graphic novels had no shortage of backstory and character complexity) riddled with inner demons, and as we learn how the nature of the character formed we become invested in the outcome of the story on a different level. We suddenly care about Batman in a way that we've never cared about James Bond, all because these writers chose to imbue their stories with theme via character.

In *The Da Vinci Code*, the hero, Robert Langdon, showed us very little in the way of inner conflict, and therefore, there was hardly any potential for a character arc. Like Bond, Langdon was pretty much perfect from page one, very much a one-dimensional character. Dan Brown will have to be content with his $300 million payday instead of a shelf full of critical awards.

The Da Vinci Code teaches us two things: the inherent power of *theme* ... and that commercial success doesn't often hinge on how well we execute the basics. If you allow the latter to rationalize your story development approach—in other words, don't try this at home—much anxiety and pain awaits. The principles of storytelling are like gravity—defy them at your own risk. If you do, you're leaping off a building without a parachute, and you better learn how to fly very quickly.

And if you recognize the former—i.e., the literary nuclear bomb that is *theme*—a set of wings might just be in your future.

PART FIVE

THE FOURTH CORE COMPETENCY—
STORY STRUCTURE

19

THE NEED FOR
STRUCTURE

I think all teachings about writing are good. Wonderful, in fact. Taken as a whole, the oeuvre of writing wisdom out there is intimidating in both its sheer mass and its inherent lack of focus. There are so many views on so many of the variables that conspire to comprise the creative writing process, as well as define the end product, that in the end the writer must decide what works for her and what doesn't. There is a wide breadth of preferences on that particular issue, especially on the issue of story structure.

Unlike screenwriting, there are no precise and rigid structural "rules" when it comes to writing novels. Especially if you don't like the sound of the word *rules*, in which case you may reject even the hint of a baseline structural paradigm. But in today's commercial fiction market there are expectations and proven techniques that *are* accepted as fundamental *principles*, and if you want to publish your novel you will have to honor them. Or at least you'll *learn* to do so when enough rejection slips collect in that desk drawer you rarely open because, like looking at your latest IRA balance, it makes you nauseous.

BREAKING DOWN THE WRITING PROCESS

At your next writing workshop be aware of how the topics on the agenda break down into bite-size segments, each of which gets the once-over from someone you've never heard of—famous writers hardly ever give writing workshops—who is nonetheless worthy of dishing it. Topics are likely to include: how to add tension to your stories; how to impress an agent; writing better titles; fun with sentence structure; tips for better dialogue; writing juicy sex scenes; how to be more creative.

Lots of little buckets of information, all valid. What's lacking at most conferences, though, as well as on the bookshelves, is an understanding of what happens when you pour the contents of those buckets into the same vessel—your manuscript.

This is the critical and largely ignored wheelhouse of writing a story, because how those elements relate and interact, how they balance and empower each other, is the key to writing a great one. You don't just need to *understand* them as stand-alone skills, you need to master the craft of melding them.

If you ever wonder how those famous authors got famous, especially if you believe your ideas and sentences are as wonderful as theirs, this is how and why.

WRAPPING YOUR HEAD AROUND THE BIG PICTURE

Earlier I proposed that the most important single word in storytelling is *conflict*.

No conflict, no story. And even with great characters in play, the ultimate commercial viability of your work depends on the story every bit as much, if not more.

Inherent to the notion of conflict is the *architecture* of how it is handled within the narrative. And that's where structure comes into play. No structure, no story, either. Because story is what turns conflict into dramatic tension. Without which, once again, you have no story. It's the full-circle truth.

This is just a slice of the Big Picture approach you need to embrace before you can write a successful story. Some writers seek that embrace as they plow through a series of drafts, others work on it during a story planning phase before they even write a draft. Either approach can work, but neither can work outside of a basic understanding of the principles of story structure. Which by definition makes *structure* the place where a writer's journey of discovery—both about the craft and about the story—should begin.

You can be the best writer of sentences on the planet, but if you don't understand story and the structure that makes it work, you'll have to settle for love letters and poetry. You can have killer ideas and craft characters that Meryl Streep would pay you to take on in the movie version, but there will be no movie version until you give that character a story to tell, one with a keen and compelling structure.

In fact, once you do understand structure and the inherent potential of story architecture—the combining of structure with concept, character, and theme, as told through effective scenes—your sentences don't have to be all that poetic. They don't even have to be much more than merely clean, functional, and coherent.

STORY IS EVERYTHING

Narrative voice is merely, well, *nice* when it happens. But it's not what agents and editors are looking for. Not remotely. Every high school and college creative class in the land has at least a few writers who can write a sentence that would make the likes of Bill Shakespeare and John Updike weep. Fluid, elegant writing is a commodity, and when it becomes the focus of your work at the exclusion of story and character, it will get you absolutely nowhere, other than an A on a community college report card. Agents and editors and producers are looking for great *stories*, well told, with solid structure at their heart.

Rarely is this Big Picture approach to writing stories addressed. I haven't seen a writing workshop yet that offers an initial exploration of what "story" even is. It sounds too entry-level, too basic. Not something you can teach in an afternoon within the confines of a hotel conference center. They assume everybody with an admission ticket has that one nailed. And everybody doesn't. In fact, as someone who reads and coaches unpublished manuscripts for a living, I can tell you that the most common shortcoming of unpublished writing is, in fact, a lack of a solid grasp of storytelling. And this isn't true because of a lack of character or fancy sentences. It's because of an epidemic misunderstanding and ignorance on the topic of *structure*.

Which means—if that's you—as you listen to the breakout session at the next writing conference on *How to Write a Better Sex Scene*, you'll do so without the essential *context* of structure. You'll get something out of it, sure, but too often you're not sure what to *do* with it. Or worse, you'll believe you *are* sure when you're actually not. If you take that workshop but still don't know how to write a structurally sound story, at best you'll end up with a broken novel, screenplay, memoir, or short story that has a great sex scene in it.

It's like trying to build a car from scratch and taking a seminar on how to repair your brakes, when you're not completely sure how the brake system interfaces with the brake pedal, or even why the brakes are necessary at all. You're there because all the cars you've ever ridden in have brakes, which seems to be all you need to know.

Doing a lot of reading is not the prerequisite to writing. You can watch an athlete or a listen to a musician or even fly in tens of thousands of airplanes, and after decades of doing so still not have the remotest clue how the athlete, musician, or pilot really does their thing at the level they do it. They make it look easy, when it's anything but.

Writing an effective story is no different.

LEARNING THE STRUCTURAL ROPES

Those athletes, musicians, and pilots—name any professional craft and this will be just as true—learned their craft from the inside out. Stroke by stroke. Move by move. Landing by landing. Beginning with theory and philosophy and history, graduating to basic physics and mechanics, evolving to basic fundamental mastery and finally, for a few, manifesting as greatness.

Such masters are the best at what they do. Not because they hit the longest and hardest or sing the best or have the best safety record, or because any specific *thing* they do is the very best in their respective field. The key to success and the gateway to a career is grasping how to combine all the variables into something that works fluidly, dependably, and compellingly.

Story structure can be taught. But nobody can teach you how to turn it into art. If you harbor the dream of doing so, understand that an initial mastery of the requisite strokes—story structure being the foundation—is absolutely essential.

AN ANALOGY FROM YOUR DESKTOP

My computer monitor likes to freeze up. Go completely blank, then come back to life as a mishmash of visual distortion. Happens three times a day.

A moment later it flashes a distorted little window telling me, basically, that I'm screwed. Something about a "display driver" I've never heard of. I have to power down and reboot the thing before I can continue.

Once back online, I begin to research the problem. The "help desks"—perhaps the most ironically named entities in all of computerdom—universally profess a solution, using jargon like this: driver, register, cache, IP address, server, bios, FTP, SML, RDF, RSS, SGML, SQL, and about a thousand other obscure terms. Do I know what these mean? Sometimes. Have I mastered any of them? Hardly.

They—the help desk jockeys and the people who write the user manuals—*assume* I have the right contextual understanding to fix my monitor. But I don't. So I just keep rebooting. Someday soon I'll have to hire someone to do what the help desk jockeys seem to think I can do by myself: replace the misbehaving driver to repair the problem. Which, I ultimately came to realize, is not an issue with the monitor at all, but with the underlying software. Or, in more writerly terms, with the Big Picture. If I understood the fundamental structure of the machine in front of me, maybe I really could make it work without being connected to someone in New Delhi.

That's what writers face. Tons of information about the parts. An assumption that we understand what it all means and how it all connects. A lack of Big Picture context. Rampant uncertainty about how to connect the parts, or even what those parts are and the criteria for their optimization.

It begins, and ends, with story structure.

DECONSTRUCTING *THE DA VINCI CODE*

Like it or hate it, Dan Brown's *The Da Vinci Code* is one of the best-selling novels of all time. We'll use it as a case study to illustrate the structural theories presented here, and perhaps to demonstrate that elegant sentences aren't what this business is all about. I'll be as specific as possible, identifying scenes and even page numbers of the hardcover edition while juxtaposing them against the standard milestone locations set forth within the principles of solid story architecture. You'll find that everything in *The Da Vinci Code* resides right where it is supposed to be.

That's no convenient accident or coincidence, either. It's a product of some combination of Brown's sense of story architecture, combined with those of his editors.

And even if the milestones don't align *perfectly* with the model—and with novels they frequently don't need to—the general shape and form of the story does.

That's the nice thing about story structure for novelists. It's a less precise and more flexible discipline than it is for screenwriters, who pretty much need to nail their story points down to a specific page. Novelists get to push and pull at the parameters, and at their book signings they don't have to cop to the engineering-driven aspect of it at all, even when it's been key to the process.

What follows in an introduction to a structural paradigm what will seem very precise, with specific locations and length parameters in place. Writers need something to shoot for, and if we come close in our stories, the balance this model creates will work its magic. It's when we omit or violate a structural element or principle altogether that we get into trouble. Dan Brown's adherence to story structure earned him that $300 million payday. The smart money says we should pay attention.

And just to be clear, Brown didn't invent this. Neither did Syd Field, who wrote the screenwriting version of this approach, which is where I first encountered it. And certainly I didn't invent it, either. I've just adapted it for novelists and have found that it applies to other forms of writing, such as memoirs, short stories, and even nonfiction work. Frankly I'm not sure who invented it. But I do know this—virtually every successful modern novel and film adheres to it. And thus, the agents and editors and producers who comprise today's market for novels and screenplays expect these principles to be in play.

Some will find these principles to be the elusive Holy Grail they've been waiting for. Others will find it validating. More than a few will find it a foreign, challenging approach that flies in the face of a make-it-up-as-you-go sensibility. Whatever your experience, though, I guarantee you this: Apply these structural principles to your work and you will be orders of magnitude closer to getting your work published.

20
STORY STRUCTURE VS.
STORY ARCHITECTURE

The critical context of understanding the difference between story structure and story *architecture* is to accept that structure is a subset of story architecture. In order to have solid story architecture you must first create an underlying structure … plus a bunch of other stuff.

Otherwise it's like trying to put clothes on a jellyfish. Trying to lay down a coat of paint on a pile of loose rocks. Trying to stuff an aroma into a beautiful urn. Or my favorite—attempting to jam the toothpaste back into the tube.

No structure, no story, and no possibility of ensuing story architecture.

ARCHITECTURE—THE METAPHOR

Let's examine the more common meaning of these two terms, this time in context to the building and construction trade. Structure is the foundation, girders, support beams, and floor plan that allow a building to stand upright. To support weight. Structure can be, and often is, bland and without art, completely void of heart and soul. Like an empty warehouse or your local DMV office. Nobody applies the term *architecture* to those places.

Architecture describes, at least in this metaphoric context, the artful aesthetic of a building. It is construction—notice here that *structure* and *construction* have the same root word: the Latin term *structura*, which is to heap up, to build—enhanced by a host of beautiful elements and adornments, from arching doorways sculpted with scrolled designs and carvings to sweeping stairways with metallic accents and surfaces laced with designs and images and textures, all of it adorned with alluring lighting and well-placed works of art, embraced with landscaping and spiced with color. And the occasional gargoyle.

All houses are structures. But only a few are *architecturally designed* houses. Those are the ones that end up on the covers of magazines.

Which is precisely where you want your story to end up. In other words … published. Only architecturally designed stories get published.

The aesthetic sum of these parts is *art* itself. All of it beginning with a structure that was nothing more than a floor plan overlaid onto a solid foundation.

THE ART AND CRAFT OF STORY ARCHITECTURE

Story structure is the sequence of your scenes that result in a story well told. Story architecture is the empowerment of those scenes through compelling characterizations, powerful thematic intentions, a fresh and intriguing conceptual engine, and a writing voice that brings it all to life with personality and energy.

Structure is craft. It can be studied, learned, practiced, and implemented. It is not talent-dependent (talent being a relative and elusive term); it is effort and knowledge-dependent.

Architecture is art. It, too, can be studied, learned, emulated, and implemented. It *is* talent-dependent, with the acknowledgement that talent itself can be cultivated and evolved through learning and practice.

Not every writer is born to be John Updike. But every writer can bring architecture to her story, provided she open herself to it. Provided she doesn't ascribe to the there-are-no-rules school of writing and immerse herself in the proven truths that successful writers validate on every shelf in every bookstore you've ever been in.

Story architecture, in this sense, is what separates a story from the crowd. It is the differentiator between nonpublished and published writing.

21
THE BIG PICTURE OF
STORY STRUCTURE

One question, rarely posed out loud, that haunts every new writer and the majority of old ones is this: *How do I know what to write, and in what order to write it?* Everything we set out to do as novelists and screenwriters—as storytellers—is part of the quest to answer that question.

Many claim there is no answer. They are wrong.

Sometimes writers are surprised—and even defiant—when they learn there *is* an answer to that question. That the answer has been there all along. That those who sell their work know it and the rest of us don't.

And then, almost without exception, they become ecstatic when it unfolds before their eyes, and in a such a way that enables them to suddenly see it in the books they read and the movies they see.

Storytelling can be as precise a craft as you allow it to be.

You can regard *story* as a cloud-like amorphous shapeshifting process that defies definition and rules—many writers do—or you can blueprint it down to the most minuscule details of plot and characterization. Interestingly enough, either approach can work. Because the central issue here isn't whether you outline or not, or whether you work your way into your story through a series of drafts. That's just a question of style and preference—a *process*—when in fact the central variable, the one that makes or breaks your story no matter how you write it, is one comprised entirely of substance. There's nothing amorphous or vague about it.

In other words, there really is a structural expectation and paradigm for your story, and if you intend to sell what you write, you can't mess with it. Some writers toil over their manuscripts and attend workshops and buy out the writing section at the local bookstore without ever stumbling upon it. Without ever being told about it. And because you can slap different labels and terminology to it, there are very successful writers out there who are using it without the slightest awareness of it. They believe it's their *gift*, when it fact they simply have an intuitive grasp of this principle.

The good news it that it's not a gift at all. It's a principle. A model. It can be learned, practiced, and applied.

Any and all *process* in the craft of storytelling needs to end up in the exact same place: a story with solid structure. How you get there is a function of *efficiency*, not its component parts or their effectiveness. And if you don't get there—which in all likelihood is because of a lack of understanding or acceptance of the principles of story structure—that is a fate of your own choosing. Or perhaps, the blind bad luck of having not seen it explained.

Your luck is about to change.

Trying to write a story without a deliberate structure is a little like trying to invent your own airplane without paying attention to something called wings. This, in a nutshell, is the most common explanation for work that goes unpublished. It doesn't matter if you outline your stories or not, or if your words make the angels weep or not, because if what you're writing isn't hitting the page in context to solid and accepted—key word there—story structure, it's doomed until it does.

You can make up your own structure if you want to, but good luck selling your work. The people buying your work—novels and especially screenplays—virtually demand that your story conforms to the known standards professionals use.

Save the experimental stuff for your lit class. This is the real world, and in the real world effective structure trumps everything else.

STANDARDS AND EXPECTATIONS

Story structure is actually a subset of story *architecture*. The difference is important because you have to have a grasp on structure before you can get a handle on architecture. Just like you'd have to wrap your head around Bernoulli's law (look it up) before you can learn to fly an airplane.

In the building trade, a finished project is more than a blueprint that leads to a big hole in the ground, a lot of concrete and steel, and a bunch of pillars strong enough to withstand a tsunami of Spielbergian proportions. It is also the fine finishes and intricate designs and delicate moldings, the textures and aesthetics that comprise the heart and soul of a space, the intangibles that make it more than a big box into which you unload furniture. When it is done, when it is a thing of beauty and function, it is called *architecture*. And it begins, at its very core, with structure.

INTRODUCING A BASIC FOUR-PART SEQUENTIAL STORY MODEL

The basic model for structuring your stories is as universal as it is misunderstood. Each of its four parts (three parts for screenplays, the middle of which can be broken into halves with separate definitions and missions) exists for different reasons and offer starkly different narrative contexts for the scenes they house. That context is the empowering juice of structure, the thing that makes it all work and answers the question, *what do I write next?* The context of each part tells you.

We will also look at the major story milestones that separate these four parts—these are as important as the parts themselves—and the various criteria that help them bring a story to full and glorious life. In other words, you'll learn what to write and where to put it in the sequence of your story.

If you want to think of four-part story structure as a roadmap, even a blueprint, that's precisely what it is. And if that offends your definition of art, you need to realize that people live and work in buildings that function, even if they are dripping with award-winning architecture. All art has structure to it. With novels and screenplays, you don't have to look hard to find it in successfully published and produced work. If proper structure is not there, chances are nobody will notice because nobody will ever finish the thing.

Already there are writers who, hearing words like *roadmap* and *blueprint*, make the leap to words like *formulaic* and *generic*. It's interesting to observe that the cousin of the word *genre*—the common description of a category of fiction—is the word *generic*. But I ask you—are mysteries generic? Romance novels? Thrillers? They all follow a fairly rigid basic story structure, and they all remain at the front of the bookstore decade after decade.

Four-part story structure is both ancient and universal.

In screenwriting it's called a three-act dramatic paradigm, and it's the first thing you learn in screenwriting school. Novelists, on other hand, can go entire lifetimes without encountering such a model. But there *is* such a model, one that's only a very slight adaptation of the one used in screenwriting.

But when you break it down, the three-act movie paradigm begins to look almost exactly like the more universal four-part model upon which it is based, and which applies to novels with equal validity. Virtually every successful novel you read and movie you see (art films get to invent their own structure; do that with your novels and screenplays at your own peril) is built on this trusted and proven structural foundation.

Story structure is to novels and screenplays what wings—and the principles of Bernoulli's law that make them work—are to airplanes.

It's also what mathematics is to software. What the human reproductive system is to childbirth … and when you consider that no two human beings come out of the womb exactly alike, even twins, you see the metaphoric wonder of structure begin to blossom.

Formulaic? I don't think so. More like *universal law*.

Generic isn't inherently bad. All human beings are generic—two arms, two legs, a torso (for better or worse), and a head. That's the structure of human beings. And yet, no two people are exactly alike. Some of us are just plain off the charts unique.

If that analogy doesn't rid you of your artistic resistance to story structure, nothing will. Because if there are seven billion people in the world with the same basic structure, and if each and every one of them is unique, perhaps you don't think you need to worry about your story being something less than art because it aligns with the accepted principles of story structure, or if there's a similar story out there in the database of literature that has the same basic premise and approach.

Chew on that and come back when you wake up and smell the royalties.

It's just the way it is. If you want to sell what you write, you need to understand and use the principles of basic story structure in your work.

THE FOUR PARTS OF A STORY

Some writers like things in nice little boxes. Others, not so much. Either way, you can look at your story like a box, of sorts. You toss in all kinds of stuff—pretty sentences, plot, subplot, characters, themes, stakes, cool scenes—then stir it up and hope that somehow, by the grace of God, it all ends up on the page in some orderly fashion that your reader will enjoy.

That's one way to write a novel or screenplay.

At the very least, you'll have to pour the box out and start over again, time after time, before any of what's inside begins to make sense to anyone but you. You can get there doing it this way ... but there's a better way.

In fact, if this is how you go about telling your story, just making it up as you go along without regard to anything remotely structural, you'll be reorganizing your box, time after time, until you do finally stumble upon the structure you are about to learn here. If you *ever* do. Because it's the only one that works. Or at least, the only one that a publisher will actually pay you for. Tough to hear, but true.

Now think of that box as a vessel holding four smaller boxes. They are numbered, one through four. Which means things just got clearer if not easier.

Instead of sixty or so little parts to juggle (scenes), you have only four big parts. At least for now. Once you figure out what each box needs to be, what the *mission* of the scenes within them will be (as defined by the part in which they reside), you'll be much better equipped to organize the sixty or so scenes they *collectively* contain.

Imagine that each of the four boxes is different in terms of purpose (context), designed to hold scenes that are categorized and used differently than the ones in the other boxes. In other words, each box has a mission and a purpose unique unto itself.

And yet, no single box contains the whole story. Each box is a subset, a *part* of a whole story. Only all four, viewed sequentially, do the storytelling job.

Each narrative scene you write is in context to whichever box it goes into. Meaning, the *mission* of the part *defines* the context of the scenes within it.

Imagine that these boxes are to be experienced in sequence. Everything in the first box is there to make the other boxes understandable, to make them meaningful. Everything in the second box is there to make the first box (where you invest the reader in the hero) useful by placing what the reader is now rooting for in *jeopardy*. The first box may not make sense until the second box is opened, and when it is, the reader is already in there with your hero, emotionally vested, intellectually involved.

This is why the first box—or *part*—has to be written properly, and according to specific criteria. Because the viability and success of the second box depend on it.

With that in place, everything in the third box takes what the second box presents and ratchets it up to a higher level within a dramatic *new* context. Because now, when done properly, we are in full rooting mode for the hero, who is acting differently, more courageously and brilliantly, than in box number two.

If you're sensing that the hero has a different experience, and acts differently, in each of the four boxes, that's precisely correct. If you didn't realize this before, congratulations, this alone will make your novels significantly better. It's called character arc (see Part Three of this book), and it is story *structure* that helps you make sense of it.

CONTEXT WITHIN EACH PART

Everything in the fourth and final box pays off all that the first three boxes have presented in the way of stakes, emotional tension, and satisfaction. That's the Part 4 mission, and it is as unique to this box as the mission of setup is unique to the first box, or Part 1.

It's like great sex. There's anticipation, followed by foreplay, followed by, well, you know, then there's the finale, also known both inside and outside of this analogy as the climax. One without the others doesn't work so well. Each phase of the experience empowers the one that follows.

Do it any other way and nobody will pay you for it.

The things that go into any given box go *only* into that box. Each has its *own* mission and context, its own flavor of stuff. Or, more to the point, its own scenes.

One of the most common mistakes writers make is putting box two behavior and context into the third box, box one behavior and context into the fourth box, and so forth. This is a writer who doesn't understand story structure, and while he may write glorious sentences about abundantly compelling ideas, he'll never sell what he writes until he does.

Such subtleties help explain the seemingly inexplicable receipt of rejection letters.

When you lay out the four boxes in order, they make perfect sense. They flow seamlessly from one to the next, building the stakes and experiences of the previous box before handing it off to the one that follows.

It's not a formula—it's storytelling *physics*. It's like gravity. It's what makes it all work.

Think of the boxes in terms of the *life* of your hero over the course of the story. Now think of that life in terms of a child growing up. Aren't the childhood years different than the teen years? The teen years different than the young adult years? Those early adult years vastly different from middle age, and then different still from the senior phase of life?

Isn't the accumulated knowledge and wisdom, hard-won through experience, the one thing that makes the living of those years, those eras, different from the ones that precede it?

As it is in life, so it is within a story. It's character arc applied to literary gravity. Defy gravity without applying the physics of an airplane and you're in for trouble. With writing, if you take something out of one box and put it into another, the whole thing can go sideways, the equivalent of jumping off a cliff. Only by observing the criteria and context of the scenes within each box will the sum of the collective boxes—the story—make sense.

Each box—each *part* of the story—tells you what it needs. It will accept nothing else. Neither will the agent or editor to whom you send your manuscript.

And *that* is the theory and opportunity of four-part story structure in a nutshell.

22

THE FIRST BOX:
PART 1—THE SETUP

The first 20 to 25 percent of your story—the first of the four boxes—has a singular, critical mission: to *set up* everything that is to follow.

That context breaks down into a handful of important things Part 1 needs to accomplish, all under the umbrella of that singular mission. The mission is *not* to fully introduce the story's main antagonistic force, but rather, to *foreshadow* it. If Part 1 does show antagonistic force at all, it shows only part of it, without explaining what it means. And it's not to show the reader the big inciting incident in the first few pages—that's called a *hook*, which is an important part of the setup.

Let's look at an example. In the first few pages of a story we might see someone following the hero, though the hero remains unaware. This presents tension and conflict, because we fear for the hero's safety. It's a great hook and it foreshadows the conflict of the story. But it doesn't *mean* anything yet. We don't understand how this conflict, this antagonist force, will thrust the hero down a certain path in quest of a specific outcome, or what the stakes of that quest will be. *That* doesn't happen until the very end of Part 1, at the milestone moment called the First Plot Point. All that's happening here during Part 1 is the *setup* of that meaning, which can include foreshadowing, the establishing of stakes, and the introduction of the hero in context to her life before the First Plot Point.

Stuffing too much story into this first box, the *setup*, can be a fatal mistake. But a common one.

Most importantly, the job of Part 1 is to establish the *stakes* for what happens to the hero after Part 1. Here is where the reader is made to *care* about what happens next.

In the case of our example, we come to understand what the hero has to lose, such as a family, a fortune, or some specific purpose in life, if this stalker grows more threatening. These are the stakes of the story, and when the reader comes to know them before fully understanding what will place them in jeopardy, our story will be more effective for it.

Despite the presence of tension, the plot doesn't even really begin to roll in Part 1 at all.

THE MISSION OF PART 1

The mission of Part 1 is to set up the plot by creating stakes, backstory, and character empathy, while perhaps foreshadowing the forthcoming conflict.

Basically, it's to introduce the hero and show us what he has going on in his life ... not for the remainder of the story, but before the arrival of the main antagonistic force (the primary conflict of the story) at the First Plot Point. That arrival often doesn't even happen in Part 1—when it does you have an early inciting incident, which is fine, but it doesn't relieve you of the obligation to insert a proper First Plot Point in the proper place—even if strongly fore-shadowed or even partially revealed. Part 1 shouldn't fully explain the conflict in terms of how it *affects* the protagonist until near the end of the first part.

Fully launching the story too early compromises your opportunity to establish these elements. It shortchanges the setup phase, which, as we've just seen, has several essential missions to fulfill before any of that happens.

The more we empathize with what the hero has at stake—what he needs and wants in his life, and what trials and tribulations and opportunities he is facing before the arrival of the primary conflict—the more we *care* about him when all of that changes.

The more the reader cares, the more effective the story will be.

With this caring aspect fully in place over the course of Part 1, it is at the *end* of Part 1 that the plot really gets its legs. That's when the hero receives his marching orders and the antagonistic force fully comes into play. It's where *meaning* is bestowed on the hero, the reader, or both. Before the end of Part 1, we aren't sure what it all means, even if it's scary or titillating.

That moment is called the First Plot Point. It is often confused with what is called the *inciting incident*, which, as stated a moment ago, may or may not occur at the plot point. Sometimes an inciting incident can be rolled out earlier in Part 1, as part of the setup. When *that* happens—when something huge and dramatic and game-changing arrives significantly before the end of Part 1—this early "inciting incident" becomes part of the "setup" of the forthcoming plot point.

An example will help clarify.

In Ridley Scott's film *Thelma & Louise*, two women shoot and kill a guy they've met in a bar but who comes on too strong once they reach the parking lot. It's not exactly an accident, more like angry self-defense that reflects pent-up anger. What was a lark shared by two feisty, unhappy women is suddenly something else entirely. It looks and smells just like a First Plot Point, but because of *where* it happens in the story sequence and how it *doesn't* meet the criteria for a First Plot Point, it's not one. An inciting incident, yes, because it does incite what happens next. It's huge, a total game-changer. But only when something else happens, something that does meet the criteria by imparting meaning to it—by defining the journey and challenge that lies ahead for the heroes—does it become a legitimate Plot Point.

The movie is a bit over two hours in length, which means the First Plot Point is due at somewhere around the thirty-minute mark. The shooting happens at 19:30, too soon to be a functioning First Plot Point. But very right-on-the-mark as an inciting incident.

Inciting *what*, exactly? For the next ten minutes the women go back into the bar and ponder what happened. It's understandably a chaotic and emotional discussion—and that's all it is, a discussion—leading to a point at which a decision is made. A decision that changes their lives forever and launches them down a path.

Did the shooting itself change their lives? Did it launch them down a path forever? Yes. But did it define those changes and the path? No. Because we don't know what their response would be. They could turn themselves in, and the outcome would have looked completely different.

But they don't. They decide to run. They do this at the thirty-one-minute mark. Which does make this moment the First Plot Point. It fulfills all the criteria for a First Plot Point, much more so than the shooting itself, and it occurs at the right place, structure-wise. By running, by not turning themselves in, the women become outlaws. They must flee and continue to evade the law, which in their mind licenses them to continue to break it. This decision at thirty-one minutes commences their story, it defines their goal, it introduces and clarifies the obstacles to that quest, and it certainly defines the stakes of their journey.

This is a common structure. An inciting incident happens early or in the middle of Part 1. In Michael Mann's film *Collateral*, for example, a body falls on the hero's taxi—an early inciting incident—but the meaning and implications to the hero's ongoing need, quest, and journey, and the inherent stakes, aren't clear until the real First Plot Point arrives. Which, unlike the previous inciting incident, unfolds as a simply yet ominous conversation between the hero and bad guy sitting in the back of the cab he is driving.

Notice how the dramatic strength or visual impact of the First Plot Point isn't a criteria. In both of the examples above, the First Plot Point is just a conversation. A moment. And yet, a game-changing, journey-defining milestone.

PART 1 IS MISSION DRIVEN

The purpose of Part 1 is to bring the character to that transition point through a series of scenes. Part 1 ends when the hero is made aware of the arrival of something new in his life, through decision, action, or off-stage news. It launches a new quest, a sudden need, a calling, a journey, which is often something very scary or challenging. It is at this moment that something comes forward to create an obstacle. There is now something the hero needs to accomplish or achieve.

If the journey was already underway in Part 1, the First Plot Point alters the nature of it or clarifies the obstacles, the stakes, and the nature of the quest. Or, the First Plot Point can be a completely unexpected and largely unforeshadowed moment in which everything changes on every conceivable level. You get to decide all this, and in context to the mission of the parts through which the story will unfold.

The very end of Part 1—the arrival of the First Plot Point moment—is the first *full* view of the story's primary antagonistic force. The bad guy, if you will. *Full* doesn't mean that the true nature of the antagonistic force is by any means complete, but rather, it's the first time the hero (and the reader) actually gets a notion of the nature and extent of the opposing force.

We may have seen the antagonistic force before, but now, at the end of Part 1, we understand what it wants, and how what it wants creates opposition to what the hero wants.

In other words, *conflict*. Conflict is the essence of effective fiction. And defining it is the primary mission of the First Plot Point, as *set up* by Part 1 of the story.

The rest of the story, Parts 2 through 4, is about how the hero moves through this new quest, encountering an escalating series of obstacles and experiencing phases of growth and enlightenment along the way.

A new journey begins at the First Plot Point. This is where the story *really* starts.

Remember the phases of life analogy a moment ago?

In Part 1 the hero is somewhat like an orphan, unsure of what will happen to him next. And like we do with orphans, we feel for him, we empathize with him. We care. The story, the quest you give the hero, is what *adopts* him going forward. It gives him purpose and meaning, a life within the context of the story. An orphan has no mission, no need other than to survive the moment. His future is unknown, left to fate. So it is within a story, though the hero may think he knows what's ahead for him.

In a novel of three hundred to four hundred pages, this Part 1 setup should take fifty to one hundred pages or so, or the first twenty-five to thirty pages in a screenplay. The longer it is, the more foreshadowing and dramatic tension (unexplained or unfulfilled conflict, which doesn't yet benefit from an illuminated purpose via the First Plot Point) is needed.

In *The Da Vinci Code*, for example, Part 1 is largely a tense chase scene unfolding within the Louvre. Robert Langdon (the hero) has no idea what's going on, who is chasing whom, or why, but we go on that chase with him, right through the first one hundred pages or so, before the First Plot Point arrives. There is no *meaning* yet, only tension.

Has the story really started here? No. This is all setup. Dramatic tension, certainly. But a defined quest for the hero, with a known antagonist in his way? Not even close. Which is as it should be in Part 1 of the story.

23

THE SECOND BOX:
PART 2—THE RESPONSE

At the end of Part 1—at the moment of the First Plot Point, which we'll examine in more detail in chapter thirty—you unveiled the real course and destination of the story: the path leading to an inevitable showdown between the hero and the opposing force that stands in the way of what he needs to do, acquire, achieve, or change in order to reach his goals. These were not the hero's goals of Part 1, but rather they are new goals as created by the introduction of the First Plot Point.

The goal could be survival, finding love, getting away from love gone bad, acquiring wealth, healing, attaining justice, stopping or catching the bad guys, preventing disaster, escaping danger, saving someone, saving the entire world, or anything else from the realm of human experience and dreams.

But whatever the hero needs, there must be something opposing the hero's quest to achieve it. No opposition, no story.

Before the Plot Point, which consists of the entirety of Part 1, that quest didn't exist. At least in the form in which it will unfold for the remainder of the story. The hero had other plans. But with the appearance of the First Plot Point moment, everything changes, *including* the hero's plans. A new journey, quest, or need is on his plate now.

In Dennis Lehane's novel *Shutter Island*, for example, the First Plot Point is when, during what is a combination of a flashback and a delusion, the ghost of the hero's wife tells him that "Laeddis is here." Everything that happened prior to this moment was a setup for what we (and the hero) experience afterwards. It's a subtle moment that occurs right on time (page 88 of the 369-page mass market paperback), easily missed. There had been a series of confusing, foreshadowing dramatic moments prior to this milestone, but they were out of context to the big picture, and without ever launching the story in its intended direction. They existed solely to serve the *setup* of the macro story, which was the ultimate resolution of the hero's grasp of his very dark reality.

Storytelling is all about conflict. Some would tell you it's all about character, but that's not accurate. Because character *depends* on conflict to illuminate itself. Every story has conflict, or it's not a story at all. Conflict is what stands in the way of what the hero needs or wants in the story.

In *Shutter Island*, the conflict is the hero's own impending insanity, preventing him from accepting reality and saving himself. Only through the pursuit of that goal do we see, and care about, the unfolding, *de-layering* of the hero's true character.

PART 2: AFTER THE FIRST PLOT POINT

Part 2 is the hero's *response* to the introduction of this new situation, as represented by the conflict itself. It's too early to have him attack the problem. Part 2 is about a reaction, through action, decision, or indecision, to the antagonistic force, and the launch of a new quest to fulfill a newly defined need.

The context of every scene in Part 2 is *response*. To what? To the new quest, goal, stakes, and obstacles as introduced at the First Plot Point. If you, the writer, have succeeded in Part 1 of the story, the reader will *care* about that journey.

In Part 2 the hero is running, hiding, analyzing, observing, recalculating, planning, recruiting, or anything else required before moving forward. If you have your hero being *too* heroic here, being brilliant, already knocking heads with the bad guys (or some other dark force), it's too early. You're in violation of structural principles if that's the case.

In *The Da Vinci Code*, Langdon spends the entirely of Part 2 simply running away from the cops who are chasing him. It's all blind *response*, without knowing who is after him or why, and therefore without a clue as to how he can turn the tables and begin to defend or attack, and expose the truth. That's what's ahead in Part 3 of the story, which is a completely different context.

At the end of Part 2, just when the hero thinks he has it figured out, when he has a plan, everything about Langdon's journey, and the reading experience, changes. This is the Midpoint of the story, which is a major milestone in its own right (which we'll cover in chapter thirty-four).

In Part 2, the hero is a *wanderer*, staggering through a forest of options and risks, not sure where to go or what to do next. He is no longer orphaned as he was in Part 1; he now has a purpose, a life, a quest, and it's just beginning.

Part 2 comprises roughly the next one hundred pages of your novel— which means, there's an entire contextual infrastructure to it … stay tuned to see what the hero does about it—or, if you're writing a screenplay, from page 27 to 60, give or take a few.

24

THE THIRD BOX:
PART 3—THE ATTACK

By now we've had enough of the hero stumbling around, acting fearful and hesitant, somewhat clueless, basically trying to figure out how to fix things and move forward and coming up empty. In other words, *responding*. In fact, the hero may not be remotely heroic at this stage.

In Part 3, though, the hero begins to try to fix things. That's the context of this quartile—to become *proactive* and downright courageous and ingenious in the quest to attain the goal. Which, by the way, continues to evolve, get stronger and more adaptive to the sudden heroics.

It is here where the hero begins to *attack* the obstacles before him. The hero starts to conquer inner demons and begin doing things a little differently than before, or at least come to understand how they have been standing in his own way. That the hero needs to change if he is to succeed. In Part 3 the hero summons courage and applies creative thinking. He leads. He moves forward.

Of course, this can't happen in a vacuum. Something—new information, new awareness—needs to enter the story to serve as a catalyst for the hero's evolution from the wanderer/responder in Part 2 toward more proactive, attacking warrior ways.

That element takes place at the Midpoint milestone—the wall between Part 2 and Part 3—and the story moves forward and shifts because of it. This is a critical scene in your story (we'll look closely at all the major story milestones later), one that many writers miss and thus leave the reader with a story that is linear, flat, and without surprise. After the Midpoint shakes things up, the plot thickens—the antagonistic force is moving forward, too—and what the hero thought would work isn't quite enough. He needs more. More courage. More creativity. A better plan.

And *that's* the next one hundred pages or so of your story (thirty pages in a screenplay). That's Part 3.

The wanderer has now become a warrior.

At the Midpoint in *The Da Vinci Code*, Langdon discovers that there is a "teacher" who can explain everything. The retreat of Part 2 becomes the pursuit of this teacher, coincident with his continuing avoidance of the police. Langdon realizes (at the Midpoint) that the *teacher* is the means of understanding and ultimate salvation. After this Midpoint realization, he's no longer running or responding, he's *attacking* the problem. Also, the subplot involving the homicidal albino assassin experiences a Midpoint context shift of its own, when the assassin is taken captive by the very teacher that Langdon is looking for. Of course, this is behind the curtain of Langdon's awareness, but not the reader's, thus taking full advantage of the power of point of view.

And then, the final piece of the puzzle arrives at the end of Part 3— the Second Plot Point (see chapter thirty-seven). And everything changes again. The Part 4 chase is on.

25

THE FOURTH BOX:
PART 4—THE RESOLUTION

The thing to remember about Part 4 is that no new information can enter the story here, from the Second Plot Point on. Everything the hero needs to know, to work with, or to work alongside (such as another character or resource) needs to have already been put in play.

Part 4 shows how the hero summons the courage and growth to come forward with a solution to the problem, to reach the goal, to overcome inner obstacles in order to save the day or even the world, to attain the fame and riches associated with victory, and to generally beat down and conquer the story's antagonistic force.

Here's a cardinal rule: The hero needs to be the *primary catalyst* in the resolution of the story. The hero needs to be *heroic*. There should be no rescuing of the hero, and the hero should never be a bit-player or an observer of the story's resolution. He is smack in the middle of the resolution, making it happen. Cardinal rules do get broken, but don't be seduced by exceptions written by Pulitzer Prize winners.

Lame Part 4 hero status is one of the most common mistakes found in unpublished manuscripts. The protagonist needs to be heroic, both generally and within the specific structural mechanics of the story itself.

Sometimes a hero can actually perish in the process. Dead heroes are sometimes big hits with readers. But before that happens, the hero needs to have solved at least a major element of the problem he was facing. When heroes die it is because they must in order to save others and resolve the story for optimum reader impact.

And that's why the orphan, then the wanderer, and then the warrior, now becomes, either figuratively or literally, the *martyr*. Because he does what must be done in order to reach the goal.

Even if the hero doesn't die—and for the most part heroes don't—he's at least willing to. And that's the essence of the martyr's soul.

In *The Da Vinci Code*, Langdon solves all the riddles that define this book with his brilliant powers of deduction. This is his heroism—he is the guy who solves the puzzle and uncovers the truth, and then steps into the role of advocate for and champion of that truth as the authorities close in.

THE WHOLE OF THE FOUR PARTS

Each part of this four-part structural model is of roughly the same length, though you can cheat the first and fourth parts to a fewer number of pages, the deficit being made up for in the middle two parts. In three-act movie structure, Parts 2 and 3 as described here are simply combined—but with the same unique contextual essences—to comprise Act 2, known in Hollywood parlance as *the Confrontation*.

And indeed it is. In Part 2 (the first half of *the Confrontation*), the hero confronts the problem by fleeing from its inherent danger, and in the second half he seeks to confront it face-to-face, and boldly, with a plan.

Rent some DVDs and read some paperbacks and witness this four-part paradigm play out before your eyes. Sometimes the contexts and milestones are subtle, but I assure you, it's all there. Four parts, four contexts, four completely separate missions for their scenes.

PART 1	PART 2	PART 3	PART 4
Setup/Orphan	Response/Wanderer	Attack/Warrior	Resolution/Martyr

As much as this clarifies the structure, the whole four-part paradigm gets even better when you throw in a whole menu of story milestones and Midpoint structural elements that help you along the way. So let's take a look.

26
THE ROLE OF
STORY MILESTONES

My approach to story structure is a little like learning surgery. In the previous chapters we took on the four major parts of a story—that's like learning about anesthesia, scalpels, catheters, and cardiac monitors. Now its time to cut into the patient and muck around a bit, see what makes the machine tick.

Because it's what's *inside* story structure that counts.

Each of the four parts of your story has specific elements—*milestones*—within their allotted pages. Each of the transitions between the parts is a major story milestone— First Plot Point, Midpoint, Second Plot Point—establishing context for the part that follows it.

But there are other milestones. Five others for a total of eight—which we'll discuss below.

Like the four story parts themselves, each milestone has a specific mission and function, and they are nonnegotiable if your goal is to write a story that adheres to the expectations and physics of standard story structure.

They are like the horn between quarters of a football game. Everything stops. The teams switch ends of the field. And then play begins again, with the same score but with a fresh clock.

Milestones are points in your story where new information enters the narrative and changes the direction, tension, and stakes. These milestones appear in the same approximate sequential place, separating the four parts of the story. Which means, every milestone is a plot *twist* (there are two minor exceptions to this, but we won't sweat them here and now), but not every plot twist is a milestone. Story milestones are like birthdays—every birthday is an anniversary of the day you were born, but not every birthday is the beginning of a new era of your life (your Bar Mitzvah, getting your driver's license, no longer having to use a false I.D. to drink).

Which is perfectly fine, by the way. You can pepper your story with plot twists to your heart's content. But you must account for the major story milestones—the ones you are about to learn here—no matter how subtle they may appear to be.

Many writers understand plot *twists*. But too few know where to put them, and why, in terms of story architecture.

THE NATURE AND PURPOSE OF MILESTONE SCENES

Milestones can be easy to miss from the reader's perspective. Because, while they are often huge and explosive—the ship hits an iceberg—they can also be nothing more than a whisper, a glimpse of a shadow, a seemingly innocent reference, a fleeting glimpse of a weapon, a peek behind the curtain.

Milestone scenes are critical, not only because they are the tent poles that support the weight of your story; they are also the lynchpins for most of the other scenes in your novel or screenplay. Without them you have no plot.

Without them, your story has no chance.

For every major milestone scene there are often several scenes leading up to it and several that spring forth from it. And *that* is what answers the question: *What do I write, and where do I put it?* The milestones tell you.

A reasonable length for a story is about sixty scenes (give or take, depending on length), some of which are strung together as sequences. So, the five major milestone scenes in Parts 2 and 3—Plot Point One, Pinch Point One, the Midpoint, Pinch Point Two, and the Second Plot Point—alone are tied into at least half of your entire story.

Determine what your milestone scenes are, and you've basically structured your entire story. When you throw in the Part 1 setup and the Part 4 resolution, which are by definition completely in context to the major milestone scenes, 80 percent or more of your story is directly connected to and dependent upon these milestones.

The milestones *are* the story.

THE MILESTONES DEFINED

Here are the story milestones you'll need to conceive, construct, and execute in your story, no matter how you go about it:

- The *opening* scene or sequence of your story;
- A *hooking* moment in the first twenty pages (ten pages for a screenplay);
- A *setup inciting incident* (optional, as the inciting incident can be the First Plot Point; this is a call the writer needs to make in planning the story);
- The First Plot Point, at approximately 20 to 25 percent through the story;
- The First *Pinch Point* (don't worry, we'll define that in chapter thirty-six) at about the three-eighths mark, or precisely in the middle of Part 2;
- A context-shifting Midpoint, at precisely the middle of the story;
- A Second Pinch Point, at about the five-eighths mark, or in the middle of Part 3;
- The Second Plot Point, at about 75 percent through the story;
- The final resolution scene or sequence.

These are the most important moments, the most critical scenes, in your story.

If you allow for three (or more) additional scenes that setup and surround these milestone moments, that's at least thirty to forty scenes. Or about two-thirds of your entire story.

You read that right. By planning for these pivotal milestone scenes, by grasping what they are and how they empower the flow of the story, and thus, understanding what types of scenes need to set them up, pay them off, and connect them, you will have launched the architecture for well over half of your entire novel or screenplay.

That's the power of story structure. It's huge.

None of these critical scenes exist in a vacuum.

You will, at any given moment in the process, be writing toward the milestones or *from* them, setting them up and then being propelled forward because of them.

Everything else in your story is connective tissue. People talking to each other, mulling over options, reacting, planning, stopping to rest, making love, analyzing, licking their wounds, studying maps, calling for help, waxing philosophical and reflecting, searching for answers.

Once you know your milestones, those connecting scenes practically write themselves. Because they have a purpose, a mission. A defined context that, because it works, tells you what kind of scene should go in a specific place. A place that melds them into the flow of the story in an empowering way.

Doing this can result in a first draft—yes, I'm actually saying this—that is worthy of submission after a quick copyedit and polish.

In fact, milestone-driven story planning is the *only* way a successful polished first-draft submission can happen.

I imagine some organic writers are throwing this book against the wall right about now. But here's the deal with an organic writing process—you *will* square off with the need to come up with these major milestone scenes as you write your drafts. Sooner or later. In your case, probably later. No way around it.

And if you don't, your story never stood a chance anyhow.

This is the inherent danger of organic writing. If you aren't even *aware* of what structural milestones need to be created, and where—your story won't work. And you may never understand why.

At least until you grasp the principles of story structure, which aren't in the least bit in conflict with the organic writing process. In fact, it empowers it.

STORY PLANNING WITH MILESTONES

You're not done with the drafting process until you nail all these milestone scenes. Nor are you done with the story planning phase until all these milestones are clear to you.

If you use your drafts as exploratory vehicles for that purpose, you condemn them to a major rewrite. Because every milestone requires a setup, and many require foreshadowing, neither of which is possible until you know where you're headed.

For example, if you're writing along with no real clue as to what will happen at your Midpoint, trusting that when you get there it will be self-evident, there's no way to foreshadow it or set it up. At least, not until the next draft. Which you can avoid, or at least make easier, if you plan all this out beforehand.

Outline or no outline, the creation of your story's milestones is the most important element of the storytelling process. More so, in fact, than the actual words on the page.

While I do advocate pre-draft outlining, and in light of the fact that the more you know about story milestones the more likely you'll be to think about them before you begin writing, I realize that it's not for everybody. Especially outlining, which is only one way to plan a story. What I *am* suggesting for *both* story planners and organic drafters is a grasp of story structure built around a handful of key milestone scenes. The more you know about those scenes and how to connect them with bridging narrative—at whatever point you know it—the closer you'll be to writing a draft solid enough to be submitted.

Here's the truth about organic writing: It's just story planning by another name. By writing drafts without a narrative or character goal, you are using your drafts as an exploratory phase or tool. In other words, you are applying the act of drafting toward the planning of your story. The reason it's actually more a *planning* activity than an actual *writing* activity—true, it's all "writing" in a general way of speaking—is that you absolutely *will* need to start over, or at least revise it to the extent you might as well start over. You can begin writing a draft that stands a chance of working until you know the plan, which includes a clear vision for these five story milestones at a minimum. Anything prior to that—be it a draft, an outline, or a pad of yellow sticky notes affixed to your refrigerator door—is just story planning by another name.

When and how you come to identify and link those milestones during the process is completely up to you.

And if you're wondering where the examples from *The Da Vinci Code* are, they're coming. In the following chapters we'll look closer at each of the milestones, and I'll reference how—and where—Dan Brown did it.

27

WRITING TO PUBLISH: THE MOST
IMPORTANT ASPECT OF YOUR STORY

I won't deny it: Coming out with a claim that one part of a novel is more important than others is always going to be fodder for a rousing critique group debate. Or, a slough of nasty comments on whatever blog—like mine—such heresy appears. I know, because it happened to me within minutes of posting such heresy. Or, as one commenter pointed out, *hearsay*.

Certainly, all the parts of a great novel come together to comprise something that is unquestionably greater than the sum of the parts. But like a good meal, there's no getting around the truth that if the first bites don't go down well, if they smell and taste like reheated leftover take-out, the rest of the meal might just end up in a Tupperware bowl.

Let's be real, a story that opens lame will never see the inside of a bookstore or make it onto a movie screen. That's why I believe that the most important section of your story is the *first* part of it. If you've ever started reading a novel or screenplay and then put it down after an hour—and who hasn't—you know this to be true.

Some call this part of a story the opening act, others refer to it as Part 1, Act I, the setup, the parting curtain, the opening salvo, the hook (not an entirely accurate description if you know your way around story structure, because a hook is a single scene or sequence), or just the first quarter of the total pages. This is what happens from page 1 until the First Plot Point, when the story hits its stride.

And to pound home this point, I'll again use an apt metaphor.

The first fifty to one hundred pages of your novel or thirty pages of your screenplay, or everything that comprises the setup, is not unlike a literary balloon. The essence of good fiction is tension, and an inflated balloon depends on tension (air pushing at the skin, trying to escape, trying to explode) for its shape and personality. The more air you put into it, the tighter the tension, and the more inevitable the forthcoming explosion.

And the hotter the air, the better.

A balloon that is so overinflated that it explodes a few feet off the ground isn't any fun at all.

The First Plot Point of your story is when the story's primary tension—its antagonistic force—makes its initial full frontal appearance in a form that imparts meaning and consequence to the story's hero, and in context to stakes you have already established. Prior to that point, you've likely foreshadowed it, or hinted at it, or at most given the reader a partial silhouetted view of it, but somewhere between pages 50 and 100 the entire story changes with a big explosion of drama (or perhaps a more subtle one that nonetheless changes everything). In essence, the balloon explodes.

The more hot air—character, theme, stakes, backstory, a ticking clock, etc.—that went into your literary balloon before you blow it up on the page, the more dramatic and effective the explosion is. But you can't put *too* much into it yet, lest the whole thing blow up in the reader's face.

In effect, at the First Plot Point your story erupts … the hero suddenly has a quest and a mission … the hero now has visible and daunting obstacles to face along that journey … the antagonistic force shows itself with an agenda of its own … we now have something to root for and against … the story has stakes … and if you've inflated your Part 1 balloon properly, the reader is invested, the reader cares.

In more writerly terms, the reader is hooked.

Imagine beginning the writing of your story without knowing and completely understanding what the forthcoming plot point explosion will entail. How could you possibly imbue your opening pages with all those elements that will effectively set the stage for the remainder of the book, and an ensuing onslaught of tension-filled balloons to follow? It won't happen, at least not until you've engineered your story—be it through planning or multiple drafts—to illuminate that understanding.

Finish strong, absolutely. But starting strong is actually more important, because it creates the context—and the tension-inducing hot air—that allows your story balloon to deliver the bang it should when it goes off.

28
FIVE MISSIONS FOR
THE SETUP OF YOUR STORY

At this point we encounter a cart-and-horse moment. Part 1 of story structure is all a setup for the arrival of what connects Part 1 to Part 2—the First Plot Point. So Part 1 and the First Plot Point (the cart and the horse) are tied together.

It's challenging to discuss one without the other. So let's first drill deeper into the structure and content of Part 1—because it comes first in the story sequence—with the understanding that it will make even more sense when we rip into a definition of the eagerly anticipated First Plot Point.

Because one cannot succeed without the other.

Part 1 has five missions to accomplish. All of them must be addressed and, in context to a setup, accomplished (synonymous with *established* in this case) before the First Plot Point makes an appearance. If you engage these five missions after that point, your story will likely tank.

THE FIRST MISSION: SETTING A KILLER HOOK

It's well known in screenwriting circles that you have only ten pages to hook the reader, who is probably an agent or even a producer who has a stack of scripts yay high that need to be covered by morning.

The same is true of novels. Those first ten pages of a script translate to the first twenty to fifty pages of a novel. In either case the best stories offer the reader—an agent or an editor—something she can sink her teeth into before she finds herself asking, "When is this thing going to kick in?"

In both cases, that something is called the *hook*.

The hook *isn't* the First Plot Point. Rather, it's something that grabs the reader very early in the read and makes her want to stick around. It *can* be an inciting incident if it comes early and doesn't fulfill the criteria of a First Plot Point. As a general rule, the earlier the hook, the better.

What is this wondrous little tease called a hook? Doesn't matter, as long as it's visceral, sensual, emotionally resonant, and makes a promise of an intense and rewarding experience ahead. It can relate to the landscape of the story, rather than the story itself. Or not, that's your call. It's a simple something that asks a question the reader must now yearn to answer, or it causes an itch that demands to be scratched.

In *The Da Vinci Code*, the hook is a dead guy on the floor of the most famous art museum in the world, with a cryptic message written in his own blood. That's something you don't see in your everyday mystery. At a glance it smells like a plot point, but it's within the first few pages and it isn't explained in terms of defining the hero's need or the story's stakes. It's just a hook, and a good one.

You should deliver a hook somewhere in your first three or four scenes. And when you do, you need to take care that it isn't an improperly early Plot Point. A hook is just a hook, dramatic as it may be.

THE SECOND MISSION: INTRODUCING YOUR HERO

Your hero should enter the story early. Long before the arrival of the First Plot Point. Your hero should appear somewhere in the first *two* scenes. Three at the most.

We need to meet and watch the hero in this pre-plot point, pre-story quest stage. We should see and feel what he is doing, what he is pursuing, what his dreams are made of. In other words, we need to have a handle on what is at stake for him once his world shifts at the First Plot Point.

In *Shutter Island*, for example, the hero, a U.S. Marshal named Teddy, arrives at an island mental facility to investigate the disappearance of a patient. We learn much about this situation, all while being absolutely overwhelmed with cryptic backstory and foreshadowing that won't make sense for another three hundred pages. The stakes are the safety of the missing patient and the subsequent illumination of what appears to be a dark conspiracy that possibly links back to the government.

In *The Da Vinci Code*, after the hook in the prologue, the first chapter introduces Robert Langdon, a humble professorial symbologist, who is summoned to help with a murder investigation. Right away there is a major twist—perhaps the second of two pre-plot point inciting incidents—that suddenly puts Landgon in the position of suspect, causing him to run for his life. The stakes are his safety and future, the discovery of the truth behind the murder, the corruption of the police, and a potential scandal that could rock the very foundation of the Western World's most prolific religion.

All of that in the first quartile.

As *your* story opens the reader needs to drop in on the lives of its cast, especially the hero. See them in lousy jobs and complicated marriages, in failing health and with frustrated plans. See them wistfully dreaming of better days to come. See them giving up. Or maybe starting over.

Or maybe they're happy as hell. At least for now. Because the First Plot Point is just around the corner, and when it arrives everything will change. Those plans, those dreams, will suddenly be up for grabs.

And at the same time, the reader needs to recognize something about *herself*. She needs to *empathize*. She doesn't necessarily need to like the protagonist all that much—that can come later when his inner hero emerges to heroically win the day.

Most of all, the reader needs to get a sense of what the hero's inner demons are. His backstory, the worldviews and attitudes and prejudices and fears that define him and hold him back. What are his untapped strengths, his secrets? These are the things the hero must later, when squaring off with the antagonistic force, be forced to acknowledge and overcome in order to step up as the primary catalyst in the story's conclusion.

It's called character arc (see chapter fourteen), and it begins in Part 1 of your story.

THE THIRD MISSION: ESTABLISHING STAKES

It is critical that somewhere in the first part of the story the reader comes to understand what the hero has *at stake*. The reader may not understand this at the time, but when the plot turns and trouble arrives she feels the weight of those stakes in the mix.

It is when the *writer* doesn't understand it at the time that the story is in real danger.

Remember, the purpose of the First Plot Point is to set the story on its ear. To begin the real story at hand. The First Plot Point changes everything we've just learned about the hero's plans. The hero now has a new objective, a new need—survival, rescue, justice, wealth, whatever—as he is launched on a new quest, all of it in opposition to an antagonistic force that dropped into his life … right at the First Plot Point.

And what makes that work is a clear understanding of what's at stake.

In *The Da Vinci Code*, we quickly realize that Langdon's liberty and safety is at stake, and that there is something much more significant and frightening at risk, as well. The First Plot Point in Marc Webb's film *(500) Days of Summer* was so quiet I almost missed it. It's a love story—and a perfect structural model to study. The deliriously happy hero hears his true love mention something vague about not being sure of her future. Of *their* future.

It changes everything for the hero. It defines his need and his quest going forward. It challenges his inner demons. It defines the stakes of his quest: keep the girl, or not. It's the story's First Plot Point, and everything that we'd seen until that moment had been there simply to set it up, and everything that follows was there to pay it off.

Stakes cannot be undervalued in storytelling. The more the hero and others have at stake as they pursue their new goal, the more tension the story will have.

THE FOURTH MISSION: FORESHADOWING EVENTS TO COME

Somewhere in Part 1 we must sense impending *change*. Often that change is a dark turn, but not always. But even if it's the dawning of a wonderful opportunity, the First Plot Point identifies some *opposition* to the attainment of a goal that is impacted by the change. And we need to have felt it coming.

Also, it isn't just the First Plot Point that is foreshadowed in Part 1. You can foreshadow the major events of the story to come, as well. The best foreshadowing is not recognized as such when it occurs—in *(500) Days of Summer* you could tell that the girl wasn't into the relationship as much as he was—but only in retrospect when something in the story harkens back to that moment.

In Lone Sherfig's film *An Education*, foreshadowing comes in the form of a peripheral character, whose behavior and subtle comments don't quite fit the crowd and the environment, and which define the potential future of the heroine. The viewer assigns no meaning to this at first—unless he happens to be a writer, that is—but later, when the other shoe falls, this behavior lingers as a memory of the warning it could have been.

Part 1 of *The Da Vinci Code*, both novel and film, has several scenes showing an albino assassin looking for what quickly becomes obvious as a religious icon, a relic that we know will connect to the death at the museum. Also, we see the pyramid structure that becomes the MacGuffin at the end of the novel.

We'll cover foreshadowing more in the next chapter.

THE FIFTH MISSION: PREPARING FOR LAUNCH

The last Part 1 goal: The pace and focus of the scenes need to unfold in context to, if not directly pointed at, the First Plot Point. A sense of foreboding or shifting winds needs to accelerate to the point at which everything changes—suddenly or subtly. Sometimes there are mechanics that need to be established, since in the real world big changes are usually preceded by little bits of business conspiring toward an unexpected result.

If you approach Part 1 of your story with these five objectives in mind, you can drive toward the conclusion of Part 1 (the First Plot Point) with the same resolution you'll bring to bear on the story's final outcome.

29
A DEEPER LOOK
AT FORESHADOWING

Foreshadowing is one of those essential little storytelling kinks—I like to think of it as an opportunity—that can be at once easier than it looks and yet challenging to pull off. If that sounds contradictory and confusing, welcome to the balancing act that is writing fiction. This nifty little storytelling skill can take your novel or screenplay to the next level.

Foreshadowing is easy when it is intentionally obvious. Just show it. It's challenging when it needs to be subtle. You hope someone notices it from the periphery of what otherwise occupies your narrative center stage.

The definition of *foreshadowing*: anything that links to, or reveals a glimpse or hint of a forthcoming story point or issue of characterization, but that is not yet recognized by the reader as a salient story point itself at the moment of its revelation.

Foreshadowing is like the aroma of cooking wafting into the next room. Sometimes you can identify the smell, other times you know only that something's cooking but not what it is.

If the foreshadowing is supposed to be obvious, make sure you attach emotion to it. That what's cooking smells good. Or is stinking up the place.

Example: A woman walks into the room. Later in the story she'll seduce our hero, but for now she's just there. Make her hot. Make the hero notice her, and make the reader notice him doing that.

If the foreshadowing is supposed to be subtle, allow it to pass without much notice.

Let's say a friend of the hero is seen talking to this woman. Since you don't want this foreshadowing to be on the nose, she's not as overtly hot in this case.

The hero notices, but only briefly, and only because his friend knows her and he doesn't. He doesn't give it that much thought, and neither does the reader. But when she shows up later, both the reader and the hero will remember that she was there, casing him out.

You can foreshadow virtually anything in a story.

Let's say, in another story, that the hero forgets a grocery list when he leaves for work in the morning because he and his wife are fighting. Showing it lying there on the table as the hero walks out the door ... that's foreshadowing. Showing that they're arguing is foreshadowing, too.

Showing us his wife, who claims she's sick and is staying home from her job that day, as she pops open a fifth of Jack Daniel's before hubby backs out of the garage ... that's also foreshadowing. This might happen with her setting down the bottle of Jack right on top of the forgotten grocery list, which is a creative way to execute it.

Having her smell yesterday's bouquet of flowers longingly and perhaps sadly, maybe touching a finger sensually to her lips as she does ... that's foreshadowing, too.

Cut to later that afternoon. The wife, three sheets to the wind, emerges from a hotel after a tryst with a lover. She holds one of the flowers in her hand. On the way home she stops at the store to fetch the groceries her hubby won't pick up because he forgot the list, which rests on the seat next to her. Then, as she pulls into the street from the store parking lot, she's killed in an accident (that would be the First Plot Point). The hero's life is suddenly very different. All of it has been foreshadowed before it actually happens.

THE ROLE OF FORESHADOWING

Notice that the foreshadowing here—the forgotten grocery list, the flowers, the lip smacking, the bottle—isn't directed toward the accident itself or its aftermath, but at the setup for that particular plot point.

Foreshadowing is *hinting*. It's a promise that may or may not be kept. It's the suggestion of tension and consequence, but without shape or form, delivered as detail, minutia, or otherwise meaningless or distracting dialogue or action.

If, while watching a movie or reading a novel, you wonder why the author took the time to point your attention toward what seems like an unimportant detail, chances are you've just been exposed to foreshadowing.

So, is foreshadowing the dropping of a clue?

It can be, but doesn't have to be. Depends on what you define as a clue. If it's an obvious piece of the puzzle, it may not really be foreshadowing at all.

Like a red high heel, size 7, found next to a body at the crime scene. That may as well have a sign on it: *Notice me, I'm a clue.*

The Da Vinci Code is full of clues in the opening act (Part 1). Some have an overt foreshadowing agenda, others (like the cryptic messages written in blood) are just clues. What *is* foreshadowed is the strange behavior of the policeman and the relationship of the body to the various da Vinci paintings near where it fell. None of that takes on meaning until much later, but it is overtly brought to the reader's attention.

If it's something that isn't obviously connected to the story, but later becomes something you remember that you now know you should have assigned meaning to—like a man buying a pair of red high heels, careful to specify he needs them in a size 7, later to end up dead with one of them lying three feet from his body, the other embedded between his eyes—that's foreshadowing, rather than a clue.

Foreshadowing is like story structure: Once you recognize it for what it is, it leaps off the page with abundant and empowering clarity.

A time and place for foreshadowing.

It could be successfully argued that the first quarter of your story is nothing if not artful wall-to-wall foreshadowing. By definition, Part 1 (Act 1 in screenplays) is all setup, so virtually anything that shows on these pages is fair game as a foreshadowing vehicle.

You can foreshadow later, too, but never in Part 4 (Act 3 in screenplays). The Second Plot Point (at around 75 percent through the story) is the absolute final opportunity to foreshadow coming events.

As the author, you need to understand how to use this tool. Heavy-handed or deliciously subtle, that's always your call. The best way to learn foreshadowing techniques is to begin to notice them in the novels and movies you consume. See how many foreshadowing moments you can detect, then pay attention to how they later link to the unfolding story. Try to differentiate the foreshadowing of plot elements vs. characterization. Both can serve a story well.

The more you see it in play, the more confident you'll be in becoming a foreshadowing puppet master in your own right.

30

THE MOST IMPORTANT MOMENT IN
YOUR STORY: THE FIRST PLOT POINT

Any time you label something the most important of anything you'll get folks crawling out from behind their keyboard to argue the point. And they may be right, especially in the avocation of writing fiction, where hard-and-fast rules about the rules are always up for grabs. It is art, after all. But I'll stand hard and fast behind this one: The First Plot Point of your story is the most important moment in it.

We've spent a fair amount of time looking at this milestone already. But in the name of clarity, let's go deeper through the use of examples.

In the film *Collateral*, the hero, a taxi driver, picks up a fare. At about 15 percent into the film, with all the requisite Part 1 elements in full raging glory (we're all over the hero's goals, his fears, and we're already rooting for him), the passenger murders someone while the hero waits in his taxi. It's huge—the body actually falls onto the roof of the taxi.

Seems like a new story from this point forward, right? You'd bet your printer that this is the First Plot Point. But it's not. It's a plot twist, an inciting incident, and a whopper.

First of all, it is a huge moment in the story, one that is very necessary to its narrative exposition. It actually could be a plot point had it appeared in the right place, but it doesn't in this case. It's too early. As is, it's part of the *setup* for the First Plot Point. Because without it, the content of the scene that delivers the First Plot Point exposition wouldn't make sense.

And the real reason it doesn't function as the First Plot Point (in case someone wants to argue that it is, indeed, the First Plot Point by design, with an intentionally early placement) is that it doesn't do the most important thing a plot point is supposed to do: define the hero's need and quest going forward, actually commencing the dance itself.

That moment happens at precisely the right place, when the hero and the killer are driving along (it should be noted that the hero is a bit upset) having a little chat. The essence of that chat is what it all means to the hero: The killer, with the help of a gun, tells the hero that he's "hiring" him to take him to further murderous appointments, and if he does a good job and stays quiet, he'll not only survive, he'll be paid $600.

That's significantly more illuminating and dramatic than the simple fact of the body falling onto the cab, monumental as that was.

The First Plot Point is the bridge between Parts 1 and 2. Which means everything that comes before it is a setup for it, and everything that comes after it is a response to it. The fact that this could hold true for other moments that seem to fulfill the criteria for a plot point can be confusing, but don't be seduced. Location is critical, because the real mission of the First Plot Point is to shift the context of the story from setup mode to response mode.

After the murder 15 percent of the way through *Collateral*, we remain in setup mode. More elements need to be put into play. We haven't met the cop yet, and he is an essential part of the forthcoming story. Only when that taxi conversation happens does the story shift gears ... from Part 1 into Part 2.

Plot points depend on two things: location within the story, and the context shift it delivers to the story. Rent this or any other movie and see. It's the best lesson in plot points—especially the first. Then apply what you've learned to novels, and you'll see that it's there, too, albeit perhaps a bit more veiled.

THE POWER OF THE FIRST PLOT POINT

Without conflict there can be no story. And since the contextual *meaning* of the core conflict shouldn't enter the picture until the reader is a quarter of the way into the story, it can be said the story doesn't really even start until Part 1 concludes with the First Plot Point.

The First Plot Point is when your story, in terms of the hero's experience within it, really begins.

The purest definition of the First Plot Point is this: the moment when something enters the story in a manner that affects and alters the hero's status and plans and beliefs, forcing him to take action in response, and thus defining the contextual nature of the hero's experience from that point forward, now with tangible stakes and obvious opposition in place.

Inherent to that definition and the story moment it defines is the call for the hero to do something he wasn't doing before—react, attack, solve, save, speak out, intervene, change, rebel, grow, forgive, love, trust, believe, or just plain run like hell. Those actions commence upon the arrival of the First Plot Point, which (I'll keep saying this, so get used to it) defines the hero's journey and goal, as well as his actions, for the remainder of the story.

It introduces conflict.

Just as essential to this sudden new journey is the presence of *opposition* to whatever the hero now needs or wants or does in response to the First Plot Point. And that becomes the story's conflict.

The First Plot Point is the moment when everything changes. Even if there have already been changes before this point. Meaning imparts change because meaning drives motivation and connects to stakes. Meaning is why people will risk their lives, kill people, or run into a corner shrieking like a little girl. Without it, a plot twist is just a twist, not a plot point.

The reader always meets the protagonist early in Part 1, dropping into his life to see where he is and where he's going. What his agenda is, his inner demons, his dreams, his worldview. She comes to understand what the hero has at stake in his life. When the First Plot Point arrives, all of this is suddenly up for grabs.

If the antagonistic force was already in the story during Part 1, something happens at the First Plot Point that makes it darker, more urgent, or more deadly, and ultimately more meaningful and frightening and consequential, thus forcing the hero to take action. Because something important to the hero is now in jeopardy, and we know what it is.

Or, with a more positive spin, the First Plot Point makes things more real and meaningful, thus forcing the hero to go after it.

Something must stand in the hero's way moving forward. Better yet, something within the hero holds him back (the conquering of which becomes a character arc) in addition to the exterior conflict at hand.

THE NATURE OF THE FIRST PLOT POINT

The First Plot Point can be huge, like a ship hitting an iceberg, a meteor striking the earth, or a murder. It can be personal, like the hero getting fired or catching his spouse having an affair or his child dealing drugs. It can be devastating, like a terminal diagnosis or a sudden kidnapping. Or a roulette ball landing on black when he put it all on red. It changes everything, and in a huge way.

Or it can be subtle, like the sudden chill in a lover's kiss. The hiring of a worthy foe in the battle for a promotion. The offer of seduction on the night of a wedding rehearsal. Again, it changes everything, not necessarily in a huge way, but in a way that alters the course of the hero's actions.

It doesn't always have to be something dark, either. A First Plot Point could be hitting the lottery, the return of a lost lover, a promotion, a second chance. But the criteria doesn't change in these happy circumstances—the hero, upon reaching the First Plot Point, still has a new quest and need, something the reader can empathize with and root for, and in the face of visible obstacles (antagonistic force or forces) that seek other outcomes.

Tension and stakes can be present from the outset, or early in Part 1 (as they are in *Collateral*). Happens all the time in thrillers. But again, notice that the criteria for an effective First Plot Point don't change, because at roughly 25 percent in, everything shifts when something new and even more sinister spins the story in a new direction.

In *Collateral*, it isn't until the killer informs the hero that he's not finished with the evening's executions, and that the hero must drive him from victim to victim if he is to survive. The full nature and implied meaning of the conflict is revealed here, thus changing the hero's need and ratcheting the stakes to new levels of urgency and risk.

WHAT THE FIRST PLOT POINT *MEANS*

The arrival of the First Plot Point means that what the hero thought was true may not be as advertised. It means safety and status quo are being threatened. It means everything must stop until this problem is addressed. It means dreams go on hold until this is solved, or it can mean that new dreams are suddenly within reach.

It means survival, or not. Happiness, or not. Justice, or not. It means that the stakes are on the table now.

The First Plot Point begins the hero's new quest in pursuit of this need. It begins a response to whatever the First Plot Point brings to the party. It brings the sudden need for safety, for understanding, for relief, for an answer, for a new approach, a new paradigm, a new set of rules.

Once you know what your First Plot Point can be, should be, and will be in a generic sense, and what it *means* to a story, you'll never again read a book or view a movie in quite the same way. It'll pop off the page or screen and slap you silly with awareness. It's always been there, but now you'll sense it coming in the setup and see it appear before your eyes at the appointed time. The wonders of story structure will suddenly manifest in a way you've never comprehended before.

Because you'll *notice* it. Better, you'll feel it. You'll finally understand that everything that happens before the First Plot Point moment is a setup for it. And that everything that happens after it is a response to it, that it is the launching of the hero's story-specific quest.

In *The Da Vinci Code*, the stakes are plenty high early in Part 1. But at the First Plot Point everything changes when we see that someone is out to kill Robert Langdon before his investigation leads him to the truth. The story really begins right there, the moment Langdon's need and purpose changes and everything shifts into an even higher gear.

The Da Vinci Code has 105 chapters. Which means the First Plot Point should occur around chapter twenty-six. Which is precisely the case. In this scene, Langdon and Sophie find a message written in blood on the face of the *Mona Lisa*, put there by the dead curator, who happens to be Sophie's grandfather. Much has happened prior to this point, but it is here that it all takes on meaning.

A plot point can be a sequence of scenes, and that's how Dan Brown does it here. Across scenes #24 and #26, everything about the story changes and clarifies, thus launching Langdon on his journey to save himself and uncover the truth of a great conspiracy.

In chapter twenty-four, the albino assassin finds what he's been looking for, which launches the antagonistic force into a higher gear. We've already seen that this is something he'll kill for, and we know that he's fronting an organization that's behind the yet-to-be discovered conspiracy.

In chapter twenty-five, Langdon confirms that Sophie isn't what she seems, and that she's there to help him escape and become her partner in the pursuit of the truth about who killed her grandfather, and why.

In chapter twenty-six, Langdon deciphers the message found on the face of the *Mona Lisa*, one that directly links—for the first time in the story—to the central dramatic premise, the theme and the goal at the end of Langdon's forthcoming quest: This is all about the Holy Grail, the "divine feminine" itself, the truth about Jesus Christ and the religion based on him.

At least in Dan Brown's story. The very audacity of this conceit is part of the reason why.

Because the reader is thoroughly, irretrievably hooked.

What is the First Plot Point in *your* story?

Does it meet the criteria? Does it appear in the right place? Does it define and shift the need and quest of the hero from that point forward? Does it create and clarify stakes? Does it imply consequences that will stem from both the hero's success and failure? Does it create sudden risk and opposition that seemingly weren't there moments before?

All this for one moment in your story. The most *important* one.

31

A KINDER, GENTLER
FIRST PLOT POINT

In the previous chapter we learned that the most important moment in your story is when everything changes for the hero. For many writers this is the single most illuminating piece of writing wisdom they'll ever hear. Because you can't write an effective story until you accept and understand this at the very core of your gonna-be-a-huge-best-selling-superstar self. In the story of your writing life, your metaphoric First Plot Point may be right here. Right at this moment as you read this.

Welcome to the rest of your writing life.

Because, if you haven't wrapped your head around this principle, chances are you'll never sell a story. But when you do fully grasp it, you'll have immersed yourself into the realm of story architecture, and that may be precisely *the* thing that gets you published.

A sudden shift. A new deal on the table. A new path for you. The only thing that stands in your way is your willingness to engage and understand.

Timing *isn't* optional.

Here's shocking news for psychotically organic storytellers: You don't get to say when that shift happens in your stories. There's a narrow little window of expectation as defined by accepted story structure principles—the First Plot Point needs to happen at about 20 to 25 percent of the way through the story. Right after you've set it all up.

This is nonnegotiable. If you do try to negotiate it, you're getting in your own way. You're messing with the physics of storytelling.

Put your First Plot Point in too early and you've shortchanged your opportunity to not only set it up, but to launch your career. The more invested the reader is in the characters, especially the hero, the more the stakes of the story have been made relevant to those characters, then the more emotional vicarious empathy the reader will experience when that most important of moments arrives.

This emotional investment is the single, most critical variable that makes your story work.

It requires ample setup time. Which it's why this is precisely the mission of everything that happens in your story prior to the First Plot Point. If an effective First Plot Point shifts the hero's journey going forward, the reader also needs to have the stakes of that journey introduced and defined beforehand.

It's like hearing about the diagnosis of a fatal disease on the news for someone you don't know vs. hearing about it with a phone call from the spouse of someone you know well. Big emotional difference.

You have about sixty to eighty pages to make that emotional investment happen. If something huge takes place earlier—and it certainly can, and to an extent that this earlier moment seems like a plot point—you're still obliged to deliver an effective First Plot Point at the proper moment, and according to accepted criteria. You need to make sure that the early inciting incident is presented in the context of setup, not that of a First Plot Point. Something still needs to happen, and in the proper place, that creates a shift that defines the hero's new quest.

Too early is one thing. Too late is even worse. If you raise the curtain on that shifting moment too late, your story suffers serious pacing problems. It'll lack a reason to be. You risk losing your reader, which in the case of an agent or editor means putting the manuscript in the return mail.

It's easy to show an example of a First Plot Point that's as much in your face as it is true to life. But not every story likes it rough. You don't have to smack into an iceberg or receive a blackmail threat or get a terminal diagnosis to deliver an effective First Plot Point moment.

Sometimes your hero's world is rocked with a whisper. A few unexpected words, a meaningful glance, the seemingly random passing of two souls on a street. A letter from someone he thought he'd never hear from again. Sometimes less is more.

The moment when everything changes.

Allow me to illustrate with a true story from my youth. I thought I was in love. Her name was Tina. We'd been dating about a month, and things were ramping up on all levels. I met all her friends. She met mine, all two of them. We shared our dreams. We liked the same things. Sexual chemistry ensued.

It was the first act, the Part 1, of our emerging love affair. And then everything changed. Subtly. Seemingly without significance. But it completely altered my Tina journey. We were walking in a park. Hand in hand, the whole sappy visual. I made some reference to the future, assumptive so. I saw her expression shift, her eyes grow distant. And she said, "If I'm around, that is."

And she wasn't kidding. From that point forward, everything changed. My quest had a different context, a new goal. I had an obstacle to overcome, and it was my own inner demons that stood in my way.

Tina was gone a month later.

Life is a story sometimes. And even then, it has architecture.

In the film (*500*) *Days of Summer*—which, as I said before, is a sparkling example of storytelling creativity, one that adheres to the contours of story architecture in subtle and illuminating ways—the First Plot Point unfolds in almost exactly the same way as my personal sob story, with nearly identical words, at precisely the proper point. Check it out, you'll see.

As for me, my love story concludes blissfully, though it took years to write that ending with a new heroine.

Her name is Laura.

32

SHADES OF GRAY:
A SOMEWHAT LIBERATING SPIN ON STORY STRUCTURE

Before we dive into the remaining elements, allow me to inject some softening context here. It's important to realize that the principles of structure are like a game plan. They *are* a game plan.

On paper they're very precise, and if you stick to them you'll always be on safe ground. But there is room for creative license, something best practiced by experienced writers who have first recognized the value of story structure and mastered its engineering.

It's like Michael Jordan shooting a free throw with his eyes closed (he did that once, and he made the shot, too). Don't try this at home; leave it to the professionals.

That said, let's put a little gray into an otherwise black-and-white proposition. It is art, after all. Even if it is just a paperback.

A PERSPECTIVE ON STORY STRUCTURE

If you've been challenged by the notion—or if you're in complete denial—that effective stories should be broken down into sequential parts, that each of these parts has a unique contextual mission to fulfill, and that each segment is separated by a critical milestone that must accomplish certain storytelling feats … if this is you, get ready for some very good news. Because the story-telling world isn't really quite as black and white as I've made it out to be.

You can't teach a new music student to ad lib. But once she's mastered the instrument, she is free to make it her own, provided her riff doesn't violate the fundamentals of musical theory. Which leaves a wide path of latitude.

If you're a screenwriter, you're still absolutely stuck with specific targets for the plot points in your stories. But if you're a novelist, you will be delighted to hear that what screenwriters must regard as a set of rigid rules really function more like a set of *principles* where you're concerned.

These principles are like traffic. Consistently disregard them and chances are you won't get a professional chauffeur's license. In fact, you'll probably get hit by a bus. But exceeding a few speed limits or cheating a stop sign now and then doesn't necessarily mean you'll end up in jail. Or dead. Or become the cause of someone else being dead.

It just means you got away with it. Sometimes you need to break the law in order to get where you want to get at the time you need to be there.

When it comes to writing fiction, stretching the limits of a principle *may* be perfectly fine. This doesn't negate the *value* of the principle; it just serves your creative needs at the time. Whether it is the right time to do so, and whether it works or not, is completely on you.

Principles still require a general sense of discipline and homage. At least, with writing, if you want to publish your work.

THE CASE OF THE WANDERING PLOT POINT

Recently I used a five-hour airplane ride to read a highly regarded thriller by a writer who lives in a neighboring zip code. As usual, I found myself deconstructing the story as I went along. Once you wrap your head around story structure, that'll be you, too. While I never doubted her, I was making sure the requisite plot points appeared within their narrowly defined range of locale, and that the four sequential parts did their generically prescribed contextual job.

Once you know this stuff, every novel you read and every movie you see becomes a bit of a clinic. Last time I just sat back and got lost in a story was when the Swiss Family Robinson was turning a confluence of vines into a foyer.

In my advocacy of story structure I encourage this deconstruction process as a means of understanding what the four parts of a story are intended to do, and how the milestones that separate them are the stuff of dramatic tension, pacing, and character arc.

So there I am, sitting in 24A somewhere between Honolulu and Seattle, waiting for the First Plot Point to appear where it should. And waiting. And waiting. Past the prescribed 20 percent mark. Past 25 percent. Getting nervous as we zip through 30 percent.

The First Plot Point in this *New York Times* bestseller finally showed up on page 118 in a 356-page novel. Do the math, that's not supposed to happen.

It got me to thinking. I need to take my musings on story structure a step further.

A plot point may not be *what* you think it is. Which means, it may not land where it should every time out.

The definition of the First Plot Point is the moment of change in the story that defines the hero's quest and need going forward, and does so in the face of an antagonistic force that the reader suddenly understands to an extent that empathy and emotion are evoked, while creating obstacles to the hero's quest, and thus creating stakes that depend on the hero's ability to overcome those obstacles.

A mouthful. Chew it carefully, because it will nourish your story. Or kill it if you don't swallow it all.

Because that is *always* what a First Plot Point does. No matter where it appears.

If you look closely, though, the essence of that definition is the grasping of what the plot point *means*, rather than what it is.

Read that again. It's subtle, and it's critical.

A husband suddenly dying because of an accident may seem like a plot point, if nothing else than by the sheer magnitude of how it changes the widow's life. But, if the story is about how she is supposed to deal with the fact that the schmuck left all the insurance money to a heretofore unknown mistress, it is the moment when *that* fact is revealed that becomes the plot point, rather than the death itself. The death was just part of the setup.

As you look for plot points in the work of others, don't be seduced by magnitude. Look for the narrative moment at which the story clarifies, when the hero's quest truly begins an informed forward motion. When the story switches from setup mode into reaction mode.

It's the stakes that the First Plot Point creates that counts, not the size of the explosion.

WHEN YOUR PLOT POINT GETS LOST

We've said repeatedly that the First Plot Point should occur somewhere between 20 and 25 percent of the way in the story. If you've perceived that to be a *rule*, that's good, because it *is* the optimal range, and rules keep us safe. But you, the novelist, do have the latitude to cheat that on either side of the target, depending on the nature of the preceding Part 1 setup sequence.

If you postpone the First Plot Point much past 25 percent of the way in the story, you'll need several twists and a deepening of the stakes prior to that point. Or, a dramatic inciting incident that hooks us and keeps things moving and building until the First Plot Point arrives. Without them an extended setup will take too long and you'll lose the reader.

If your intended plot point comes much earlier—if you're choosing to violate the rule—make sure you create another milestone moment, one that deepens the stakes of the story and that adheres to the oft-repeated definition and mission of a First Plot Point—at the appointed location. In this case, because you have an early plot point, wait until about 25 percent of the story to do so, making sure it changes the course of the hero's quest from what it was.

The rationale behind the plot point theory connects to pacing. As you monkey with the principle in your own work, make sure pacing isn't the sacrifice.

A plot point may be a sequence of scenes, vs. a specific moment.

Sometimes the First Plot Point isn't a sudden *moment* at all. It can also be the consequence of a sequence of scenes or story points, all condensed around the prescribed vicinity where the plot point should occur.

Sometimes when it's tough to nail down a plot point in a story you're reading or a movie you're seeing, it's because *several* things happen that *could* be the plot point. For instance, take the earlier example about the dying, cheating husband.

The husband is seen cheating. The husband dies. The lawyer tells the wife that the insurance policy doesn't bear her name. The mistress shows up at her house demanding all the jewelry—including her wedding ring—that the dead husband has left her in his will.

Obviously, the widow has a new quest and need, and she's in reaction mode. A plot point has definitely occurred.

But where? Which moment defines this story's First Point Plot?

The plot point may occur as a *sequence* of scenes that occur from around 20 to 28 percent of the story. Each scene changes the nature of the widow's quest, spinning the story in a new direction, but only after they're all on the table do we fully understand what they mean.

So, which scene is the plot point itself?

Answer: It doesn't matter. At least not for the reader, because the sequence *as a whole* achieves the goal. The writer knows—my money is on the lawyer's revelation that the mistress is the beneficiary—but post-execution it is the *effect* of the scenes in the sequence, rather than the mission of any single scene, that counts.

Relax. Just tell your story.

But do so from within the context of understanding how and where story structure comes into play. This will keep you safe and keep the story moving forward. Just like a musician can't go off riffing a solo until he understands the underlying melody. Just like an athlete can't successfully freelance a play until he understands where the rest of the team will be on the field. Just like an actor can't ad lib dialogue unless she fully appreciates the context and intention of what was written for her in the script.

Don't sweat the percentages. Sweat the stakes, the dramatic tension, and reader empathy. If you're simply in the neighborhood, story architecture will protect you.

But if you disregard its principles, be aware that this is a tough neighborhood, indeed. Once lost, you may never be found.

At least, your story won't be found in a bookstore, that is.

33

EXPANDING YOUR GRASP
OF THE PART 2 RESPONSE

Part 1 is over. The First Plot Point has changed everything. The story begins *here*.

Welcome to Part 2. Now what?

As complex as the context of the Part 1 setup is—you need to tell us everything while actually telling us nothing—the context of Part 2 is comparatively simple: Everything about Part 2 focuses on the hero's *reaction* to the new journey you've just launched for him. And that includes his reluctance to accept it.

What would you do, in real life, if everything changed? If someone was out to get you? If the world were about to crash around you? If your dream shot was suddenly within reach? Would you immediately jump in and try to seize the day? Would you be the hero right off the bat? Would you make the best decision the first time out? Would you try to make it all go away overnight?

Probably not. No, first and foremost you'd seek shelter, answers, advice. You'd run. You'd hide. You'd shield yourself and those you love from danger. Seek information. You'd find a safe haven to take stock of what just happened. Explore options. Regroup.

That's what Part 2 of your story is all about. All of that, and more.

Of course, the specific response of the hero depends on the nature of the changes wrought by your First Plot Point, and the stakes you've put into play. The hero's choices here need to make sense, the reader needs to understand and respect the decisions and actions your hero makes in those first tension-filled moments after the First Plot Point. Even if he is driven by knee-jerk, longtime inner demons.

If the hero's lover tells him that he is not the one, he retreats in pain. He seeks an explanation. He tries harder to win her back. Or perhaps tells her to buzz off and leave town.

If his lover or someone else tries to kill him, he defends himself. He hides. He reports her to people with badges. He seeks to understand. He makes a plan. If the airplane the hero is in loses an engine and begins spiraling to the ground, he screams. Then he prays. Then he comforts the person next to him.

What the hero doesn't do is rush the cockpit and take over. That comes later. For now, the hero is still very human. And his reactions need to be in context to that humanity. It's Part 2, and the mission here is to show the hero's response.

Part 2 is all about *reaction*.

If you've done your job in Part 1, the reader already cares for and empathizes with the hero as he faces this new antagonistic force and the call to a new quest. And because you've established stakes by now, the reader feels the risk and the potential loss or gain within her own core.

In which case the reader is completely hooked. That's why you wait until now to unleash the darkness. The reader needs to care before she feels the hero's fear.

You have twelve to fifteen scenes or scene-sequences to construct over the course of Part 2. All of them come from within a context of response. If you're tempted to have the hero start saving the day, back off—it's too early for that. You can allow him to try, but it can't work.

Not yet. It's too early.

If he does try, he must learn something from that failure. The antagonist seems to only be growing stronger, getting closer. The hero faces his own shortcomings—his inner demon—during this first failed Part 2 effort to bring about a solution. What he learns from that attempt, about both himself and the antagonistic force, will be applied to his next attempt to fight back in Part 3.

The Da Vinci Code's Part 2 response.

There's no missing the fact that Langdon is doing nothing other than reacting to what Dan Brown setup in his Part 1 of *The Da Vinci Code*.

Meanwhile, from another point of view, we see the cops who are after Langdon, increasing the tension because not even Langdon knows what we know, or how close they are.

Remember, the First Plot Point is the revelation that there is a conspiracy, and that someone has been killed because of it. And that the authorities think Langdon is responsible. So he must react. He must run.

In Chapter 27, we see the cops discuss Langdon suddenly fleeing the scene.

In Chapter 28, we see Langdon react as the cops find him.

In Chapter 29, the tension increases when we see the albino assassin discover what he's looking for, which will bring him closer to Langdon.

In Chapter 30, Langdon and Sophie shake the guard and make their escape from the Louvre.

In chapters 32 through 42, which is occasionally interrupted to switch to other points of view that show us what Langdon cannot see, we witness Langdon and Sophie doing nothing other than running. And while they run, they talk and talk and speculate about what they've seen, what it might mean.

In Chapter 43, Langdon arrives at a bank to attempt to get inside a safety deposit box in response to one of the keys he's discovered. This is still a reaction—he's just following his options and his instincts without a target in sight.

In Chapter 45, they're on the run again, because someone at the bank called the cops. This guy can't catch a break.

In Chapter 47, they've stolen an armored truck. And guess what … they're still running.

It's all 100 percent reaction. Every Langdon and Sophie scene, which are intercut with scenes showing the cops closing in.

Langdon has no real idea who is after him, or why. He's just responding to what the story has thrown at him.

Classic Part 2 context.

The Midpoint scene, which separates and transitions Part 2 into Part 3, is at Chapter 51. That's out of 105 total chapters, which makes it very close to the actual midpoint. In terms of pages, it occurs on page 213 out of 454 pages in the hardcover, also very close to the targeted location for this critical story milestone.

Location of milestones isn't an exact science. Having them present and functional is.

PACING AND SCENE SELECTION

Pretty much anything you concoct in the way of Part 2's desperate retreating strategies or doomed attempts to strike back will eat up more than one scene. You'll need a *sequence* of scenes, each linking to the next to logically build toward something, which in turns links to the following dramatic sequence.

With three things to go for here—a retreat and regrouping, a doomed attempt to take action, and the reminder of the nature of the antagonistic force at the Pinch Point (see chapter thirty-six)—those scene sequences pretty much consume the twelve to fifteen scenes you have to work with in Part 2.

Just as you were heading toward a destination called the First Plot Point for the entirety of Part 1, you are also heading for a destination during all of your Part 2 scenes. The context of this Part 2 journey is response, and the dramatic destination is the Midpoint, where once again something new will enter the story and change the nature of the game, both for the hero and the reader.

If you have a scene or two of immediate reaction to the high drama of the First Plot Point ... if you then have a scene or two in which your hero regroups, retreats, or otherwise takes stock of his options ... if you have a scene that sets up the Pinch Point ... then the Pinch Point itself ... then a scene or two responding to the Pinch Point ... followed by a few scenes leading up to the Midpoint scene ...

Guess what? You've just defined, in a generic sense, about ten of those twelve to fifteen scenes that comprise the entirety of Part 2! The principle of story structure has just answered the question, *"What do I write next?"* Because, once you have your big concept and a solid First Plot Point in your head, Part 2 is, to a significant extent, already blueprinted for you. And with your very intimate knowledge of the story and your understanding of a) where you are in it; b) what needs to happen at the moment; and c) where it's going in context to the bigger picture ... you should no longer be staying awake nights wondering what comes next.

You already know. In fact, sleep may be problematic for quite another reason—you'll be up all night writing.

A final note of reassurance: Your ability to fill in the blank spaces will grow as you progress into the story. The story won't quite write itself, but what the story needs will become increasingly clear as you move forward.

The more you know about story structure, the truer this becomes.

That's what happens when you write from a context of understanding the generic model of story architecture—knowing the mission and contextual purpose of what must happen, and then where to put it. As you fill in the blank spaces with specific scenes early on—in a flow chart, beat sheet or outline, or in your head ... however you work—your inner storyteller will be suggesting ideas for future scenes as you go.

If no ideas manifest and you do indeed understand these principles, perhaps your idea really isn't compelling after all.

The trick is to know where to place those elements—not too early, not too late—to maximize pacing and dramatic tension. Once you understand story structure, and whether you're outlining or writing organically, it's much harder to make a mistake.

34

WRAPPING YOUR HEAD
AROUND THE MIDPOINT

A funny thing happened on the way to the ending of the story. Everything changed. Right in the middle, in fact. A big fat unexpected twist.

Or not. The Midpoint context shift can be as subtle as a distant look in a lover's eye.

The Midpoint is one of the three major milestones in story structure. It is easily defined and an extremely flexible tool to use. In fact, that's precisely its undoing for newer writers and those who don't write from a context of solid story architecture—it's *too* easy. Which makes it easy to skip altogether.

Definition of the Midpoint: new information that enters the story squarely in the middle of it that changes the *contextual* experience and understanding of either the reader or the hero, or both.

In other words, the curtain parts. The character or the reader suddenly knows that which wasn't known before. This new knowledge can pertain to previously existing yet hidden information, or completely new information. That's your call. Either way, the sudden injection of this new awareness changes the context of the story, and thus the reading experience. New weight and dramatic tension has been added.

A Midpoint is very much like a plot point in several ways. It can indeed be considered a plot twist. And yet, unlike other plot twists, which can appear without concurrent relevance or meaning to the story, a Midpoint changes things through meaning. Through the revelation of what's been, until this point, behind the curtain of awareness, the Midpoint empowers the hero in the transition from Part 2 wanderer to Part 3 warrior.

A TENT-POLE MILESTONE

Think of the First Plot Point, the Midpoint and the Second Plot Point (which we'll discuss in chapter thirty-seven) as three thick poles that hold up the tent of your story. Omit any one and the thing is lopsided, susceptible to blowing over in a stiff wind and unable to support the weight of the narrative canvas.

Infrastructure is everything, both in circus tents and in storytelling.

The Midpoint's delivery of a morsel of narrative information may not change the story per se, but it does change the hero's and the reader's *understanding* of what's been going on. Because if you've done your job thus far, chances are neither really sees the whole picture.

If the hero is privy to the new information already, though, the Midpoint curtain parting will certainly change his course of action. Which means you'll need to twist that previously known information in an empowering way. Remember, the difference between Parts 2 and 3: The hero evolves from response mode into attack mode.

An example of this would be the knowledge of a cheating spouse. The hero is aware of this, and has been responding to the news, which appeared at the First Plot Point. The Midpoint here could be the discovery that the person his wife was cheating with was none other than his own brother, who has been by his side commiserating the entire time.

Suddenly the hero is empowered. Actions taken from this point forward aren't reactive in nature, they're proactive. The hero now knows who to go after.

The Midpoint can be described as a catalyst. It activates new decisions, behaviors, and actions stemming from a new perspective.

MIDPOINT EXAMPLES

In *Coma* by Robin Cook, the hero is running around trying to determine who is killing off patients in her hospital, making it look like routine surgeries gone south, for the purpose of selling their organs on the black market.

Terrifying. In Part 2 of the story she has brought her superiors in on the hunt, hoping for their support. After all, it's their hospital.

Meanwhile, someone is trying to kill her to stop her from discovering the truth. At the Midpoint, Cook pulls back the curtain to reveal—to the reader only, not the hero—that the people behind it all are, in fact, her superiors at the hospital. The same folks to whom she'd gone for help. Everyone is in on it but her. Which is an entirely new context of dramatic tension.

Meanwhile, she continues to confide in her boss in the belief she has an ally, when in fact she's handing the bad guys everything they need to whack her.

Later she learns who is behind it all, but that's actually the Second Plot Point of this story. At the Midpoint the curtain parts only for the reader. In Part 3, her empowering knowledge is her attack on a piece of diversionary information provided by her bad guy boss, which only buries her deeper.

Another example, this one from a rather generic love story: Two people are planning on getting married. At the First Plot Point, the girl confesses to the guy that she's been having doubts and wants to put the whole thing on hold. Everything changes. Suddenly the hero has a new need and quest ... a classic First Plot Point.

Then, in the response that makes up Part 2, the guy tries to find out what's wrong and up his game. By-the-book story structure so far.

Then, at the Midpoint, the curtain parts. He finds out that she's been seeing another guy on the side, which changes the context of his understanding, and thus informs his ensuing attack on the problem in Part 3.

Same story, higher tension, more urgent stakes, with a powerful new context for both the hero and the reader.

It's almost impossible to change context for the hero and *not* the reader, but changing it for the reader before it changes for the hero is a great way to really crank the tension in your story.

Either way, the Midpoint kicks your story into a higher gear.

In *The Da Vinci Code*, there are two possible Midpoints. Which is perfectly fine provided the intended functionality is in place. Dan Brown chose his own application of the principles—and so can you.

In the last chapter, I said that the Midpoint moment occurs in Chapter 51, slightly before its assigned position (out of 105 chapters … that's close). But there is another possible Midpoint moment in Chapter 55 (slightly after the middle of the story). Structurally this gets the job done, though not according to the traditional paradigm. This illustrates that the reader may not be completely sure which scene is the milestone itself. The *author* needs to know, but when you pepper your story with new information and twists, as Brown does, the reader may be easily fooled.

In Chapter 51, Langdon and Sophie end the blindness of their running (which eats up all of Part 2) by determining that their new destination is Professor Teabing, who is, in fact, "The Teacher" they have sought all along. This changes the context of the story from blindness to hope, from random fleeing to directed attack.

In Chapter 55, the curtain again parts for both the reader and the hero when we learn what, specifically, this Holy Grail thing is all about. It's not a cup that used to hold homemade chablis, and it's not a metaphor: The Holy Grail is Mary Magdalene, specifically, her womb.

Bam! This is huge. This is new context of the first order. Because it immediately explains why the church is a bit pissed off about it all. Why they have, in the conceit of this story, sought to suppress this truth for two thousand years. Why there is a secret sect of assassins who seek to snuff out anyone who gets too close. And, why there is another secret sect that wants to use this news toward their own goals.

These two Midpoint milestones change the context of the story, and thus, both the hero's and the reader's experience going forward. They throw everything into a higher gear, with more precise and urgent stakes and a specific destination where the showdown will take place.

35
COMMENCING
THE PART 3 ATTACK

They don't call them heroes for nothing. But thus far, through the Part 1 setup and the Part 2 response, we haven't felt many heroic chops coming from our protagonist. In fact, we've watched the hero respond to his calling and the forces that oppose it—especially the forces that oppose it—with very human decisions and actions that are, for the most part, something short of bold.

It is the humanity of his agenda in Part 1 (stakes) and the commonality the reader feels toward the hero's response in Part 2 (empathy) that hook the reader into your story. This is where we cement the relationship between hero and reader, because the reader a) sees part of herself in this character; b) can feel what the hero is going through; and c) is strapped in for a vicarious ride that allows her to escape her boring real-life existence. That's why she's reading the story, and it's important that you deliver on these counts.

Now it's time for your hero to step up.

Because now we're in Part 3 of the story, and this is when the hero needs to get down to business.

While Part 2 was about the hero's response to the First Plot Point, Part 3 is a full-on proactive *attack* to solve the problem at hand. It's a pretty simple mission, really, but one with a few subtleties that empower it.

Most notably, the information conveyed at the Midpoint milestone.

You may already have shown the hero attempting to do something proactive back in Part 2. In fact, that's not a bad way to create momentum and tension—taking a swing at whatever is attacking you would be part of a rational response.

But none of that worked very well back in Part 2, did it? At least it shouldn't have. In fact, it mainly showed how committed and powerful and cunning and sinister and complex the antagonistic force in your story really is. The tension goes up because the reader knows the hero is going to have to do better, to summon much more courage and force, to smack down the bad guy who stands in his way.

BAD GUY, OR ANTAGONISTIC FORCE?

I keep referring to an *antagonistic force* in reference to the thing that stands in your hero's way. That can take many forms—a bad guy, a sinister organization, the weather, a crappy boss, aliens who want to enslave earth, a cheating spouse, a hidden secret, an inner demon.

But not all stories are about squaring off with evil. Just as many are about finding love or solving a problem for the betterment of mankind. About a chance for redemption and justice. And not every hero is a basket case burdened by inner demons worthy of a William Friedkin movie (Google that one if you're under forty).

But in every story there *must* be opposition to what the hero wants and needs to accomplish in response to the game-changing First Plot Point—which launches the hero on a new path. It is that opposition or obstacle that is the antagonistic force. It's usually a person—the bad guy or girl, or someone who is not so bad but has a different agenda blocking the hero's way—but it can be a force of nature or some social pressure.

Or the IRS. We can all empathize with that.

THE PROACTIVE NATURE OF PART 3

Whatever the antagonistic force in your story is, it's about to confront and test the emerging hero in your protagonist. Part 3 is where the hero literally fights back, hatches a plan, enlists assistance, demonstrates courage, shows initiative.

This is when he steps up. He evolves from responder to attacker. From wanderer to warrior. In Part 3 your hero gets downright proactive. Not always with success—however, he is learning from each failure—but with newly energized courage and intention.

Just as importantly, this is where he begins to really fight against his inner demon.

Back in Part 1 you established some inner dialogue or programming for the hero that holds him back, and we've seen that weak link in play as a factor in whatever influenced or foiled the response efforts in Part 2. But a good hero sees and acknowledges his own flaws, and here in Part 3 he begins to adjust and accommodate. He gets over himself in order to do what he must to reach his goal.

As in Part 2, these twelve to fifteen Part 3 proactive attack scenes—beginning at the Midpoint and leading into the Second Plot Point, which arrives at about the 75 percent mark—must once again show the reader, front and center, what stands in the hero's way. And that flash of opposition should be pure and dramatic.

In fact, you need to devote an entire scene to it.

The Second Pinch Point—smack in the middle of Part 3.

A reminder of the story's main antagonistic force, called a *pinch point*, takes place squarely in the middle of Part 3. This is yet another demonstration of the nature, power, and very essence of the antagonistic force (this is actually the *Second* Pinch Point). And it's more frightening and unwavering than ever.

And like the hero, the antagonist has evolved, too. He's learned how the hero is fighting back, he's overcome his own weaknesses in pursuit of his own quest. This is how tension and pacing increases, because everybody's picking up his game by this point.

We'll cover these pinch points in more detail in chapter thirty-six, but for now put placeholders in the middle of Parts 2 and 3 for them.

In Part 3 of *The Da Vinci Code* ...

Langdon and Sophie spend the majority of Part 2 dodging those who are trying to kill him. Running. From the cops, and from the guy behind the curtain—the albino assassin. But in Part 3 Langdon begins to wise up. He's *chasing* leads into dark places instead of escaping into churches as refuge.

At the Midpoint the story shifts from fleeing from the cops to rushing *toward* a resource—Teabing—that can help them solve their problem.

They are now being *proactive* instead of reactive. They are *attacking* their problem. For the first time in the story, Langdon and Sophie are taking action that will come to bear on the solving of the problem, rather than simply trying to figure out what the problem is before it kills them.

36

PINCH POINTS

Must be the name: pinch points. People struggle with getting their head around it. Sounds like some form of ancient eastern message therapy. Or something kinky, maybe.

Actually, the pinch point is the most simplistic and efficient of the story structure milestones.

THE FUNCTION OF PINCH POINTS

By now it's clear that your story must have an antagonistic force—a bad guy or bad girl—and that its first full frontal appearance in the story occurs at the First Plot Point, which closes out Part 1 of your story.

That antagonistic force defines the nature of the hero's ensuing need, quest or journey. It needs to remain, at least contextually, front and center in the story at all times after Part 1.

But sometimes context isn't enough. The reader needs to see that ominous force in its purest, most dangerous and intimidating form. Or, if it isn't dangerous and intimidating, then at least the reader needs to feel it for herself, rather than through the eyes of the hero. The reader needs a reminder of the danger, the stakes and the implication, the unseen monster we know is waiting under the bed.

After the First Plot Point, the obstacle to the hero's quest is always there. As the hero begins responding to his new quest, the antagonistic force tends to drop into the background. But sooner or later the reader—if not the hero— needs to meet that antagonist again, to look in its eyes and understand what it wants and the power of that desire. That moment is called a pinch point.

PINCH POINTS, DEFINED

Definition of a pinch point: An example, or a reminder, of the nature and implications of the antagonistic force, that is not filtered by the hero's experience. The reader sees for herself in a direct form.

There are two pinch points in your story. The only difference between them is where they appear in the sequence of the story.

Let's say you're writing a love story. At the First Plot Point, the hero's girlfriend dumps him like an empty can of Red Bull. A nice buzz, now she's done. The reader is not sure why the girlfriend is running away, but the hero's need and quest from that point forward is to win her back. And because he doesn't know why either, his first mission is to find out.

The antagonist here is the girlfriend. The antagonistic force is her disinterest in him. This blocks the hero's need to get her back.

During Part 2 the reader experiences the antagonistic force through the perceptions of the hero. The reader feels his pain, empathizes with his confusion, and invests in his hopes. We've all been there, and it sucks.

At the First Pinch Point, though, the reader needs to see the antagonistic force for herself. Not just hear it discussed or referenced, not just remembered ... she needs to *experience* it through the eyes of the hero. Or at least the consequences of the opposing force as they affect the hero. Or, in some stories, an exposure to the antagonist is for the reader's perception only, completely separated from the hero's perception. While the reader sees what the hero is facing, he continues to *respond* to it, largely unaware.

A good pinch point in this example might be a quick cutaway scene showing the girlfriend in Aspen, wrapped in the arms of another lover against a backdrop of falling snow through a picture window in their suite at the Ritz-Carlton.

That's it. Nothing more is necessary. Just show us the girl with someone else.

Location is everything ... in real estate and with story milestones.

A pinch point can be very simple and quick. It can be one character reminding the other of what's going on. A glimpse of an approaching storm—take that literally or metaphorically, one that will apply to your story—and the havoc it is capable of bestowing on all in its path.

It can be a kidnapper beating the captive just for the fun of it. Or, the kidnappers playing the screams of their victim over the phone to pressure the person paying the ransom.

The simpler and more direct it is, the more effective it is. If the antagonist roars, let us hear the roar. That's all a pinch point needs to accomplish.

The First Pinch Point comes squarely in the middle of Part 2. The second squarely in the middle of Part 3. The three-eighths and five-eighths marks of the story, respectively.

A pinch point may require a setup scene, it may not. That's why this isn't a formula, it's a format. You get to choose.

In the movie *Top Gun*, the antagonistic force is the hero's backstory: He's trying to get out from under the military disgrace of his father, and in doing so he becomes a maverick (his pilot nickname) who plays loose with the rules, sometimes at the peril of his peers, not to mention his career.

In the setup sequence for the First Pinch Point, we see a flying exercise (a mock dogfight) in which the hero messes up by being careless. The actual pinch point moment occurs in the locker room right after, with a simple thirty-second conversation in which a rival says to him: "It's not your flying. It's your attitude. You may not like the guys flying with you, they may not like you ... but whose side are you on?"

The hero and his co-pilot then discuss this in hushed tones, admitting that, yeah, this is the problem all right. It's also the pinch point—we've just witnessed the antagonistic force of this story in its full glory, and we are reminded of what it is capable of doing and the stakes of it doing so.

In Clint Eastwood's film *Million Dollar Baby*, an old boxing trainer is driving his female boxing protégé through some southern rural real estate late at night. They are talking, and the hero suddenly goes all soft and personal and tells the trainer a story about her dad and a dog, a life-long pet, that he had to put down.

Just prior to this pinch point scene is a scene that exists for the sole purpose of setting it up. At a gas station earlier in the day, the hero has some meaningful eye contact with both a dog and the little girl it belongs to, and we can see the wistful memories playing right behind her eyes. When the pinch point scene arrives, we get the metaphoric meaning of her little story quickly. And in case we don't, she adds an epilogue by saying, "I got no one but you."

Her little trip down memory lane—the dog that needed to be put down by a loving master who, despite the agony of doing so, loved it enough to spare it further misery—isn't random, either. Later this becomes precisely what the trainer must face when the hero is beaten within an inch of her life and left paralyzed and brain dead. The pinch point scene—which foreshadows the story's dark conclusion—is short and powerful in how it reminds us all of what this story's thematic purpose and the hero's obstacles are. She is alone. She has no one but the trainer, and he has no one but her. If they aren't there for each other, neither will survive to seize this final chance at redemption.

Pinch point, theme, foreshadowing, and setup … all in one two-scene sequence.

In *The Da Vinci Code*, the First Pinch Point occurs on page 158 of the hardcover, in Chapter 37. Langdon's search for answers finally leads him to the Knights Templar and their search for the Holy Grail. Which is precisely the heart and soul (an ironic way to put it, actually) of this story's antagonistic force—the church's hiding of the nature and location of "the Holy Grail" and the willingness to kill to protect that secret. Notice that this comes at 35 percent of the way through the story, which is close enough to the optimal target, the 37.5 percent mark.

The Second Pinch Point also arrives right on cue—albeit a bit early, like the first one—in Chapter 64. The assassin clocks Langdon from behind, just as Langdon is opening yet another box containing a cryptic clue.

This couldn't be more in line with the definition of a pinch point. The assassin represents the antagonistic forces of the story, as he's a killer who's been searching for the very thing Langdon has just found. What better reminder of an obstacle, for both the hero and the reader, than having it hit you over the head.

Dan Brown may not use the terms plot point and pinch point—you don't have to either—but he certainly understands story structure. Like his story or not, you can't argue with the results.

A TASTY ANALOGY

Think of a diet that requires you to eat three big meals per day for the purposes of *gaining* weight (the metaphor here is your story needing to gain momentum and dramatic tension). You *must* eat those three meals. However, that doesn't mean you can't or shouldn't grab a snack between those three major meals. And it doesn't mean those snacks should be anything less than fully nutritious.

Snacks or no snacks, you still need to sit down to those three big meals.

Same with the First Plot Point, Midpoint, and Second Plot Point. Those are your three big meals. Don't skip them if your goal is to add dramatic tension and jack the pace to your story.

The pinch points are like nutritious snacks between those meals—mid-morning and mid-afternoon. They're good things. They give you energy, they nurture you. You wouldn't eat them too soon after a major meal, nor would you eat them right before a major meal. No, they're smack in the middle of the gap between those meals.

As for any other snacks (moments in which your bad guy does his thing), well, remember that in this analogy you're trying to *gain* weight ... so go for it. The more dramatic calories you stuff down the reader's throat the better.

37

THE SECOND
PLOT POINT

I n chapter thirty we defined and explored the First Plot Point, which is the most important and pivotal—literally—moment in your story. We've been referring to it ever since, as all things dramatic and wonderful flow from it.

One might assume that the Second Plot Point, then, is the second most important milestone in a story. And while a case could be made for that opinion, the Second Plot Point doesn't always pack quite the same narrative punch. But it is a major milestone, and as such it deserves our rapt attention and utmost writerly respect.

Because a story will tank without one.

Definition of the Second Plot Point: the final injection of new information into the story, after which no new expository information may enter the story other than the hero's actions, and which puts a final piece of narrative information in play that gives the hero everything she needs to become the primary catalyst in the story's conclusion.

At this point the story shifts into *resolution* mode, based on this new information or some decision or action on the part of the hero or the antagonist.

Here's a better definition: it's when the final chase scene starts.

THE VALUE OF THE SECOND PLOT POINT

The information delivered at the Second Plot Point changes the story (it has that quality in common with the First Plot Point) in such a way that the hero's quest is accelerated. There are new doors opening, new strategies to be hatched, new risks with more immediate rewards.

At the Second Plot Point you can often smell the ending just around the bend. You sense the story is turning that corner, that it is now a freight train that cannot be stopped. And yet, you're not sure what it will hit, or precisely when.

At least, if you're the reader. If you, the writer, aren't sure yet, you're in a deep pile of trouble at this point.

The Second Plot Point separates Part 3 from Part 4 at about 75 percent of the way through the story. Which means the hero transitions here from an attacking warrior to a hell-bent, selfless, heroic, and even martyr-like champion of all that is good. Or at least *necessary* in terms of solving the inherent dramatic problem at hand.

At the Second Plot Point the hero learns something that will take him one step closer, the final step, in fact, toward doing whatever needs to be done in Part 4 to bring the story to a satisfactory closure. Like the Midpoint, the Second Plot Point can deliver information that is not yet known or fully understood by the hero, but in such a case it still launches the final push toward the resolution. It's the writer's call—either the reader or hero, or both, need to know that the game has changed, and that at this point there are no more revelations ahead. What's on the table is all there is to work with from this point forward.

In Dennis Lehane's *Shutter Island*, the hero hooks up with a woman in a cave who appears to be the missing patient he's been sent there to find. The hero has been through a lot and has concocted some theories of his own at this point, and this woman—who, it turns out, is completely imaginary within the hero's delusional fantasy—sets him straight and, as a result, sends him out to save his partner from a lobotomy at the hands of the evil doctor, all of it going down at the dark and scary lighthouse we've seen glimpses of before.

The chase is on, the fuse is lit. The hero now knows everything, and won't be stopped in his quest to make things right. Classic Second Plot Point stuff.

In *The Da Vinci Code*, the Second Plot Point shows up in Chapter 75. It's when Langdon, in his heroic wisdom, cracks the message hidden in the codex, which revealed every last secret to be had about the code Leonardo da Vinci had so cleverly hidden in his paintings. In other words, the point of everything.

But that's not all. We learn that the folks Langdon thought were helping him are, in fact, bad guys. As it turns out, Teabing is the guy behind the entire caper, including sending the albino assassin to find the secrets of the code.

This is the last piece of new information in the story. From this point on, Langdon has everything he needs (or at least, everything he's going to get) to uncover the truth and ultimately deduce the location of the Holy Grail itself.

This pivotal shift is the Second Plot Point, and it occurs right where it is supposed to be found in a solid story.

THE PRE-SECOND PLOT POINT LULL

Here's a little screenwriting trick that works great for novelists, too. Even if you've been going to movies for years you may not have noticed this, but you certainly will going forward.

There is an all-hope-is-lost lull that occurs right before the Second Plot Point appears.

In George P. Cosmatos's movie *Tombstone*, the Clanton gang is driving the Earps (as in Wyatt Earp) out of town. There's a tense and sarcastic farewell as the Earps ride away in wagons with long faces, after which the villain sends a henchman out to finish the job, to kill Wyatt and his brother.

The pace draws slack. The lights dim, the music goes funereal. All is lost for poor Wyatt and his crew. This is the pre-Second Plot Point lull, a moment when all seems lost.

Then, in the following scene at the train station (which is the Second Plot Point), we see only the elder Earp brother on the train waving to Wyatt standing on the platform. But wait, wasn't Wyatt leaving town, too? Could it be that something is up his heroic sleeve?

The Clanton henchmen arrive, but Wyatt takes them by surprise and informs the survivor that there's a new sheriff in town—literally, I kid you not—and that the poor schlub is to go back and tell his cronies that hell's a-comin'.

There may as well be a flashing graphic saying: Second Plot Point! Second Plot Point!

In James Cameron's *Titanic*, the Second Plot Point is the moment the ship sinks. Clean out of sight, leaving the two lovers floating among a field of debris and screaming survivors. Everything that happens after that is Part 4 of the story, which becomes a burning fuse leading to the inevitable conclusion, followed by an epilogue that bookends the movie's prologue.

There certainly wasn't much of a lull prior to that moment. In fact, what we get is one of the most spectacular—and expensive—CGI effects moments in movie history.

In *The Da Vinci Code*, the lull prior to the Second Plot Point doesn't exist, either. Maybe Brown was too busy doing estate planning with his accountant, who knows.

Which goes to show that this lull is totally optional. The other elements of story structure ... not so much.

PLANNING FOR THE SECOND PLOT POINT

If you write organically, the Second Plot Point can give you fits. And if you write this way without a solid understanding of story architecture, it will in all likelihood derail your story. Because chances are there won't be one. At least that an agent or editor will recognize as such.

Why? Because you really need to understand what new information you're saving to unleash here in order to make this milestone both powerful and meaningful.

It's the last piece of the puzzle, the final ingredient. You can still surprise the reader in Part 4, you just have to use what's already in play rather than insert new information.

THE BEGINNING OF THE END

Part 4 is the beginning of the end of the story. You have ten to twelve scenes to wrap it up, using your Second Plot Point as the springboard for those sequences. That moment can be difficult to describe, even generically, because it can be just about anything.

In a love story it could be the hero quitting a job that cost him his marriage, and now he has to find his long-departed ex before she hitches herself to a new 401(k).

In a thriller it could be the arrival of the fleeing hostages at a port in the storm, where they are able to place a call to the authorities, leaving Part 4 to the business of keeping them alive until help comes. Which won't matter, because the hero will dispatch the baddies by herself before they get there, anyhow.

The Second Plot Point is one of those three major tent poles—along with the First Plot Point and the Midpoint—that are supporting the weight of the story. Everything else sags from one of those poles or rises toward one.

And like the first two poles, if you spring it on the reader too soon the tent becomes lopsided. Wait too long and the suspense and dramatic fabric of the final act (Part 4) will be compromised.

And if there's one place you want your story to be strong, it's at the end.

38
THE FINAL ACT

There are more than a few writers and teachers out there, many of them orders of magnitude more famous than I am (not hard to do), who don't like to compartmentalize or even attempt to define the sequential parts and essential milestones of a story's structure. Too formulaic, they say. Takes the fun and creativity out of it, they claim. A write-by-the-numbers strategy for hacks, a vocal few plead.

When they do talk about story structure, they tend to dress it up with descriptions that are less engineering-speak in nature—"the hero's journey" … "the inciting incident" … "the turn"—and are more appropriate to a lit class at Oxford. Makes them sound—or more accurately, feel—more writerly. Or perhaps they just aren't used to accessing their left brain for this very right-brained thing we call storytelling.

What's interesting is that the stories these writers create, especially if they're published, and especially the stories they use as examples in their teaching, follow pretty much the same structural paradigm. And given that this isn't an exact science, that puts them in this left-brained ballgame whether they want to wear the uniform or not.

None of how story structure is labeled out there in workshop land is inherently wrong, nor does it really matter. What you call it is far less important than how you implement it. And even before that, the extent to which you understand it.

Thank God for screenwriters. Because they call it like it is. In fact, most of them think Oxford is a loafer.

What this has to do with Part 4.

I prefer to call story structure what it is: four parts, four unique contexts and discreet missions for the scenes in them, divided by two major plot points and a Midpoint. Call them plot twists if you want to, the folks at Oxford won't know. Throw in a compelling hero's need and quest. Then formidable obstacles that block the hero's path. A couple of pinch points. A hero who learns and grows, someone we can empathize with and root for. Scenes that comprise the connective tissue between them all.

Then execute all of it in context to a fresh and compelling conceptual idea, a clear thematic intention, an interesting worldview, and a clever take on the plot.

I dunno, it all sounds pretty creative to me.

In other words, a blueprint for storytelling. One that, when understood and marinated in artful nuance and dished with clean writing, becomes nothing less than the Holy Grail, the magic pill, of writing a novel or a screenplay.

Not remotely easy. But perhaps for the first time, eminently clear.

Then we come to Part 4: the finale of your story. And guess what?

There is no blueprint for it. And no rules, either. Well, okay, there's one.

THE GUIDELINE FOR AN EFFECTIVE PART 4

The one rule of Part 4—the resolution of your story—is that no new expositional information may enter the story after the Second Plot Point that commences it. If something appears in the final act, it must have been foreshadowed, referenced, or already in play. This includes characters—no newcomers allowed.

Aside from that one tenet, punishable by rejection slip if you dismiss it, you're on your own to craft the ending of your story. And in so doing, the enlightened writer observes the following guidelines and professional preferences.

That's why they still call this art. You're free to experiment as you please. But if you don't follow these few guidelines, you do so at your own peril, and will likely remain unpublished.

THE HERO AS CATALYST

The hero of the story should emerge and engage as the primary catalyst in the Part 4 resolution. He needs to step up and take the lead. He can't merely sit around and observe or just narrate, he can't settle for a supporting role, and most of all he can't be rescued.

I've seen all these things, many times, in unpublished manuscripts. I've rarely seen one in a published book or produced movie. It happens, but never in a title anybody remembers.

THE HERO AND PERSONAL GROWTH

The hero should demonstrate that he has conquered the inner demons that have stood in his way in the past. The emerging victory may have begun in Part 3, but it's put into use by the hero in Part 4. Usually Part 3 shows the inner demon trying for one last moment of supremacy over the psyche of the hero, but this becomes the point at which the hero understands what must be done differently moving forward, and then demonstrates that this has been learned during the Part 4 denouement.

The hero applies that inner learning curve, which the reader has witnessed over the course of the story, toward an attack on the exterior conflict that has heretofore blocked the path.

A NEW AND BETTER HERO

The hero should demonstrate courage, creativity, out-of-the-box thinking, even brilliance in setting the cogs in motion that will resolve the story. This is where the protagonist earns the right to be called a hero.

The more the reader *feels* the ending through that heroism—which depends on the degree to which you've emotionally vested the reader prior to Part 4—the more effective the ending will be. This is the key to a successful story, the pot of gold at the end of your narrative rainbow. If you can make the reader cry, make her cheer and applaud, make her remember, make her *feel*, you've done your job as a storyteller.

If you can cause all of those emotions to surface, you just might have a book contract on your hands.

IF YOU ARE WRITING A SERIES

If your story is a stand-alone, you don't have to tie off all loose ends in Part 4. Only the major ones. Again, this is your artful call.

But if you are writing a series, loose ends are important. You need to be very clear that your novel or screenplay is required to resolve the *story-specific* issues you've put in play at the First Plot Point, even if there are series-specific issues left dangling. The primary plot-at-hand itself must be resolved.

What lives on to be published another day is usually character-focused. For example, in the Harry Potter series, the hero solves a specific problem in each installment, the unraveling of which is the stuff of the individual book. But the overriding unresolved drama of Harry finding the bad guy who killed his parents goes unresolved—though it *is* moved further along—in anticipation of the next installment.

Simply ending a book in a series without resolving anything is a major mistake of many new novelists. The book must stand *alone*, period. The only way it has a chance of catching on as a series is if the first book works.

And when it does, each and every subsequent installment is subject to this guideline: You need to tell a unique story in each one, a story that unfolds parallel to the overarching premise of the series, and you need to resolve it—completely—before moving on to the next manuscript, where the overarching premise awaits.

And then something amazing happens ...

Here's the real magic of Part 4. If you've done your job well in the first three-quarters of your story, if you've plotted with powerful milestones that are in context to a compelling and empathetic hero's quest and evolving arc, chances are you'll intuitively know how your story needs to end when you get there. Or, if not intuitively, then after some serious introspection and long walks in the woods with a digital recorder.

And by "get there," I'm not suggesting you write the first three parts and then see where you are. Just shoot me if that's what you think I mean.

Fact is—and this is for anyone who thinks what is recommended above sounds like organic storytelling development—unless you develop your story over the first three quartiles using the principles, parts, and milestones as benchmarks, you'll be more lost in Part 4 than you may even have realized. Only by having an executed story plan as a baseline for the perhaps somewhat slightly more organic unfolding of Part 4 does this process stand a chance.

That said, it's better to plan Part 4 ahead of time, too. Even if you get a better idea for how to end your story along the way, this provides the richest landscape for that to happen.

What I'm saying here is that you should strategize and plot all your main story points *beforehand*—even if you aren't yet sure of your ending—and in the process of developing the first three parts you'll find that the final act begins to crystallize as part of the process.

If you engage in story planning through a series of drafts, rather than an outline, you'll need to write enough drafts to finally understand what Part 4 should be. What the best way to end your story turns out to be. Same process, different tolerances for pain.

But there's risk in that. If you are a drafter instead of a blueprinter (notice I didn't say outliner, that's a different process yet, one of several viable ways to plan a story), the likelihood of you settling for mediocrity is orders of magnitude greater. The prospect of rewriting the first three hundred pages again does that to a writer.

Too many stories end badly.

And yet they somehow get published and even succeed to some degree. That's because the rest of the story, the structure of it and the compelling essence of the character, triumphs to an extent that the ending doesn't make or break the story at all. It just is. And often—pardon my very valid cynicism here—because there is a famous author's name on the cover.

Bad endings are far more common with established authors than they are for new ones because new authors rarely publish a book in which the ending isn't one of the best things about the reading experience. A bad ending—unsatisfying, flat, illogical, or just plan wrong—will get you rejected faster than misspelling the editor's name.

That said, it's *always* better that your ending is solid. Your goal should be to make it a home run, especially if this is your first novel or you're a new screenwriter. Because the reverse is true, as well—a killer ending might soften the editorial reader to things that only a proven pro would get away with.

Story structure empowers an effective ending. If you can't craft one after a requisite deep immersion into the infrastructure of the first three parts, you haven't yet gone deep enough.

THE FINE PRINT

Every once in a while you'll read about a neophyte swimmer getting into trouble in deep or fast water, and then, when a more experienced swimmer paddles out to help, he fights off the rescue with all his waning strength.

The thing about panic and resistance is that it can get you killed. What can kill you even quicker is not even knowing that you need rescuing.

The analogy hits home because every now and then, more often than you'd think, I encounter writers who just won't accept the unimpeachable truth and validity of story structure. They fight it off as if their writing dream is being mugged. They reject it as formulaic and therefore unworthy. Maybe they once heard a famous author—one who doesn't even realize the extent to which he is applying these principles in his work—talk about the spiritual, magical way he writes stories, sometimes actually bragging about all the rewriting he does to make it right.

Make no mistake, a rewrite is always a corrective measure. Nothing to brag about.

Virtually every published novel and produced screenplay is, in fact, a natural product of solid story architecture. Regardless of how it got there. To believe otherwise is like saying the aesthetic beauty of the halls of Versailles has nothing to do with poured concrete foundations and seamless masonry. With *architecture*. Or that, back in the day, there wasn't an actual blueprint for it all. Or that the pouring of those foundations was a no-brainer to the extent it didn't warrant intellectual energy of any kind.

These architectural atheists swear that writing a novel or a screenplay is, or should be, a process of random exploration, that their bliss resides in following characters down blind alleys and allowing them to set their own pace from there, with no real knowledge of where they're going.

I read this all the time in writing forums. Almost exclusively from unpublished or self-published authors. The overwhelming majority of published authors know otherwise, even if they apply different language to it … which they usually do.

This is like saying the joy of playing golf is wandering randomly around the course, crisscrossing fairways, club in hand, hitting balls at assorted greens as you please. I don't dispute the inherent kick in such an approach. Hey, random creativity can be fun ... so can finger painting. There's an innate kick in a lot of things: drugs, alcohol, sex with ex-spouses, Russian roulette ... but that doesn't make them smart or ultimately productive.

Methinks these folks are confusing process with product.

If you're only in it for the process, hey, knock yourself out. Just don't expect to get published within this century.

Writing without bringing a solid grasp of story structure to the keyboard is like doing surgery without having gone to medical school. It's a recipe for frustration and inevitable rejection. Because the patient's gonna die.

Just because you've watched every episode of *Grey's Anatomy* doesn't mean you're ready to do an appendectomy. Just like having read everything Tom Clancy has ever written doesn't qualify you to write a publishable techno thriller.

Story architecture is nothing short of the Holy Grail of fiction writing. Or if you prefer, the ante-in. Tom Clancy and every other author in the bookstore understands this. Even if they write from the seat of their pants.

How they write isn't the issue.

What they *know* about what they write is.

You can write like Shakespeare in love and have the imagination of Tim Burton on crack, but if your stories aren't built on solid and accepted structure—which means, you don't get to *invent your own* structural paradigm—you'll be wallpapering your padded cell with rejection slips.

I'm not saying you *must* outline your stories. That's not what story structure means. What I am saying is that you do have to apply the principles of story structure to the narrative development process, outline or no outline. Organic or totally left-brained. At least, if you want to publish. That's just a fact.

That said, allow me to backtrack just a nudge or two.

If you're a screenwriter, the confines of the structural box within which you live are as inflexible as a Donald Trump prenuptial agreement. Obey them or die trying to be the next Tarantino, who inexplicably got a free pass on all this stuff. If you're playing the odds to be the Next Great Exception, you might consider some reality therapy.

Screenwriters don't mind the box into which they are stuffed, they accept it and go creatively hog wild within its comfy black-and-white confines.

But here's the good news for novelists: Life is easier for us. All of the structural guidelines and story milestones put forth here are offered as *principles* as opposed to commandments.

When I've specified a place to insert a milestone, you get to insert the word "roughly" into that specification. When I've identified the length of a certain part of a story, you get to chop or add to a reasonable extent.

Stick close to these guidelines and you'll be treading a proven and safe path. One that leads directly to a bookstore near you.

Disregard them completely, and you won't sell your story. Period.

Advocating for story architecture is like teaching your kids about the world—you tell them to do as you say, not as you do, you tell them about the golden rule and the law of attraction and the mystical consequences of karma, and you do your best to explain that good things happen to good people who live by these creeds.

And when it doesn't … well, that's life, and it's not always fair. Doesn't mean it's not a valid principle. There are many more examples of trashed dreams from not observing these principles than there are of success stories from choosing to be an exception.

Lessons in hand, you watch your children leave the nest to live their lives according to their own whims and appetites. Sometimes you win, sometimes … not so much.

There are no guarantees in the art and craft of storytelling. Where teaching story structure is concerned—sometimes they publish, sometimes they don't. You can't make someone live in a box, even if the sides are somewhat flexible and porous.

The only life raft coming your way in this sea of choices is one of your own construction. Or should I say, *choosing*.

Chances are it has the words USS *Story Structure* stenciled on the side.

39

THE SINGLE MOST POWERFUL
WRITING TOOL YOU'LL EVER SEE THAT FITS ON ONE PAGE

A bold claim, that. But I challenge you to read this list—which really does fit onto one page (you can download a printable one page version at writersdigest.com/article/story-engineering-downloads)—and then argue that you've seen a more empowering checklist of must-haves gathered in such a condensed space.

There's enough stuff here to fill up a bookshelf full of how-to writing books. If you don't know what these questions mean, by all means go to that bookshelf and settle in.

If you do, get busy, your bestseller awaits.

This is a listing of everything you need to know about your story before you can successfully finish it, stated in the form of a question. There was a time when I would say this is everything you should know about your story *before* you write it, but that only applies to folks who want to write a first draft that's basically a tweak or two away from being submitted.

Sounds crazy, I know, but it happens. I've sold three or four drafts using this approach.

For drafters—those allergic to story planning and who fight to the death for their defiance of outlining—this becomes a checklist of things you're looking to discover (and answer) in your series of inevitable drafts. The more answers you can stuff into your next draft, the fewer subsequent drafts you'll need to write.

And if you leave only a few of these untouched, no draft you write will ever be final. Only abandoned. Yeah, it's that powerful.

Photocopy this list or print it out and keep it in a safe place. Frame it and put it next to your computer. Whatever works. Because when you fully understand what these questions mean to your story, and how to integrate the answers into it, you're there.

What is the conceptual hook/appeal of your story?
- Can it be expressed as a "what if?" question?
- Can you answer that question?
- Does your initial "what if?" question immediately inspire subsequent "what if?" questions that begin to suggest plot points and story segments?

What is the theme of your story?
- Is your intention to sell a point of view, or merely explore it?
- Does you story inspire multiple themes?

How does your story open?
- Is there an immediate hook?
- What is the hero doing in his life before the First Plot Point?
- What stakes are established prior to the First Plot Point?
- What is your character's backstory?
- What inner demons show up here that will come to bear on the hero later in the story?
- What is foreshadowed prior to the First Plot Point?

What is the First Plot Point in your story?
- Is it located properly within the story sequence?
- How does it change the hero's agenda going forward?
- What is the nature of the hero's new need/quest?
- What is at stake relative to meeting that need?
- What opposes the hero in meeting that need?
- What does the antagonistic force have at stake?

- Why will the reader empathize with the hero at this point?
- How does the hero respond to the antagonistic force?

What is the Midpoint contextual shift/twist in your story?
- How does it part the curtain of superior knowledge ... for the hero ... and for the reader?
- How does this shift the context of the story?
- How does this pump up dramatic tension and pace?
- How does your hero begin to successfully pursue or attack his need/quest?
- How does the antagonistic force respond to this attack?
- How do the hero's inner demons come to bear on this attack?
- What is the all-is-lost lull just prior to the Second Plot Point?

What is the Second Plot Point in your story?
- How does this event change or affect the hero's proactive role?
- How does your hero become the primary catalyst for the successful resolution of the central problem or issue in this story?
- How does that role meet the hero's need and fulfill the quest?
- How does the hero demonstrate the conquering of inner demons?
- How are the stakes of the story paid off? Who wins, and what does he win? Who loses, and what does he lose?
- What will be the reader's emotional experience as the story comes to its conclusion?

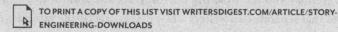 TO PRINT A COPY OF THIS LIST VISIT WRITERSDIGEST.COM/ARTICLE/STORY-ENGINEERING-DOWNLOADS

The astute reader will notice that these blocks of questions correspond to the four parts of story structure. And how, upon closer examination, the list envelops all of the four elemental components of the Six Core Competencies (concept, theme, character, and structure), leaving the other two (scenes and writing voice) to your brilliant execution.

40

THE SIX MOST IMPORTANT
WORDS IN STORYTELLING

To publish your story, you must wrap your head around, and master, six important words, each of which opens a can of literary worms to become a concept. These words are integral to the Six Core Competencies, as they establish qualitative targets and empowering tools that support each of those elements and skills.

It's sort of like singing: You must first learn to carry a tune, and then you must learn how to perform.

A better clarifying metaphor ...

The six most important words at the end of this chapter are to the Six Core Competencies what athleticism is to sport-specific skills.

They are the foundational literary essences you need to apply to whatever story you are working on. They are the stuff of *talent*, the qualities that separate two writers who possess exactly the same degree of knowledge and practice, yet one makes it and the other doesn't. If *knowing* and *delivering* sound like the same thing to you at this point, consider this: In some sports you must apply a foundational skill as a fast or tireless runner in a sport that may or may not be all about running, but is required to play the game. Like basketball, tennis, baseball, football, soccer, rugby.

First you must learn to run. Then you must learn to play the game. Run better, play better.

If you can master these six *talents*, and do so concurrent with mastering the Six Core Competencies, you will write better stories than if you don't.

That's a lot to get your head around.

I hope nobody told you this fiction writing stuff would be easy. Just like nobody told your local hometown football hero that making an NFL team would be easy, either.

Professional athletes constantly practice fundamentals behind the scenes. They watch videos, hire personal coaches, build upon a base of fundamentals with skill-specific strengths, and the result is a career.

These six most important words are like spring training for writers. They define a fundamental base of talents that you must bring to all the requisite storytelling skills. No matter what your story, you need to keep them in mind at all times as you write.

THE SIX MOST IMPORTANT WORDS IN STORYTELLING

These aren't words as much as they are realms … dimensions … essences … fundamental qualities. Notice they have nothing at all to do with how well you write *stylistically*. Writing style is just the uniform that the literary athlete—you—puts on. And the uniform means squat when it comes to winning or losing.

Writing voice isn't what will get you published (though it can and often does get you rejected, which is why it is one of the Six Core Competencies). *Storytelling* power will.

So, here are those ever-important words:

Compelling

Will anyone care about your story? Is there a hook, a draw? Is there inherent emotional and intellectual appeal? What question is your story posing to the reader, and is the answer *compelling* enough for anyone to care?

Hero

Yeah, you know you need a protagonist, blah blah blah. But is your lead character actually heroic? In what way? Or is the word *hero* a label rather than an adjective? Does the reader empathize with what he needs to do? What is at stake for him? What does he need to conquer, both internally and externally, to reach his goal? Why does the reader care about that goal? What is heroic about the hero's ways and the means of getting done what must be done in your story?

Conflict

Nobody wants to read about a walk in the park. Really, they don't. What opposes your hero's quest? What does this conflicting force—usually a bad guy, a villain, but not always—want or need? What is at stake for him or it? Most importantly, how does this conflict exert the force of dramatic tension into the story line, into each and every scene in the story?

Context

The most overlooked and taken-for-granted nuance in storytelling. What is the contextual subtext at any given moment in your story? How is the past influencing the moment at hand? How is the inherent conflict of the story exerting context into the moment at hand? What forces influence the characters as they speak, take action, make decisions? What is the thematic context of the overall story, and how does it manifest in the moment at hand?

This is truly advanced stuff. Master it and you'll find yourself on a bookshelf somewhere. Context and dramatic tension—often synonymous, but not always—are what makes your scenes work.

Architecture

That sound you hear is me once again beating this drum. Does your story unfold with a proper setup? With the properly placed and paced revelation of the hero's new quest and need following that setup? Has the context of the hero's new journey, in a personal sense, been clearly established? How does it affect what is said and done going forward? Are there shifts and surprises, valleys and peaks, both in terms of narrative exposition and dramatic tension?

Resolution

Does the end of your story deliver an emotional payload to the reader? Does it make sense? Will it linger once the final page has been turned? A killer resolution forgives the sins of softness in the story, but only if the hero is empathetic, the conceptual heart of the story rich and compelling, the thematic gift of the story penetrating, and the technical execution of the story optimized to make your ending the best it can be.

The better you understand and execute these six fundamental attributes, the quicker you'll sell your work. Possibly for real money.

Because once these are captured and clarified, there are no bounds to your potential as a storyteller. Every writing dream you've ever dared to imagine can be yours.

You wanted a magic pill ... here are six of them. But remember, they need to be digested simultaneously, and in context to the Six Core Competencies of Successful Writing.

41

OUTLINING VS.
ORGANIC STORYTELLING

Writing is a two-party democracy. To the left are those who write stories from their heart, or according to the other side of the aisle, from the seat of their pants. On the right are those who write stories from a meticulously constructed outline.

Sprinkle in a few moderates who dabble in both, and you pretty much cover the gamut of how writers get stories out of their heads and onto a page.

The two sides don't talk to each other much. At least about writing. And yet, the debate rages on.

Organic writers claim outlining robs them of spontaneity and creativity. That the only way a story can come alive is to discover the characters and allow them to set the course of the story. To listen to them.

Outliners, for better or worse, think that's just plain nuts.

The discussion divides a room quicker than politics and sexual preferences. How can you craft a story that foreshadows and builds toward a delicious ending, say the outliners, without knowing what that ending even is?

How can you keep a story fresh and spontaneous, say the organic writers, if you're merely painting words over a previously constructed outline? What if you get a better idea along the way?

The answer to both arguments is … you can't. At least not until you bring the principles of story architecture to the table before you write the story. Or at least, in *either* case, that you're willing to change literary horses midstream.

And then, outline or no outline, all things become possible.

To outline or not to outline … that's the wrong question.

The issue isn't about outlining. The issue is simply the degree of foundational story architecture awareness that a writer brings to her process.

Without story architecture, both processes ultimately fail. Stories will come out convoluted, one-dimensional, poorly paced, and ultimately rejected. With story architecture in the mix, the story emerges as a well-oiled machine. The only question then becomes: Is your story compelling or not?

Because even story architecture can't save a bad idea or weak execution. Even if you outline it to death. You can lead a horse to engineering school, but you can't make him an artist.

THE INFRASTRUCTURE OF STORIES

As much as some organic writers don't like to admit it, there is indeed a basic architecture for successful stories, with specific milestones that must appear at quite precise places. Successful organic writers understand this, which means that as their stories pour unrestrained out of their heads onto the page, they do so in alignment with those principles.

Outliners who construct story blueprints without such an awareness suffer the same fate. Their manuscripts are merely fruitions of a broken structure, and while they may get to a "final" draft before their more organic counterparts, it'll be just as lacking in what publishers are looking for.

Both sides of the debate are missing the boat if they don't know what follows what, and why.

THE VERDICT

On a more half-full note, bringing a keen understanding of story architecture to your writing process is more than empowering; it's essential.

To write a successful story, you can't wing it and expect to get to the Promised Land. That doesn't mean you need an outline, it means you need a foundational core competency in story architecture. No matter how you write. Once you have it, you can wing it all you want. Your stories will come out in the right sequence with proper pacing. Or, you can get there by constructing outlines that yield stories in which everything is in the right place at the right time.

How you get there is up to you. If you get there is up to your grasp of the principles story architecture.

Outlining is optional. Story architecture isn't. Debate over.

PART SIX

THE FIFTH CORE COMPETENCY—
SCENE EXECUTION

42

THE ESSENTIAL NATURE
OF SCENES

Everything we've covered thus far deals with storytelling theory, criteria, and the inherent elements of telling an effective story. The collision of ideas and the principles that will allow them to come alive within a story that works. By way of analogy, if that story were a house or an office building, all of this stuff could exist on a two-dimensional blueprint. In fact, it would have to—nobody in his right mind shows up at a construction site with a dump truck and some lumber without a carefully conceived architectural document in hand. A blueprint that includes schematics, measurements, and the infrastructure of plumbing and electrical systems, up to and including an artist's rendering of the final product for the pre-sales brochure. After that planning and design, the building is finally ready to be constructed, all without a single variable unattended to and leaving no doubt whatsoever that it will stand up against a stiff wind.

This essential level of structural certainty is attained without a single nail being hammered.

But sooner or later you have to park the truck in front of a vacant lot, hire some folks, dig a hole, pour some concrete, and get busy putting up walls. Once you have those walls in place you can worry about what color to paint them and what kind of tile and granite you prefer—that's *writing voice* in this analogy—but for now you're focused on foundation, studs, flooring, joists, and shingles. As you should be. You're all about assembly, fitting things together, getting the weight-bearing physics right while realizing the architect's structural and aesthetic vision.

Writing a successful novel or screenplay, or any type of writing for that matter, is no less complex or dependent on structure and process.

As a writer, you *are* that architect. You are also, at some point after the blueprint galvanizes in your head and then on paper, the general contractor, laborer, plumber, electrician, roofer, truck driver, interior designer, painter, carpet layer, appliance installer and, eventually, broker.

To accomplish all of this post-blueprint work, you have but one primary tool in your toolbox of literary assets—scenes. Sure, you've got ideas and you've got a huge pile of words ready to go, but none of that means a thing at this point without *scenes*. Scenes are what you use to hammer your story home.

You may think that words are your primary storytelling tools. But they're actually more like paint and plaster rendered onto an infrastructure that won't crumble under its own weight. If your conceptual idea is weak, your character less than compelling, your theme flat or missing altogether, and if it's all in the wrong order, Shakespeare himself on his very best day can't save you. At least until the broken infrastructure has been fixed.

And for *that* you need a story architect, not a wordsmith. You must be both.

A STORY IS THE SUM OF MANY SCENES

A long-form story (a novel or a screenplay, even a memoir or some forms of nonfiction) is a sequence of separate, discreet, yet dramatically connected scenes. Sometimes those scenes are linked by narrative glue that doesn't itself qualify as a dramatic building block—think of this as mortar—but for the most part a screenplay or a novel consists of somewhere between forty and seventy scenes, each of them a one-act play with a beginning, a middle, and an ending. An ending that, in the case of a screenplay or a novel (as opposed to a true one-act play), thrusts the reader forward into the subsequent scene with an escalating level of tension, logic, and exposition. A book you *simply cannot put down*—this being your goal—is a book with great scenes that propel you toward other great scenes.

A scene must present a dramatic scenario, with something at stake. A scene is, in that way, a microcosm of the larger story in which it appears.

A scene has a beginning, a middle, and an ending, yet you don't necessarily have to show the reader all of them. Rather, a scene should have an outcome, and that outcome is a carefully conceived and designed evolution of the story moving toward a higher, further goal. And yet, it is capable of delivering its own punch and vicarious ride.

You can be a master architect where the four elements of storytelling—concept, character, theme, and structure—are concerned, but if you can't build a decent scene your manuscript will never get into the hands of the editorial folks who have the power to green-light it. Your ability to craft compelling scenes is critical to your success, and thus this aspect of writing is one of the Six Core Competencies you need to master.

THE GAME OF STORYTELLING

Sportscasters can understand and talk about a given athletic pursuit or a specific game with every bit the acumen of the folks on the field playing it. And yet, they wouldn't think of stepping between the lines and joining them.

Writing scenes is actually playing the game of storytelling. The other stuff, important as it is, is the equivalent of analyzing a game without ever putting on the pads. Winning depends not on your requisite knowledge of the rules and grasp of the fundamentals—little leaguers can master fundamentals—but on effective, professional-level *execution* via a sequence of narrative scenes.

As for your writing skills … it isn't always the fastest or more athletic player who wins, or even becomes a champion. It's the player who has the most heart, the player who won't quit, and the player who gets the most out of what she knows and has been given. To which she is always striving to add.

Even if you struggle with the words and consider yourself an average writer of sentences and paragraphs, it is your scenes that will make or break your story. And your career. You can polish the words later, and you can rest easy knowing that if your story is compelling enough because the structure, content, and context of your scenes are stellar, there are basements full of underpaid editors who are charged with doing anything and everything—up to and including rewriting you if necessary—to make your writing publishable.

But if the scenes aren't effective, no matter how pretty your words, the story will tank.

WHAT COMPRISES A SCENE?

A scene is a unit of dramatic action or exposition (which includes narrative review, overview, or connective tissue) that stands alone in location and time. If you *change* location or time—such as skipping ahead an hour, or to the next day, or even going backward in time—it's a new scene. Even if you blend that into what appears to be a seamless narrative.

If your story is a wall, scenes are the bricks. If your story is a staircase, your scenes are the stairs. If your story is a song, your scenes are the verses.

Scenes can be delivered as a single chapter, or your chapters can contain several of them. A book with seventy-eight chapters can have seventy-eight scenes, or it can have 178 scenes, though in that case many of them would be quick visual hits that deliver a piece of narrative information. There are no rules in this regard; it's always the writer's call. And thus, the nature, volume, and impact of your scenes define your level of craft.

If your chosen strategy is to have multiple scenes within a chapter, it's good to skip a line of white space whenever you change location or time—in other words, when you change scenes—if for no other reason than to clarify to the reader that you have indeed moved on to the *next* scene. Obviously, when you jump to the next chapter, that scene transition takes care of itself.

Sometimes, though, a scene can transition *without* a skipped line of white space, using a simple sentence as a sort of narrative glue. Consider the following example, which cuts in at the very end of one scene and transitions directly—and clearly—into the next one:

> ... and after doing precisely what she had asked of him, he
>   quickly departed the premises and got into his car.
>   After a ten-minute drive he arrived at the house he once oc-
>   cupied with his wife, hoping she wasn't there. When he saw her

> car in the driveway—the one he bought just a year earlier; this was
> the first time he'd laid eyes on it since the divorce—his heart sank,
> prompting him to drive past after slowing only a bit, abandoning
> his original intention to leave the package on the porch.

This is one scene melding directly into the next without the use of a skipped line. Even without that white space, there is a shift in both time and place, and thus the reader is presented with two scenes, not one.

Now let's look at the very same transition, only this time using white space (a skipped line) instead of a transitional sentence.

> ... and after doing precisely what the instructions had explained, he
> quickly departed the premises and got into his car. He had only
> one more thing to accomplish in order to put it all behind him.
>
> The first thing he saw upon turning the corner in his old
> neighborhood was his wife's car parked in what was once his
> driveway. He had bought it for her just a year earlier, and this
> was the first time he'd laid eyes on it since the divorce. His
> heart suddenly sank, prompting him to drive past after slow-
> ing only a bit, abandoning his original intention to leave the
> package on the porch.

Notice how the narrative that ends one scene and opens the next is a bit more descriptive than in the prior example. The reader needs to be *ushered* from scene to scene, one way or the other.

Both examples illustrate how scenes in a novel can sometimes play like edits in a movie. In nearly every story there are quick moments like the ones described above, coexisting with longer, meatier one-act dramas that deliver dialogue, subtext, and characterization, all the while becoming the vehicle for critical story exposition.

In either case, though, there is a specific principle that serves to keep a writer focused and efficient in the delivery of scenes. In fact, it is one of the most empowering and critical of the many principles that reside within the Six Core Competencies model.

Blow this one, and you put your entire story at risk.

43
THE FUNCTION
OF SCENES

Every scene in every story has specific duties and obligations it must live up to. This is the province of craft, and while certain principles are indeed in play, execution is a function of author choice and taste. Storytelling is nothing if not a provider of great latitude, often with enough rope for the author to hang herself.

And thus are A-list writers distinguished from the rest.

These obligations—think of them as purposeful *functions*—exist on two distinct levels. One of them is obvious—you learned it in freshman creative writing, perhaps to your detriment—the other is one of the most powerful pieces of storytelling advice you will ever hear. And while it's not all that complicated, it is the temptation to *make* it complicated that trips up writers who don't realize the effect of it. It's called ...

MISSION-DRIVEN SCENE WRITING

Imagine a scene that shows a character sitting in a room. You describe the room. You describe what the character is wearing. You write about the chair. Maybe you wax eloquent about the clouds and the soft ambient embrace of a furnace warming the place from an early winter chill. Norman Rockwell could show up at any moment. It's all so visual, so very Joyce Carol Oates. You go on and on about this—we've all read these books—and then, when you've described enough of what the place looks and feels and smells like, you decide to end the scene.

If that's all there is, you've quite probably made a major storytelling mistake. If you make it twice in one manuscript, the acquisitions editor on the other end will hurl the thing against a cubicle wall.

Why? Because every scene needs to deliver a piece of story information, also known as *exposition*. A scene that merely describes a place, or even something about a particular character, yet nothing really ever *happens* in the scene—no decision, no information, no action, no change or forward motion to the story whatsoever—the scene violates one of the most basic and empowering of storytelling principles.

Every scene has a *mission* to accomplish. Or it should have. And that mission—in *addition* to lovely descriptive language about setting and place—is to move the story *forward*. Not to take a snapshot of it.

That said, here's the golden little secret that is rarely spoken aloud, and just as rarely broken: Optimally, each scene should contain only *one* such piece of exposition. The mission of each scene is to deliver a single, salient, important piece of story to the reader.

Less is more here. More than one bomb going off, or even a little mouse trap clicking shut, is often too much for one scene. It's always your call when doling out the details of a story, but make it carefully, and in full view of this principle.

Iconic thriller author James Patterson is famous for his mission-driven scene and chapter strategy. He not only devotes each scene to a single, energy-infused mission of narrative exposition, he makes each of those scenes a new chapter. His novels often contain well over a hundred chapters, each a mission-driven scene, with some as short as a single page. This has created a trend in commercial fiction, one that makes the story more easily accessible to readers of every level.

How *you* do this is a question of choice and taste.

You can make the scene experiential in nature, and therefore longer, allowing the reader to experience each and every breath of the moments in which the new information is revealed. Or you can get right to it.

ENTERING THE SCENE EARLY

Before we jump to the other realm of scene function, let's focus on this mission-driven approach a moment longer. Because it begs the question of how to set up and deliver the piece of narrative information that is the subject of your scene's mission.

Your scene won't work until you are crystal clear about its mission. A scene should never wander around in search of meaning and mission ... you need to *know*. And when you do—*only* when you do—can you then craft a delivery that allows the reader to linger and tease as you please.

Oscar-winning screenwriter William Goldman, who wrote *Butch Cassidy and the Sundance Kid* and *All the President's Men*, suggests writers should enter scenes at the last possible moment. This is called *cutting deep into the scene*, and it's a powerful technique for pacing. While this is solid gold wisdom, it must be interpreted. For it to work, the writer must be absolutely clear on what the mission of the scene needs to be.

Why? Because part of the scene strategy could be a deliberate attempt to stretch the tension of a scene to great lengths, and in excruciating detail, rather than cutting directly to the moment at hand. And when that's part of the mission—to take the reader for a vicarious ride—it defines how the scene needs to unfold.

We don't always need to see the car pull up, see the hero ring the doorbell, see his fiancée answer, see them chatting awkwardly over drinks ... before he dumps her. All that stuff is obvious and void of drama or interest. Just cut to the couch and let the tears—and possibly the airborne china—commence.

Quentin Tarantino has done this drawn-out, experiential scene structure masterfully twice, in the opening scene of *Inglourious Basterds* (a nine-minute gut-wrenching scene that arguably earned Christoph Waltz a 2010 Oscar for Best Supporting Actor), and earlier in the famous Christopher Walken-Dennis Hopper interrogation scene in *True Romance*, a scene that still holds up as one of the most tension-filled, dialogue-crisp units of dramatic action ever set to film.

Both scenes had a single piece of information to put on the narrative table. Both scenes could have been executed in as few as thirty seconds. But Tarantino, who by virtue of these scenes branded himself as a master of scene construction, chose otherwise, and for good reason. His mission was to drive us crazy with empathetic tension. And to get there he added layers to the second realm of scene construction—drawing out the moment in great detail—which defines the delivery of the mission-driven nature of the first realm.

Be aware, though, that you can't stuff too many of these heavyweight scenes into a story. They work best at a major milestone—especially the Midpoint—and should give way to otherwise crisp pacing and the latest possible scene entry strategy.

To be an enlightened writer, you must understand precisely what each scene needs to accomplish, and that part of the goal involves the reader experience. Cluttering the scene with too much exposition—anything beyond a single piece of story information is too much—will water down pacing. Even if there are two or more things to put on the table for the reader, create separate scenes to get it done.

A change in scenery and time always calls for a new scene, but nothing says you can't make two scenes from one setup, especially if there are two important pieces of storytelling at hand.

With this as a crystallized mission, your challenge and opportunity becomes how to *optimize* the scene for maximum effect. How to make it the best possible reader experience, in service of the larger story, that you can. Not only through tension, anticipation, fear, titillation, and empathy, but also by including the ambiance of setting and place to an extent that is appropriate to where the scene resides in the story sequence.

Which brings us to that second level of scene function.

SCENES AS NARRATIVE LANDSCAPES

Setting is *not* narrative. Action and exposition *are* narrative. And yet, setting and place—such as an era, a city or geography, or a specific culture—are vital elements of the craft of empathetic storytelling. If your morsel of narrative is delivered on the steamy streets of Hong Kong, then by all means make the reader smell the dead fish wafting from a nearby alley. Just don't make the scene *about* the dead fish.

In addition to delivering this golden goose of story exposition, you are obliged to make sure each scene contains a handful of other basic qualities, and to understand that the nature of those qualities *evolves* over the course of your story. In other words, your scenes may look different in the first part of your story than they do in the last.

Each scene unfolds in a *place*. An environment, both micro and macro. If that place is germane to the storytelling—and *only* if it is germane to a better understanding of the story—you should give the reader an appropriate look at it. Too often, even in some published work, a writer will drivel on about how something looks, attempting to imbue something as mundane as overcast skies or a postal worker's freshly pressed uniform with poetic sheen. Not a good idea. Less is usually more when it comes to visual description.

We've all seen how the butcher looks after a long day behind the glass counter. We don't need a museum docent's visual analysis of the blood spatter on what was earlier that morning a clean white apron. Don't insult the reader with the obvious. Only go into detail when specifics serve characterization or impart meaning, nuance, or content to the unfolding of the moment or the larger context of the story.

Then again, if your hero *is* that butcher, and this is the first scene in which the reader has seen him at the office, and if his subtext and journey is somehow related to his work experience—such as, he has a thing for knives—you might conclude that a moment of focus on the room, including that apron, is appropriate. Later in the story, on the seventh visit to the butcher shop, the reader doesn't need that level of detail.

As the writer, you get to make that call.

CHARACTERIZATION WITHIN SCENES

In addition to setting and place, each scene is an opportunity—and an obligation—to illuminate character. Even if that illumination only serves to maintain a context you've established earlier. When character unfolds alongside action and narrative exposition, the scene becomes a vehicle for all three.

Some scenes, especially early in a story, are actually all *about* character. Showing the reader an aspect of character becomes your mission for that scene, and thus remains true to the principle of having a clear and singular expository mission as the objective of the scene. It is when there is only character *without* a narrative pass to throw, and when this is by default rather than by design, that you have a scene that an editor will suggest you delete. In fact, you can count on it.

Bottom line: Your story should be moving forward at all times. Even a flashback needs to move a story *forward*, if nothing else than by virtue of the reader's new understanding as facilitated through that flashback.

Exposition is how the story moves forward, not through setting or even characterization.

Every scene is an opportunity to impart the details and subtleties of characterization. If it's early in a story, adding more detail and eloquence may be appropriate, including an allusion to backstory and inner landscape. But if those layers have already been introduced, later scenes shouldn't go overboard or become redundant in showing them to the reader.

Nelson DeMille shows us such a scene as the opening hook in *The Lion*. DeMille's novels, while strong on plot and theme, are exceptionally dependent on character and writing voice (the guy is hilarious, even in a serious story, precisely because his heroes are testosterone-infested wise-asses). Such is the mission of the opening scene.

We meet our hero, U.S. security specialist John Corey, while on a routine observation in New York City in the company of a green-behind-the-coif FBI agent, who is his driver for the day. Quips and *bon mots* ensue. They're following a known terrorist—that's the hook, the reader empathizes with the hero and his quest by the bottom of page 1—and for the entirety of the first two scenes, some twenty-three pages, DeMille is heading toward two very clear and yet experiential missions.

In the first scene (which is also the first chapter), the reader doesn't get a glimpse of this scene's mission until the final paragraph. The mission of the scene is to inform the reader that Corey can't get his nemesis out of his head, a killing machine known as The Lion, even as he is chasing lesser villains. The secondary mission is pure characterization, but that realm is always incumbent upon a scene, and in an opening scene can almost trump the exposition goal, which is the case here.

In the second scene, Corey follows the minor league terrorist to an Atlantic City casino, then confronts him in a rest room with what is nothing less than unprovoked assault, sending the guy to the hospital. The mission of this scene is to show the reader who the hero is—a terrorist-hater, a badass, a rebel who doesn't pay attention to rules or authority, and a guy with a score to settle—through the physical confrontation. Characterization through *action*. And that action was the mission of the scene.

Both scenes are completely mission-driven. There isn't a moment of goal-less wandering, as if the writer were just skimming top-of-mind thoughts (which is precisely what happens when a writer doesn't know, from page 1, where the story is going). The first scene has no action at all, other than following an Iranian gentleman around, simply to facilitate the introduction of the story's antagonist, which is a worthy mission provided there is a piece of salient story information as well, which there is. The second scene's mission is to show the reader the assault on the Iranian in the casino restroom, to which the reader may assign significant meaning, all of it by DeMille's design.

Later chapters get very exposition-specific. But each and *every* scene— which is the case in virtually every published novel and produced screenplay—has a mission at its core. In your search for writing knowledge, you will learn how to spot what it is at first pass.

THE CUT-AND-THRUST TECHNIQUE

Everybody wants to write a story that the reader can't put down. Or a script that rivets viewers to their seats. Accomplishing that is the sum of everything we've discussed thus far, as well as what's next. But while that's all big-picture stuff, there is one scene-specific thing you can do that makes it tougher to close the cover and turn off the light. You need to write scenes that propel the reader into the next scene with a sense of urgency and anticipation. Which means you need to end your scenes with a question—figuratively speaking—that demands an answer.

This is called the *cut-and-thrust* technique (I first heard this from my agent, and to be honest I'm not sure where it originated). It involves the final paragraph in a given scene or chapter, sometimes the final line itself. It is a moment of surprise, where something new is introduced, something unexpected and compelling. That moment may or may not be the conclusion (or resolution) of the scene, but it virtually demands that the reader keep going, if nothing else than to find out what it means and what happens.

In a good thriller or mystery, virtually every scene ends with some degree of cut and thrust. In my own novel *Whisper of the Seventh Thunder*, I end many scenes this way. Some of the better ones (in terms of immediate impact to help illustrate the nature of an effective cut and thrust) are listed below. Notice how you don't need to read the scene itself to sense how these final moments propel the reader forward. Remember, each of these examples is the last line or so of a scene.

- He would write it for Lauren, to honor her memory, the consequences of blasphemy be damned.

- Lauren led him out of the cave, stepping through the stone archway into what would prove to be an altered reality for them both.

- What if, the voices whispered, Lauren had been right?

- Her final words were, "I'm gonna make you a big star, Gabriel Stone. Nothing about your life will ever be the same."

- The tiny smile vanished, replaced by a cold fascination.

- His theory would be tested tonight.

- "Whether Gabriel Stone knows it or not, he's part of something God put into writing over two thousand years ago."

- She was smiling, as if she knew something no one else could.

- When he returned to the table, NSA agent Sarah Meyers was gone. But the card remained, tucked under an empty cup.

- He leaned against the iron bars and pretended to hold a mobile phone to his ear, watching the limo in the reflection of the glass in front of him.

- Which meant the Columbia Center project could proceed as planned.

- The line went dead.

- Larsen knew the name. He had already found him. By his own order, Gabriel Stone would be dead by this time tomorrow.

- As he tumbled back into the void, he heard someone say they had no idea how he made it out of there on his own.

- He would kill Gabriel Stone himself, face to face.

- Closure sometimes required a bullet to the brain.

- As the darkness enveloped him, Gabriel prayed the one-touch dial connection he'd enabled as he fumbled in his pocket while undressing had gone through.

- "We have to get out of here," she said. "Now."

- She turned and looked at him, her eyes moist. "So you see, I have questions for you, too."

- He felt a chill wash over him, as if something evil had licked the base of his neck.

- Gabriel recognized the face, then the clothes. As he stared, the dark haired woman from the library said, "Hello Gabriel." And then she smiled, raising a gun to eye level.

- Other than the men in this room, no one who knew the truth would be alive to tell it.

- But Sarah was gone. As was the laptop and the DVD.

- And then he heard the voice of an angel.

- Then Simon Winger closed his eyes as he raised a gun to his temple and pulled the trigger.

- From a plush chair across the room, Charlotte Brenner touched her fingertips together and smiled.

- But Charlotte Brenner was gone.

- He leveled the gun and fired a bullet into Daniel Larsen's chest.

What's obvious here is that to employ this technique you have to be solid on two immediate things: the mission of the scene, and the mission of the following scene.

You can't create an effective cut and thrust until you are.

SCENES: COMMERCIAL FICTION VS. "LITERATURE"

The word *literature* is a loaded gun. All writing is, at some level, a form of *literature*, just as all oceans, rivers, and lakes are a form of water. But there definitely is a supposed qualitative definition of the term—more categorization than value-assessment—and too often meaning is assigned to the term that implies literature is better and of more value than what is otherwise considered to be more commercial fiction.

If you've ever read *Moby-Dick*, you know this isn't necessarily true. The value in reading about a mythic whale swallowed by a boring plethora of words is up for debate. *Better* is always an opinion, and often one held by folks who smoke pipes and are paid to tell us what we should and shouldn't value in our reading.

Sometimes, though, writing *literature* vs. commercial fiction is a choice a writer can make. A stylistic target. Dennis Lehane—he of the commercial *and* critical home runs *Mystic River* and *Shutter Island*— deliberately went this route in his historical novel *The Given Day*. The fact that this book sold only a fraction compared to his other works isn't the point. What is the point is that the composition of these books—literate vs. commercial—is somewhat different. And it has to do with *scenes*.

Both styles have plots, even though it may be hard to find them in a *literate* novel or an art house film. Plot is conflict, and conflict implies character. So far it's the same game. The difference is a question of emphasis.

In what professors and some critics call true *literature*, it's perfectly okay for the mission of a scene to be character-focused, almost to the exclusion of even a hint of story exposition. You can have chapter upon chapter of character moments and dissection, without ever really sensing what the hero needs or wants, or what stands in his way. The mission of the scenes is to illuminate character, while action and forward-motion is optional and sometimes rare. In commercial fiction the exact opposite is true.

Of course, story (through plot) must eventually show up, but only true fans of literate novels are still with the hero at that point. I'm not judging, I'm just clearing up the mystery that surrounds what makes a book commercial and what makes a book an icon of literature. When a writer can do both—as Lehane does regularly—then it's all a marketing strategy. And the smart money stays away from the word *literature* at all costs.

Like everything else about writing, including the nature and mission of our scenes, we always get to choose.

44

A CHECKLIST
FOR YOUR SCENES

One of the biggest risks of writing organically involves your scenes. Writing a scene without knowing precisely what comes after it (i.e., the *next* scene), and even more precisely how that scene fits into the bigger story picture, is like nailing together a staircase without knowing where it will go in the floor plan of the house, or even if your house has more than one floor at all. This approach is not only dangerous to the health of your story as a whole. A scene written organically—without a mission—is already being fitted for a casket.

In order to cut deep into a scene without all kinds of unnecessary setup business, you have to know the scene's sweet spot. To optimize the inherent dramatic potential of a scene, you have to know not only the mission, but also the micro-structure of the scene itself, including how it will conclude. And you can't possibly create an effective cut-and-thrust transition until you understand the same things about the scene that comes next.

A writer needs to know more about the scene in question than the reader ever will. To assist you in wrapping your head around your scenes, the following is a generic, criteria-driven questionnaire that you should use as an acid test before you begin writing a scene. Or, if you're struggling with a scene that you've started but already know doesn't work, use these benchmarks to get you closer to where you need to be.

- What is the mission of your scene?

- What is the primary piece of story exposition that the reader will receive in this scene?

- Does that piece of expository information move the story forward? How?

- Does the new information require any foreshadowing or setup from prior scenes?

- What is the precise moment—in action, dialogue, or other narrative context—at which this information will be exposed in the scene?

- What is the latest moment you can enter this scene without compromising either the information itself or the potential for a dramatic experience that becomes the vehicle for that delivery?

- Is your plan for the scene designed like a short story, with its own tension and stakes and flow?

- What is the reader experiencing—feeling, understanding, clarifying, or other emotion—as the scene unfolds?

- What is the level of anticipation during the scene, as paid off by the moment when the morsel of story exposition is exposed? Or, if it's a deliberate surprise, how have you tricked or set up the reader to make that moment as jarring as possible?

- How are you demonstrating character in the scene? Is characterization driving exposition (in other words, is the mission of the scene to show the reader something about the character), or is exposition driving character (how the character reacts and handles the news)?

- Is the scene efficient? Does it drive gracefully and fluidly toward its payoff moment (the mission)? Or does it mark time needlessly?

- Does the mission of the scene stick close to the linear spine of the story line? Or is it a side trip that an editor might ask, "What's this have to do with this story?" even though you originally believed it to be interesting? (Note: *interesting* isn't the point … storytelling momentum and relevance *is*.)

- Does your scene end with a cut and thrust? Does that transition align with the mission and content of the next scene? Is the transition in keeping with how you've established earlier transitions?

- If you have more than a single scene within a chapter, have you separated them with a skipped line of white space? If not, have you transitioned from one scene to the next in a manner that is clear and smooth?

- Does your scene open with something clever, poignant, surprising, or intrinsically interesting? Have you avoided redundant or unnecessary descriptions of setting, place, character appearance, or other issues of ambiance?

Keeping these issues at the forefront of your scene planning will not only help you craft crisper, more efficient, and effective scenes, but they'll also come to bear on the pacing and stylistic impact of the story as a whole. Just like a brick in a wall, each scene has its place and function, and if you want it to stand out among the others, you need to be proactive about how that plays to the reader. A moment of creative inspiration applied to a scene without completely understanding how it might impact the story as a whole can bring the whole thing to a screeching halt.

Know your scenes before you turn them loose in your story. Don't spoil them with *too* much window dressing or agenda. Love your scenes, and they'll love you in return.

PART SEVEN

THE SIXTH CORE COMPETENCY—
WRITING VOICE

45
FINDING YOUR VOICE

By far the most common entry-level mistake in the writing game, the thing that can get a perfectly good story rejected by an editor on the first page, is *overwriting*. A writing voice that is overly laden with energy and adjectives, that tries too hard, that is self-conscious in a way that detracts from the story, that is obviously the work of a writer trying to poeticize a story that doesn't stand a chance.

Bad writing voice is like wearing a clown suit to the Oscars. Chances are you won't make it past the lobby.

Of course, one writer's clown suit is another's tuxedo. Which is to say, you may believe your eloquence is palatable and beautiful, and you may feel the need to stuff all this fat into your sentences because you don't feel they're muscular enough as is. It's always an opinion—yours and the editor's, and finally the reader's—but it's a critical one.

The mailrooms of the big publishing houses are full of these manuscripts. Writers who try to trick up their sentences. Who reach for contrived eloquence. Who attempt to liberate their inner poet. Who overtly imitate someone famous who writes that way (J.D. Salinger has inspired more rejected manuscripts than any writer in history). Generally stinking up the place with strings of words that detract instead of enhance.

Overwriting will get your work rejected faster than a ridiculous *deus ex machina* in the final act.

That's not to say *stylistic* writing, a voice full of attitude and personality, is a bad thing. Hell, I'm doing precisely that right here. But it's how I write, and its seasoned with several decades worth of professional experience (including the scars to prove it) in fine-tuning. Shooting for a level of personality in your narrative is always a risk.

To mitigate that risk, carve this into your forehead: *Less is more.* Just don't minimize your writing voice to the point where it sounds like copy from a metropolitan telephone directory. Somewhere between a love letter scripted by a drunken, suicidal poet and the world's driest technical copy awaits a level of style that suits you. And just as importantly, suits your story or manuscript.

Your journey as a writer, as a storyteller, is to find it.

IT'S CALLED WRITING *VOICE*

The essence of your writing voice is one of the Six Core Competences. Which means you have to get it right before you can turn pro. That word—*pro*—is critical here, because while it may be simplistic or positively John Updike-like, it absolutely, unequivocally, needs to be *professional.*

Where that bar resides is, once again, an opinion. One thing, however, is always true about this—the further you move in either direction from a safe and clean middle ground, the higher the risk your work will be perceived as less than professional.

Writing voice, in my humble opinion, gets too much airtime at writing conferences filled with people who are actually in need of mentoring on their storytelling. It remains a staple of academia—high school in particular—but it's actually the least challenging of all the Six Core Competencies when it comes to publishing your work.

You don't have to write like J.D. Salinger or John Updike to get published. Pick up any random published book from a shelf at the mall and you'll see this to be true. While there is a huge variance in style among those authors, they all have one thing in common: They've met the bar of professionalism. Which in today's commercial market means clean, crisp, efficient writing that doesn't stink up the place with too much *effort.*

Think of writing voice as you might regard a singer's voice. Not everybody making records sounds like Josh Groban or Maria Callas. Some of them sound like they woke up from inadequate anesthesia during an appendectomy. Any singer, though, can mess up a song with too many melodic gymnastics. Think Adam Lambert trying to trick up the national anthem. Great voice, but the crowd at Wrigley Field wouldn't approve.

THE AROMATIC BENCHMARK OF VOICE

Writing voice is like air: If you can smell it, something is cooking, and it may not be appetizing to everyone. In fact, something may be rotten. The scent of a Chihuahua slowly roasting on a spit over an open flame may play well in the North Hamgyong Province of Korea, but it turns stomachs in rural Massachusetts. And yet, in both corners of the planet, everybody loves a clean, fresh breeze totally void of scent.

Less is more. The more personality and humor and edge you are looking for, the truer this is.

Attempting to imbue your writing with noticeable narrative style is always risky, because you're hoping and assuming that whoever is reading your work will be attracted to that particular style. The safest bet—one placed by a bevy of best-selling writers that includes Dan Brown and John Grisham, Stephenie Meyer and James Patterson, and a whole bunch of other authors who are too often and unfairly accused of *not being all that good* because their writing bears no stylistic scent—is to write cleanly and crisply. To write *simply*. Sort of like that breath of fresh air, the hallmark of which is that it doesn't smell like anything at all. It's just, well, pleasant. It flows. It goes down easy.

At the very least, it's *professional*.

The personality and voice of your writing should be natural, not something contrived. It can take years to find your natural writing voice, and when you do you'll never fear the color purple—as in, purple prose—again. Because only when you are writing naturally, without forcing it and without abusing adjectives (in *Elmore Leonard's 10 Rules of Writing*, he advises writers to remove every single adjective from their manuscripts) will the scent of your narrative be as subtle and functional as it needs to be to attract a buyer.

Consider the novelist Colin Harrison. Harrison has been called the "poet laureate" of American thriller writers, but not because of what that tag implies. You'd think someone with that on his nametag would be positively Shakespearean with his words. But eloquence isn't your goal as storyteller—*essence*, as conveyed through tonality and attitude, *is*. And nobody does that better than Colin Harrison.

Here's the first paragraph of Harrison's novel *Manhattan Nocturne*:

> I sell mayhem, scandal, murder, and doom. Oh, Jesus I do, I sell tragedy, vengeance, chaos, and fate. I sell the sufferings of the poor and the vanities of the rich. Children falling from windows, subway trains afire, rapists fleeing into the dark. I sell anger and redemption. I sell the muscled heroism of firemen and the wheezing greed of mob bosses. The stench of garbage, the rattle of gold. I sell black to white, white to black. To Democrats and Republicans and Libertarians and Muslims and transvestites and squatters on the Lower East Side. I sold John Gotti and O. J. Simpson and the bombers of the World Trade Center, and I'll sell whoever else comes along next. I sell falsehood and what passes for truth and every gradation in between. I sell the newborn and the dead. I sell the wretched, magnificent city of New York back to its people. I sell newspapers.

There are only four adjectives here. Two in each of two sentences. That's it. And yet, this paragraph screams attitude and personality. It is a soaring, melodic example of writing voice, one that is completely in keeping with the dark city detective thriller that it is, only written by a master linguist. Use this as a model of writing voice that's way out there from the boring, vanilla middle of the stylistic continuum, and allow it to inspire your musings at that level.

Just don't imitate the guy. Or anyone, for that matter. Editors can smell a rip-off a mile away.

Less is more. Even when you're shooting for more. Just keep trying things, checking in with how it works, and listening to the feedback. Allow your writing voice to evolve, unforced but certainly subject to the highest standards you can bring to it.

Many of us become writers in the first place because we have been told for years that we have *a way with words*. That can actually be a curse in this game. Just make sure that the words don't have a way with you and your career.

Novels—and especially screenplays—don't sell because of writing voice. But they do get *rejected* because of writing voice. What sells are great stories, told well. *Well*, in this context, being a balanced mastery of the Six Core Competencies, which includes a writing voice that smells like money.

THE VOICE OF DIALOGUE

If you write fiction, by definition you write dialogue. Which means that dialogue, for better or worse, is part of your writing voice, and will be judged as such by an agent or editor long before it stands a chance of reaching the reading public.

For some writers this comes very naturally, and for others—even those who don't struggle in the slightest with their narrative prose—their dialogue sounds like it came from the script of a bad third-grade play.

Writing great dialogue is very much like narrative prose—it cannot be taught. But a *sense* of it can be *evolved*, and for that to happen you need to develop an *ear* for it.

If you have the ear, you can write it down in your stories.

DIALOGUE AS REALITY

The overwhelming fault in dialogue from many newer writers is dialogue that doesn't sound genuine. It's just not how real people in the real world talk.

You have to begin by throwing all that you know about grammar and the physics of a respectable sentence out the window. Because people just don't talk that way to each other. Never have, never will.

Some people speak via certain shorthand. They don't say half of what they mean, yet they are perfectly understood. Others speak indirectly, and still others imbue their communications with agenda and unspoken subtext.

Dialogue is also specific to variables such as age, culture, geography, relationships, and agenda. When Mike Rich, a very white guy from a very upscale part of town, wrote the screenplay for *Finding Forrester*, his spot-on street dialogue was attacked by some as having been brushed up by someone else, someone who had lived the life of his inner-city protagonist. But Rich did what all writers need to do—he jumped into the contextual heads of his cast and allowed them to speak as they really would, not as a white guy who has never seen a crack pipe might think they would. This took work, which Rich legitimately claims with pride. The actors and the director get less credit than the screenwriter relative to the keen ear employed in the dialogue, which made the scenes ring true.

Let's look at two examples of the same moment, a contrived slice of dialogue created for this purpose. One is how a newer writer might do it, the other how it might actually sound. This reflects the writer's own point of view and awareness—nobody *chooses* to write dialogue that is off the mark—and thus defines the challenge at hand. You can't settle for *you* in your character dialogue, you have to get outside yourself and make it *real*.

Two old friends who haven't seen each other since graduation run into each other at halftime of an NBA game.

> "Hey! Holy cow, man, how are you?"
> "I'm fine, you?"
> "Yeah. You look ... successful."
> "Doing okay. How about you?"
> "Can't complain. How long has it been ... like, a year?"
> "Three. Are you married?"
> "Engaged. You?"
> "Divorced. Hey, that's how it goes sometimes."

Yeah, that pretty much sucks, I know. But that's what lands on too many desks of too many editors. Not because the writers are bad, but because they don't bring an ear to the dialogue. They can't seem to imbue characters with a realistic ambiance and edge.

This would play better:

> "Dude! 'Sup, man?"
> "God, you look ... what are you, like, running the show over there?"

"Can't complain, livin' the dream."

"You look like Donald Trump's son or somethin'."

"Better hair."

"Hear that. What's it been, like, a year?"

"Ya think? Try three. LeBron was still learning his crossover. You married yet?"

"Nope. Still chillin'."

"Dude."

"I know. You? Don't see a ring or a tan line."

"Divorced. Thank God for prenups, the bitch."

"Dude. Sorry to hear."

"Don't be. My new girlfriend looks like Trump's daughter ... it's all good."

Writing dialogue with *street cred* isn't the point. Rather, make sure your dialogue adds to the reading experience by transporting the reader into the moment, and via nuance and subtext, into the agendas and lives of the characters involved.

The best way to develop an ear is to listen. Not just to real life—which is the mother lode of all dialogue—but to snappy, rich dialogue from every book you read and movie you see.

Avoid *on-the-nose* dialogue when you can—something your conservative aunt might say on her first trip out of Iowa, ever—that doesn't add any color or personality whatsoever. (Unless, of course, that's really how your character talks in the story, which you might want to take a look at.) Dialogue is a great—and inherent—opportunity for characterization, and like many of the creative choices you face, to not seize it is to choose mediocrity.

And while your narrative voice can be pleasantly mediocre in context to a killer story, your dialogue should never warrant that same description.

46

THE BEST WRITING
ANALOGY I KNOW

In sports they say *you can't coach speed*. When they draft otherwise
equal football prospects, a tenth of a second in the forty-yard dash is
the difference between a multimillion dollar first-round contract and an
undrafted walk-on.

When you get to the more advanced levels of any game—and rest
assured, if you're trying to publish your work you are trying out for
the major leagues—the best a coach can do in either case is to work
on eliminating poor technique that hampers performance, allowing
the athlete to make the most of his natural gifts of speed. If you aren't
already at a professional level of ability, they won't even let you into
the tryout.

Athleticism is a gift bestowed by DNA. It is a natural essence, and
folks from all levels of it continue to find success. It's just that the ones
with less of it on their plate have to work a little harder, perhaps with a bit
more intensity and creativity, to compete at a professional level.

You don't need to be the fastest to make the team or to have a career.
But you do need to play at a professional level of skill, and you do need
to find your niche.

So, is writing talent a *gift*? We certainly hear writers described as
talented all the time. But in our case it's not a gift of DNA at all. Any more
than innate, core intelligence is something we are born with. Certainly,
in that realm, our natural intellectual capacity and quickness influences

what we bring to the avocation of writing, but it isn't anything like the world of athletics.

Nobody is saying that Nora Roberts is any *smarter* than you are, at least in terms of raw horsepower. As a storyteller ... the numbers make her smarter than all of us.

So, why is *this* my favorite writing voice analogy? For one simple reason—*you can't coach voice*. Not to a significant or meaningful extent. Any more than you can teach someone to carry a tune or run the one-hundred-yard dash in under ten seconds. As far as coaching goes, once you get the bad habits and flaws out of the way, there's really no way to make someone a better writer of sentences than they can make themselves. Coaching is all about clearing the path and optimizing the moment with what you've got.

As with athleticism, you *can* work to eliminate technical flaws from your writing style, beginning with putting a cap on overwriting and an addiction to adjectives and adverbs. And certainly, the more you read the kind of work you seek to do yourself, the more you engage in study about it, the more you'll clear the path toward reaching your maximum potential. That's all this book really is. It's a set of principles that help you get bad ideas, unprofessional habits, incomplete notions, and outdated techniques out of the way, allowing the best story you have in you to surface, while creating a benchmark for the best sentences you can bring to it.

Nobody can teach you to be clever. To be funny. To be ironic. To spin a sentence that sends a reader into a frenzy of contemplation or that mirrors the human experience with a fresh lens that clarifies while it invigorates. To be *talented*. These are the realms of writing to which we aspire, and yet, despite how many people crowd into the writer's conference room, we are quite alone on that path.

One thing is certain, however. If you allow yourself to stop growing, if you stop seeking to learn and improve as a writer, you will certainly stop growing. You will have declared that your cap has been reached, and if you're not already in the game at that point, you'll never get in.

I like to think of writing as analogous to life itself.

We are all different now than when we were younger. And we will be different years from now than we are today. Those changes manifest in many ways—outwardly through our appearance and the evolution of our health, and inwardly through our worldviews and the values we apply to everything we do.

It's no coincidence that so many people mellow with age. They're simply at a higher level of life's learning curve. They're different. They're *better*. Because mellowness is acceptance of what is, and the ability to not let it get to you anymore.

This is life. And this is precisely what *writing* is all about as an avocation, a passion, and a career. How you change over time as a writer, how you grow—gracefully or bitterly or boringly—and what you choose to give back and experience is completely up to you. The more proactive you are about that journey, the more it gives back to you.

If you seek to improve your writing voice, immerse yourself in the world of writing. Your own and that of others. Be conscious of what you see there as a peer, as well as a consumer. Use every word you see in print, every frame of film that shines down on you from a screen, as a laboratory for your work.

And then—most importantly—listen for your true voice to emerge. Like a muscle, it needs to be pushed and practiced, to be allowed time to become part of the growth process. You can't see a muscle grow, yet you can look back and realize you are stronger today than you were before.

So it is with your writing voice.

It will come to you, first in a whisper, and finally with a proud and stubborn shout. And once it announces itself and declares who you are as a writer, allow it to take over from there.

And know that, without a corresponding growth in your storytelling skills—in the other five core competencies—your new muscular, evolved writing voice will take you absolutely nowhere.

Writing professionally is an all-or-nothing proposition.

47

MORE MUSINGS
ON VOICE

H ere's the bottom line about writing voice. Any redundancy is deliberate, because this can't be pounded into the head of a newer writer too
often, or with a big enough hammer.

We are writers. We must compose the songs we sing. We must choreograph the dances we perform. We must design what we ultimately
seek to build.

We are unique among artists in these things. Composers need not
carry a tune. Choreographers need not perform. Screenwriters and directors need not be actors or set designers. Architects need not even be
present as their creation is being built.

But we, as writers, are alone with all dimensions of our craft. We are
the sole determinants of words as we compose, choreograph, and design
stories. We are judged according to both, story and voice, separate and
together, on how their sum exceeds the whole of their parts.

Writing voice is but one of the Six Core Competencies you must master.
Deficiency in any one of them bars you from what you seek to achieve.

With regard to voice, though, this is ironic if not paradoxical. Because many come to the craft of writing for the sound of their own voice,
if not the utter joy of it. And yet—and here is the paradox—it is at once
the most likely of the elements that will bar you from the inner circle
of the published, while being least among the criteria that allows you
entry to it.

Allow me to explain.

It takes an agent or an editor many dozens of pages to determine the merits of your *story*. It takes only a few pages to assess the rhythm and melody of your writing voice. Those first pages expose the writing as that of a professional, someone who is publishable … or not. If it compels, if it flows or doesn't overwhelm, it passes muster as acceptable.

And that's *all* that is required of voice. Any allure of a stellar writing voice beyond that point is a case study in diminishing returns. You don't have to write like a poet to sell your story. You simply need to write *well enough* to get through the door into a crowded hall full of storytellers.

From then on, your *story* is what determines your fate. At that point, once you can hang with the pros, sentence for sentence, little if nothing else matters.

So many writers focus on their *words*.

As they should, if their writing voice has not yet matured and found its unique pitch. If it even remotely smacks of awkwardness or the timidity of a neophyte. If it tries too hard. And yet, despite that focus, and as we discussed in the previous chapter, voice is virtually impossible to teach. All the grammar lectures and sentence modeling in the history of the world won't get you there.

Writing voice must, in effect, be *earned*. Discovered. Grown into. It must evolve into a signature cadence and tonality, with colors and nuance that imbue it with subtle energy and a textured essence of depth and humanity.

Effortlessly. Simply. Cleanly. Without the slightest hue of purple.

It must become something that is completely and totally *yours*.

There is only one way to earn it.

And it isn't a function of talent.

You must write. Practice. Constantly. Intensely. Humbly and aggressively. And you must do it for years if that's what it takes. Because it refuses to be rushed. Your writing voice will grow into its own comfortable shoes, on its own terms and in its own time. And once there, you will know you are home.

And then, from that point forward, it's all about your storytelling.

You don't have to write with the spectacular gift of a prodigy or even the seasoned wit and cynicism of a salty veteran. You just have to be *good*.

But your storytelling—as demonstrated through a mastery of the Six Core Competencies—must be *better* than good.

Good is a commodity. Good is everywhere. Good chokes the in-boxes of every publishing company and movie studio that has ever hung out a shingle.

What is good and what is better than good is always a judgment call. The paradox never ends. Because often the harder you try to be good, the more you'll come up short.

Good writing is effortless writing.

An adequate, clean, professional-level writing voice is your ante-in. It's what gets you a shot at having someone care about your story. It's what allows an agent or editor to read past the third page to actually *experience* your story.

In effect, it could be said that when an agent or editor *ceases* to notice your writing voice, you are there. You are in the game.

And your ace in *that* game is your story.

PART EIGHT

THE STORY
DEVELOPMENT PROCESS

48
GETTING IT WRITTEN

Whether you're a plotter or a plodder, a planner or a pantser, organized or organic … we are all faced with the very same daunting question: *What do we write next? And how do we know?*

The answer to that last question is now in your possession—the principles of story structure, in context to a vision for concept, character, and theme, the sum of which become your guide on this journey, beginning at page 1. They may not put specific words into your head, but they do delineate the objectives, context, and criteria for the scenes in your story according to where you are in the storytelling sequence. And if you remain true to them they will always lead you to a story with all of its requisite parts in place. Whether anybody will like it or not remains at issue, but the principles will prop you up in that regard, as well.

From that outrageously complex question—*how do we know what to write?*—springs other key questions and issues as you progress through the story development process. Such as:

- Where are you in this story?
- What will further the dramatic tension best at this point?
- Have you characterized in parallel with exposition?
- Is your next idea the best creative choice among the options?

Addressing these questions effectively requires that you even know what your story options *are* at any given point, something you can't effectively do until you completely understand where the story is headed. The principles, at least in terms of the contextual relationship of the parts to each other, tells us *that*, as well. You are always either setting something up, responding to what you've setup, attacking the problem, or resolving the problem. The available resources of concept, character, and theme are there to make those four phases of the story dramatic and meaningful.

To say that it's *that simple* would be a significant understatement, but in a way, it *is* that simple. Because, if you're creating the story and its scenes in accordance with the principles we've discussed here, you really don't have any other options. And if you think you do have another way to write your story, if you're inserting newly invented types of scenes and off-the-wall contexts for those scenes, you might already be lost and not even know it.

At least until an agent or editor or script reader tells you.

THE MOST EFFICIENT STORYTELLING TOOL, EVER

Notice I didn't label it the *best* tool ever, even though it might be. Every writer must decide *that* for herself. But what I'm about to share with you—a specific technique for discovering and fleshing out your story—is highly efficient, and if you apply it correctly, if you possess the patience and vision and creativity to pull it off, you can use it to develop and sequence your story *before* you begin drafting it, even without even writing a single scene.

The tool is called a *beat sheet*.

This skeleton of the story allows you to develop a vision for each and every scene in a story—and in doing so, a vision for the story as a whole—then commit it to paper as a note, sometimes using just a single word for each scene. This is done prior to writing any of the scenes. In a beat sheet—so-named because it identifies story beats or moments—you hone the story, trimming here, adding there, growing one scene, evolving another, making sure all the while that they fit within the principles of story structure, and that they make optimal dramatic sense as they unfold.

That's hardcore *story planning* at its purest.

Why does it work? Because the search for story is as inevitable as it is inescapable. Your search for story resides at the very heart of your process, regardless of what it is.

Another way to develop your story is to just sit down and write the darn thing. To draft it organically. To make it up as you go along, relying on your knowledge of story structure and instinctual storytelling chops to lead you to the best creative decisions when you come upon them. We've discussed this before, and why it doesn't work efficiently. With an organically grown draft, you have to use subsequent drafts to *find* the story. That's usually a lot of extra drafts before you stumble upon it.

Using a beat sheet can actually result in a first draft that *works*, that is a polish away from being something you can submit with confidence. It takes a certain type of writer to pull this off, but the good news is that the more you know and accept about these principles of story structure and the other core competencies that make it work, the closer you'll be to recognizing the inherent value of this process. At least to some level.

FINDING YOUR STORY'S BEAT

The use of a beat sheet is a means of avoiding all the disasters that ensue when you write a story by the seat of your pants.

Toward that end, let's go into more detail of how to use a beat sheet. A beat sheet is a list of short, bulleted descriptions that define each scene in your story. They may not even be scenes at first, just moments and ideas. If you have sixty scenes in your story, create a beat sheet with sixty entries that describe the mission and the content for each scene. Each entry on the beat sheet describes what the scene does in context to story exposition. It explains *why* it is there.

You can do this using a flowchart on a computer or a bunch of circles drawn on notebook paper. You can put up sticky notes on a wall or arrange cards on the floor. All work equally well, because all these approaches allow you to *see* your story as a whole sequence before you write it.

And when you can see it, you can fix it. You can optimize it. You can move forward from structural planning to creative planning with confidence and passion.

I saw a documentary on the Blue Angels, the flying aerobatic team, and I was fascinated by the process those elite pilots go through to prepare for each air show. The relationship between the six F/A-18 Hornets is critical to success, and in this case survival. Before every performance, the pilots gather around a table and go over the precise sequence of the maneuvers together … *verbally*. Nothing high-tech about it. They close their eyes and listen while the lead pilot narrates each move they'll be making together, and in the sequence they'll be making them. His words calmly yet crisply define what's coming, how to move the stick and adjust power, and how to transition from move to move. He not only rehearses what they'll be doing together, but how. The rhythm of it. The nuance of it. These pilots intimately understand the story of their routine from beginning to end. And what the crowd experiences as a result of that intimacy is a thing of power and beauty that defies the complexity and intensity of the process that makes it happen.

The development of your story—striving to know each and every moment in your head—will benefit from such an approach. Those who argue that it results in an inflexible story that isn't open to inspired creative adjustment and better ideas forget that this is all taking place on yellow sticky notes, which are much easier to revise than a four-hundred-page manuscript any day.

And, that this is precisely what you're doing when you pants a draft, without the safety net of knowing you're only going to have to throw away a yellow sticky note instead of a whole section of narrative.

THE PRE-DRAFT BEAT SHEET

If you complete a beat sheet *before* you write the draft, you'll execute what is in essence a detailed story *plan*, and will do so in context to a working knowledge of story architecture, with each part and each story milestone functional and in the right place. Even if you end up changing things as you write—and you almost certainly will—you'll do so in context to a whole that already works, rather than considering changes that upset the balance and rhythm of the entire structure.

Each scene you identify will be pre-wired to be the right content in the right place, leaving you free to execute it at the highest level of brilliance and efficiency (pacing and dramatic impact) possible.

THE POST-DRAFT BEAT SHEET

No matter how you've developed your story, sometimes you come to the realization that it isn't working as well as it should within the draft itself. Sounded good in your head, but on paper it's lacking. When this happens, rather than addressing the manuscript in repair mode, it is more efficient and effective to lay out your story as a beat sheet and see if a better flow manifests from that process. If there's a better way to write it, the beat sheet will expose it to you.

This, by the way, is the backdoor to story effectiveness for organic writers. When you sense it isn't working, overlay a beat sheet that tells the exact same story and see where it can improve.

You'll do this once, and only once. Because when you experience the creative power and efficiency of viewing your story as a whole, it's hard to go back to an organic approach. Welcome to story planning ... which you were doing anyway within your draft.

The beat sheet becomes a blueprint for an outline.

Even if you hate the notion of outlining, you need to realize that it doesn't hate you. There is no downside to outlining that isn't a figment of your imagination, perhaps an intimidation factor, especially when the outline is simply an expansion and evolution of a beat sheet. If you're an experienced and confident storyteller, you can even skip the outline phase altogether and write your draft from the beat sheet itself.

Expand each bullet on your beat sheet to a descriptive sentence, then evolve it into a summary paragraph about the scene in question. If you've had enough creative vision to express it as a specific story beat—and not just a placeholder "needs to achieve thus and so" entry—you will have no trouble expanding the bullet into a sentence or paragraph. You may find yourself writing a short description of the scene itself rather than the next beat of the story. The process is that powerful ... one beat will lead you to the next, and before you know it the movie of your story is already playing in the theater of your mind.

To get a better feel for this, let's look at two flavors of beat sheet—generic and story-specific, from the same story. One, usually a pre-draft version, describes the *mission* of each scene in a generic way, such as "introduce hero here." The other, useful as both a pre-draft and post-draft process, reveals the *specific* content of the same scene. So rather than "introduce hero," the beat might read "we meet Jack at work."

What follows here is an entire generic Part 1 sequence of a novel or screenplay, with an assumption of twelve scenes required to get the job done prior to and including the First Plot Point. The number of scenes expands as necessary as the beat sheet develops. It doesn't lock you into anything you later decide isn't the best idea.

These are just bullets that express what needs to happen in the story at a certain point, and in a certain order. For organic writers already breaking out into hives at this notion, be reminded that this is *sequencing* only—something you'll have to execute sooner or later—and that it leaves you free to explore and flesh out options for the narrative that drive toward expositional goals.

The beat sheet is as much an exploration tool as it is a vehicle of execution. A draft *can* do both, as well, but it requires orders of magnitude more time and effort, and can actually stifle the creative process in the same way that a huge ship takes longer to turn in the open sea than does a speedboat.

To better grasp this, you need to know the through-line (also known as the elevator pitch) for the story itself, which is something you absolutely must know before you begin any beat sheeting or outlining.

Here's the elevator pitch for our example generic beat sheet:

> What if a man finds out his wife is having an affair, and in the course of trying to learn more about it she is murdered, with all signs pointing to him as the killer? He must escape the police and the actual killer long enough to prove his innocence and expose the truth.

The beat sheet for Part 1 of this story (the setup), expressed as a sequence of generic story possibilities, might look like this:

1. Prologue—preview of forthcoming problem.

2. Intro character and his life prior to facing problem.

3. Show character's present pre-First Plot Point life, what his stakes are.

4. Off-stage flash of approaching antagonism (foreshadowing).

5. Hero's first hint of inner darkness.

6. Hero timidly confronts that darkness, we see it's his Achilles' heel.

7. Hero is warned to stay away, doesn't know what this means.

8. Hero confronts the impending jeopardy without knowing the stakes.

9. Hero is falsely reassured.

10. Hero doesn't buy in, goes stealth to see for himself.

11. Major darkness thrust upon him, everything changes.

12. Hero finds himself unjustly accused (this is the First Plot Point).

It's interesting to note that this generic Part 1 beat sheet could be applied to any number of stories, some having nothing at all to do with the above elevator pitch.

Which brings up an interesting application. When, as an exercise, you deconstruct *another* story and create a *generic* beat sheet for it that you already know works, you can then apply similar story needs and sequencing to *your* story to find inspiration for—here's the answer to that question—what to write next.

Inspiration is never a rip-off of someone else's idea. If it worked for another story in form, perhaps something similar in form that leverages a parallel dramatic premise can work for your story, too. Especially if you're struggling with what to write, and in what order.

Once you've completed a generic beat sheet, you can make it specific to your story by adding a little more information and focus.

THE STORY-SPECIFIC BEAT SHEET

Here's that same premise, only this time with specific scene ideas rather than generic needs. Same beat sheet, same sequence, but now it's actually the beginning of a story plan.

1. Man and woman in hotel room, wildly making love; we see her wedding ring on the counter next to the man's wallet. This is a prologue—we aren't sure who is who.

2. We meet our hero, who runs a successful retail boutique founded and owned by his wife. She's the face of the business; he does all the hard work.

3. We see that she gets all the glory and money, while he gets little credit or appreciation. But the employees know. There's trouble afoot.

4. Wife says she's got a meeting downtown. Kisses him, leaves, but goes to hotel rendezvous with lover. One of the other employees sees her there.

5. That employee tries to tell the hero what's up, but without betraying the wife, who is the Big Boss. She has a crush on the hero herself (foreshadowing).

6. Hero follows his wife a few days later, but finds nothing wrong.

7. Hero confronts his wife with his suspicions, she denies. They argue.

8. Hero goes to hotel, shows bellman his wife's picture, he recognizes.

9. Confronts wife, she says this was where her meeting was. More anger.

10. Employee assures him his wife's lying. She saw her with a lover. There are seeds of an attraction between them, especially on her part (foreshadowing).

11. Days later, hero follows his wife to a different hotel on a tip from the employee, breaks into room ... finds his dead wife inside. Touches things, incriminates himself carelessly. Calls the police, then ...

12. Employee finds him waiting in lobby, whisks him away ... says police are already looking for him, they think he did it, he's been framed by his wife's lover, and she'll help him until he can prove his innocence. She'll explain how she knows all this later.

These twelve story beats represent the first sixty to seventy-five pages of the manuscript.

Of course, in the end it's the psycho employee who killed the wife, trying to get the hero for herself and blame the wife's lover for it. Hijinks ensue.

Remember, you should always be developing a beat sheet in context to an existing idea or concept, hopefully a powerful one.

And if you aren't, this can be a way to land on one, which then requires further development before it becomes a viable story sequence.

THE EVOLUTION OF A BEAT SHEET

The list of bullets becomes a fluid and growing tool as you add and discard story ideas that deepen the stakes, heighten the pace, focus character, and set up an ultimate showdown that pays off the character arc along with the reader's empathetic and emotional investment.

If you've tried to write a story organically and realize it has holes and pacing problems, you can use a retroactive summary beat sheet to determine if, in fact, your choices were the best options at any specific point in the sequence, something you really have no way of knowing in the moment of organic composition. Also, until you know what you're writing *toward*—either a plot point or the ending itself—it's impossible to inject any foreshadowing, which is critical to tension and pacing.

The beat sheet is a tool for backstopping the creative decision-making process.

When you combine this tool with brainstorming, deconstructing similar stories, and maybe even drafting a few chapters, you'll find yourself able to envision an entire story without having to write an entire manuscript. But however you do it—and there are many variations on this approach—you must make this creative process your own.

The process itself can be as flexible and organic as you want it to be. You may just find creating a beat sheet to be the most empowering thing you can do toward assembling and writing an effective and publishable story.

49

THE PANTSER'S GUIDE
TO STORY PLANNING

Over the course of the debate about story planning vs. organic, seat-of-the-pants story development, I've come to realize several things. Most notably, that we are all in the same boat, planners and pantsers alike.

First, pantsers don't want to hear about it. For some reason the very notion of planning out major story points before you actually begin working on the manuscript is judged as either offensive or unworkable. At least for them. This is, in my view, much like someone claiming they can't fly in an airplane ... because they've never set foot in one. And so they choose to drive.

The truer statement is that they *won't* fly in an airplane. They settle for a five-day train trip—the very definition of inefficiency—to get across the country. It's a choice, a preference, rather than a statement of fact.

Great analogy, that. Multiply the time it takes to get there via air by a factor of ten, and that's about the same ratio of completion efficiency in comparing story planning to beginning a story with no idea where it's going. Both vehicles get you there in one piece. It's just that the long way might cause you to miss the very thing you came for.

The fact is, *everybody* who writes a story engages in some form of story development.

There's no escaping it, no matter what you prefer to call it.

If you develop your story on the run, organically, if you just sit down and start writing with no clue what comes next, and then when you get to the end of a chapter you just keep writing and making stuff up from your gut, chapter by chapter ... that, too, is story planning. Even if you don't like the term.

In that case pantsing, or organic storytelling, is your *chosen* methodology. And we all must live with the consequences of our choices, in writing as in life.

Pantsing actually *can* work.

It's like exploratory surgery vs. a targeted operation. The exploratory surgeon doesn't know what she'll find inside, and when she gets in there she does what seems right, making precise and critical judgments in real time. The pre-planning surgeon, however, enters the operating room with a stack of MRIs, blood tests, and a certainty about what's waiting for her, and she goes straight at it, with a minimum of blood loss, patient trauma, and time under anesthesia.

Good analogy, there, too. Because until you know what you're doing and why, you're putting your story in jeopardy. We can kill our patient even though our intention was to help.

Even if the result is the same—the same tumor is located and extracted— the pantsing surgeon takes a lot more time, and at greater risk, than the planning surgeon.

In this analogy, both doctors know precisely what they're doing. So both procedures will work. But that's not always the case with writing a story. Sometimes the author has no real idea what he's doing. The more you know about what makes a story work, about what goes into it, what goes where, and why, the more compelled you will be to execute at least a minimum level of story planning before beginning the actual narrative process.

Conversely, the less you know about story structure, the less likely you are to plan, because you don't even know *what* to plan.

Whether you plan it or pants it, if the requisite story milestones and the dramatic arc don't unfold properly, the story will fail. The key, then, is recognizing that there is a proper unfolding to be had. And the rejection of that notion is the undoing of many pantsers.

Organic writers sometimes drop names of successful authors who swear by the pantsing process. But here's the deal—those famous folks are in complete command of the principles of story architecture. They are like pilots who don't require a flight plan because they get it, they can handle anything that comes their way. And even though it's not written down, rest assured those pilots know precisely where they're going before they take off.

THE FATAL FLAW OF PANTSING

You can't finish what you never started. And until you know the ending of your story, you can't start writing a draft that will actually work. You can write exploratory drafts, but until that outcome has become clear and has been tested against the criteria, the draft is always destined for a major rewrite.

Let me say that again. If, for example, you've unleashed a story organically that wasn't written in context to a target outcome, and then 60 percent of the way through it you finally come to realize *how* it should end, and at that point you *begin* pointing your narrative toward that goal ... your story won't work. It can't.

Your only viable option at that point, now that you know the ending, is to start another draft. One that puts all of the moving parts and contextual elements and foreshadowing into their proper place. Retrofitting rarely accomplishes the goal, and when it comes close, it's usually less clean and elegant than a complete rewrite. It's impossible for story milestones to be in the proper place until you know your ending.

But there's good news for writers that are scared to death of this truth.

You actually can do both.

You can continue to write your stories organically—to *develop* them organically—but with a wildly improved chance of success if you'll understand, plan, and implement nine specific things ahead of time.

In the grand scheme of things, that's not all that much. But they are the nine most important things you need to know about your story, whether you figure them out ahead of time or during the writing itself.

They are essential, unavoidable (and if you do avoid them your story will fail), and they don't discriminate between planners or pantsers.

I'm not suggesting that planning out all sixty to ninety scenes of your story is the only path toward success for everyone. Some planners do just that—I'm one of them—but even if you write organically you can slash your writing time by more than half by writing fewer drafts and significantly boost your odds of success if you plan these nine key elements first.

THE NINE THINGS YOU SHOULD KNOW BEFORE YOU BEGIN WRITING

This reminds me of an old Steve Martin joke: How can you be a millionaire and avoid paying taxes? Okay, first you get a million dollars ...

Insert nervous laugh here.

The nine things you need to know before you begin writing break down into two categories: the four sequential *parts* of your story, roughly defined as quartiles, and the five essential story milestones (story points) that chart your course over those four parts.

Again, if your story is to work, you *will* discover these nine things. Either within a plan, or within a draft that will require significant rewriting.

The suggestion here is that you should discover each of them *ahead* of time. With only five story milestones to shoot for, that's only five scenes to plan ahead of time, instead of the outrageous suggestion to plan all sixty or so scenes. Then, with these five key moments in mind, go ahead and pants the rest of them. When you do, the organic process you apply to the draft will turn your metaphoric car into a high-speed bullet train.

Not quite nearly the speed of sound, like that airplane, but orders of magnitude more efficient than writing blindly from the jump seat of a car.

The four contextual parts of your story ...

This will be a bit of a review. But if you're a committed pantser, chances are you will benefit from it because you've probably discounted much of the structure approach at first blush. Fact is, though, you can't really go deep into these four contextual story parts until you know the five story milestones that wall them in.

This is what you'll be shooting for when you do. Each of the four parts of a story is comprised of about twelve to eighteen scenes, and eat up about 25 percent of the total length of the story.

- **Part 1: Setup.** Scenes that introduce the hero, the context, and the stakes of the story, all before something huge happens (the First Plot Point) that really ignites the hero's journey, need, and quest, which is what the story is really all about.

- **Part 2: Response to the hero's new journey.** Whatever his life course and need was before, it's either put on hold or altered because of a new calling or need, as presented and defined by the First Plot Point.

- **Part 3: Attack on the problem.** Whereas the hero has been reeling and reacting and fleeing and rebounding, at the Midpoint of the story he begins to fight back, to move forward to seek a solution.

- **Part 4: Resolution.** Wherein the hero conquers his inner demons and becomes the catalyst for the resolution of conflict and the meeting of his goal.

These four parts define the *context* of the scenes that populate them. For example, if you're in Part 2 (reaction/response) and you write a scene that has your hero acting perfectly heroic, and successfully so, it won't work as well because it's out of context and will ultimately sabotage the flow of the entire narrative. That's a subtlety that's next to impossible for a newer writer to apply instinctively in a make-it-up-as-you-go moment.

The five milestone story points ...

In looking at those four contextual story parts, it's clear that you also need to understand the *transitions* between them. If Part 1 is a setup for the arrival of the First Plot Point and Part 2 is a response to it, then obviously you need to understand what a First Plot Point even *is*, where it goes, what it does, and why it works.

The same is true of the other four major story milestones. Your story won't work until they're functional and in the right place.

Here are those five moments that your story depends on:

- the opening hook
- the First Plot Point
- the Midpoint (context-shifting transition)
- the Second Plot Point
- the ending

Some of these can unfold as tight sequences of scenes, especially the ending. And there are other suggested transitions, moments, and context shifts that reside between these parts, many of which are rendered instinctual when you're writing in context to the major milestone transitions.

Where's characterization in all this?

The answer is—it's all over it. The four contextual parts are a roadmap to the presentation and flourishing of your character in context to the dramatic need and action you're giving him. If you implement your characterization outside of these guidelines, your story won't work as well as it should.

Sometimes people reject what is true simply because it's new. They're not comfortable doing it that way. Exercise and diet, for example. Relationships. Money management. All of these life challenges depend on certain principles, and you can reject those truths until you are blue in the face, and you can do things your way if you want (the singles condo complex is full of them), but you won't get near any of those goals until you live according to certain principles.

Same with your stories. Pants if you choose, but do so with an awareness that there are, at a minimum, nine things you need to understand when you do. Or you will either most certainly fail, or stumble upon them instinctively without ever really knowing how it happened. All nine of these story ingredients and principles can be developed ahead of time. Brainstorming, percolating, trying out scenarios and sequences using note cards and conversations over drinks ... all of them are a viable means of discovering what dramatic conventions serve your story and your character best.

50

FROM HOW WE DO THIS
TO WHY WE DO THIS

I n the creation and evangelizing of my story development model, the Six Core Competencies of Successful Writing, I like to tell people that there is nothing in the realm of storytelling that doesn't fall into one of these six buckets.

By now you're familiar enough with the Six Core Competencies: concept, character, theme, story structure, scene execution, and writing voice. Four elements and two skills. They are stated here in no particular order—you can start with any one of them and you must end with *all* of them—and you need each to be solidly crafted and rendered if you hope to write something that is of salable quality. Leave out or deliver weakness in only one—*any* one—and your manuscript will get you a "nice try" and a rejection slip.

And yet, there are many who master the core competencies and still struggle. Who don't find an audience at all. The core competencies define a set of tools and lead toward a process, but they cannot infuse your work with *art*.

The Six Core Competencies are the stuff of *craft*.

What remains, the final elusive factor—other than luck, which you can create through a combination of craft and perseverance—is something that cannot be taught. It must be *discovered*. And, in a full-circle realization, the means of discovering it resides in your grasp of the Six Core Competencies.

ONE LAST ANALOGY

I have a condo in the Phoenix area. Being an ex-minor league pitcher, I remain a rabid and analytical baseball fan who soaks up as much spring training as possible. Every year I see hundreds of sturdy young men take the field in hopes of one day making a major league roster. Every athlete on that field arrives with the basic core competencies of the game of baseball well in hand. Almost all of them are worthy of playing baseball in the big leagues, but only twenty-five break camp with a contract. Some stay there because they are *known*, taking the spot of someone who may be more gifted. They are proven and reliable, while not especially spectacular. Some get there because of providence—another player gets hurt and a door opens. Some earn their way to the top through performance. And some, despite out-performing the players ahead of them, remain anonymous in the minor leagues.

In this way, baseball is life. Just as writing is life. The parallels are, for me at least, remarkable and sobering.

As with baseball, selling your writing is a competition. Your basic mastery of the requisite skills is only the ante-in, the invitation to attend spring training. Once there, you need to be *better* than the other guy, who probably brings the same level of mastery of the core competencies of the game that you do. You need to have something about your game that stands out. Writing that is not just good, but *exceptional*.

Writers who consistently make the best-seller lists, who make a career out of telling stories, do one thing better than the rest of us. You know their names. You could argue that writers who simply get themselves published in the face of incredible odds and stiff competition—names you don't yet know—do the same.

Maybe they got lucky, maybe they didn't. But always, they developed an instinct for storytelling that makes them stand out in the moment when it counts.

And *that*—storytelling instinct—is what separates and elevates them. Even if their sentences are pedestrian and their concepts cliché. Successful storytellers put it all together with a value-adding panache and intuitive insight that defies definition or description. With high art. They *get it*, and they deliver it with a distinctive narrative sensibility that exceeds the sum of its six core parts.

These writers *seize the moment* better than those with lesser careers, and in a way that is beyond emulation. It is second nature to them. Even if it takes them years to pound it onto a published page, which it often does.

Your goal, using these Six Core Competencies as a toolbox and a process, is to develop such an instinct for yourself.

Nobody can teach you how to do that. But the Six Core Competencies can arm you with the awareness, tools, criteria, and insights to get to that point.

So, as you strive to master the Six Core Competencies, as you absolutely should if you hope to get that spring training invitation, bear in mind that doing so is only your admission ticket. What must be summoned forth from there cannot be imparted through a book or a workshop, as can the Six Core Competencies. It must be discovered, summoned, and nurtured within you.

And so we are stuck with that paradox.

The Six Core Competencies cannot get you published without the benefit of instinct. And yet, instinct cannot manifest in your stories without them. A wonderful, hopeful paradox that allows the dream to survive the odds. Because there is a *way* to get there.

Instinct is the elusive magic that happens when art collides with hard-won craft. Until you master the Six Core Competencies of storytelling, instinct will remain dormant, unrealized potential. It will wait for you, but you have to dig it out from deep within.

There is only one way to find instinct. You have the tools in hand. Everything you've ever read or studied, or *will* read or study, can be placed in context to this holistic storytelling awareness. The world is your workshop, and it's time to start taking notes.

What's next on this journey is to go after it. Keep digging. Keep finding these core competencies in the stories you absorb as a reader or viewer. But more than that, you must write your way to the point at which that instinct manifests within you. Only then, after perhaps millions of words have been spent, can it make its way onto the page.

Or maybe, by using these principles, you can hit a home run in your rookie year.

WHY WE DO THIS

We are lucky. *Very* lucky. We are writers.

Sometimes that may seem more curse than blessing, and others may not regard what we do with any more esteem or respect than mowing a lawn. To an outsider this can appear to be a hobby, or maybe a dream that eludes most.

But, if that is how they view you, they aren't paying enough attention. If you are a writer—and you are if you actually write—you are already living the dream.'Because the primary reward of writing comes from within, and you don't need to get published or sell your screenplay to access it. Sure, that dream is worthy, and it can be validating. But trust me, published writers agonize over their work in very much the same manner that you do, and in their quest to tell a great story they have the same hurdles, fight the same battles, and experience the same variance of emotional experience. Some of them don't have a clue about how they get there, they still believe in the storytelling fairy that whispers words to their subconscious and speaks directly to their characters.

Whatever. Recognized or not, every writer has a process.

You are already among them.

You are a writer. And now, you are an enlightened writer. Take a moment to celebrate that fact. And then get back to work. The rest is out of your hands.

The inner reward is the gift of life itself. Writers are scribes of the human experience. To write about life we must see it and feel it, and in a way that eludes most. We are not better people in any way—read the biographies of great writers and this becomes crystal clear—but we are alive in a way that others are not. We are all about *meaning*. About subtext. We notice what others don't. If the purpose of the human experience is to immerse ourselves in growth and enlightenment, moving closer and closer to whatever spiritual truth you seek—hopefully have a few laughs and a few tears along the way—wearing the nametag of a writer makes that experience more vivid. We're *hands-on* with life, and in the process of committing our observations to the page we add value to it for others.

Even if all we seek to do is entertain. Whatever we write, we are reaching out. We are declaring that we are not alone on this planet, and that we have something to share, something to say. Our writing survives us, even if nobody ever reads a word of it. Because we have given back, we have reflected our truth. We have *mattered*.

So, go out there and write with passion and insight. But always write with pleasure and fulfillment in the knowledge that you matter. And whatever your writing dream, keep the Six Core Competencies close at all times.

They will set you free of the self-imposed limits others suffer. The ceiling is gone, vanished forever.

Live the dream. Write your story. Then *become* one.

INDEX

ABOUT THE AUTHOR

Larry Brooks is a critically acclaimed best-selling author of six psychological thrillers (including *Darkness Bound*, *Pressure Points*, *Serpent's Dance* and others), in addition to his work as a freelance writer and writing instructor. He is the creator and editor of Storyfix.com, one of the leading online instructional writing sites.